First edition published by Parragon in 2012

Parragon
Queen Street House
4 Queen Street
Bath BA1 1HE, UK
www.parragon.com

Created by Moseley Road Inc.
Editorial Director Lisa Purcell
Art Director Brian MacMullen
Written by Jo Rose
Edited by Edward Sczesnak
Designed by Terasa Bernard, Brian MacMullen
Production by Holly Lee, Danielle Scaramuzzo

ISBN 978-1-4454-8971-1

Printed in China

THE BOOK OF SAINTS

A HISTORY OF SAINTS FROM THE TIME OF CHRIST TO THE PRESENT DAY

Table of Contents

INTRODUCTION:
Who Are the Saints?

"God creates out of nothing. Wonderful you say. Yes, to be sure, but he does what is still more wonderful: he makes saints out of sinners".

So wrote Søren Kierkegaard, the Danish philosopher, in his journal on 7 July, 1838. The notable lives profiled in *The Book of Saints* are much of a piece with this observation. For here are stories of ordinary human beings becoming extraordinary by turning their lives over to God. The warrior who lays down the sword, the well-born government official exchanging a life of vice for one of virtue, the dark soul emerging from the depths of despair to proselytize thousands: the lives of the saints, far from being "saintly" in the way the term is often misunderstood, are lives full of action. They are lives of sacrifice, hard work, suffering and struggle.

Saints accomplished great things. They took on corrupt governments, battled entrenched orthodoxies (occasionally, within the church itself), and fought superstitious ignorance. They healed the sick, baptized the enslaved, and often travelled thousands of miles under some of the worst conditions imaginable. And they endured unimaginable persecution, very often at the cost of their lives. Or as Saint Teresa of Avila put it, "We always find that those who walked closest to Christ were those who had to bear the greatest trials".

Christians have venerated saints almost from the beginning of the religion's existence: the very first saint, Stephen, appears in the Bible. Most of the earliest saints were martyrs, faithful Christians who suffered the death penalty under Roman laws rather than recant and practise Roman paganism. Over the centuries, however, Christian authorities have canonized, that is, officially recognized, many different kinds of saints.

They came from every stratum of society. Saint Katharine Drexel, for example, who founded the Sisters of the Blessed Sacrament, dedicated her considerable fortune of some twenty million dollars to her religious work. Saint Martin de Porres, beatified by Pope Gregory XVI in 1837, grew up in poverty, the illegitimate son of a Spanish nobleman and a black former slave. Saint Bernadette Soubirous was a French miller's daughter. Apostles, virgins, martyrs, monks, mystics, royalty, and peasants, as varied as the saints are, share one trait: they all lived lives of heroic virtue in unswerving devotion to their faith.

Geographically, the saints are every bit as diverse, hailing from every continent and a host of nations: there is scarcely a corner of the globe

LEFT: Virgin and Child with Four Angels *(1510), by the Netherlandish artist Gerard David, places Jan van Eyck's well-known composition of Mary and the Infant Jesus against a tableau of contemporary Bruges.*

that hasn't produced at least one outstanding saint. And although *The Book of Saints* includes the stories of more than 150 worthwhile lives, there are over 10,000 saints recognized in the Roman Catholic Church alone – this volume can hope only to hint at the vast, glorious array of Christianity's many saints.

The earliest saints date from the period before the Great Schism (about 1054 CE), a period of comparative unity within the Christian Church prior to the advent of the two main branches, the Western Church and the Orthodox (Eastern) Church. The lives of these saints, apart from their intrinsic interest, provide a distant vision of a nascent, more hegemonic religious institution, one that, as events eventually unfolded, would never come fully into being. As a result, observant readers will note, differences occasionally arose between the two churches regarding the attribution of a particular saint's feast day. Where this is the case, *The Book of Saints* provides both.

Not every Christian admits their spiritual efficacy, but undeniably saints – in their earthly lives, at least – played enormously significant roles in the history, development, and theology of Christianity, and, by extension, the general history of humanity. It is therefore difficult to overstate their importance, whether spiritual, theological, or simply historical.

"Yet not I live, yet Christ liveth in me" (Galatians 2:20). All of the saints profiled in this volume aspired to lead a more Christ-like life. That they did so – and that they succeeded in moving Christianity forward to the considerable extent that they did – is a testament to their enormous bravery in the face of difficult, perilous, often life-threatening circumstances. Considered in this light, these examples of profound moral courage are every bit as relevant to us today as they were to the early Christians hundreds of years ago.

Saints are often the subject of our great works of art and many stunning images decorate churches throughout the world. This image of John the Baptist (1505), by the Umbrian painter Pietro Perugino, is part of a large double-sided altarpiece the artist was commissioned to render for the Basilica della Santissima Annunziata in Florence.

Saints Peter, Martha, Mary Magdalene, and Leonard *(c. 1514–16) by Correggio contains emblems for each of the four saints: keys (Peter), a dragon (Martha), ointment (Mary Magdalene), and fetters (Leonard).*

Saints of Martyrdom

During the first few centuries AD, Rome outlawed Christianity and persecuted its believers. Christians who suffered the death penalty rather than deny their faith became martyrs. Their names, death dates, and occasionally brief biographies filled the pages of the first martyrologies. Confounding the empire's intentions, martyrs likely helped to spread the faith – such devotion so impressed some Roman citizens that they, too, converted. Eventually, the Roman emperors converted to Christianity, thus entwining church and state and ending official persecution. Yet devout missionaries, seeking to convert others, often encountered hostility – sometimes paying the ultimate price. Even in traditionally Christian countries, violent political regimes have in recent centuries martyred many of the faithful; in 1992, for example, Pope John Paul II beatified a group of 25 Catholics who died in Mexico under the brutally anti-Catholic regime of Plutarco Calles (1924–28).

The veneration of martyrs is one of the oldest and most widespread aspects of Christian faith; by the fourth century, churches had started to collect their relics. During the Middle Ages, virgin martyrs like Saints Barbara and Lucy or the legendary Cecilia were especially exalted. Today some of the more fabulous aspects of the martyrs' legends have been questioned, yet the sheer bravery of even the least legendary martyr, evidencing unwavering faith while suffering terribly, deserves commemoration.

Saint Stephen

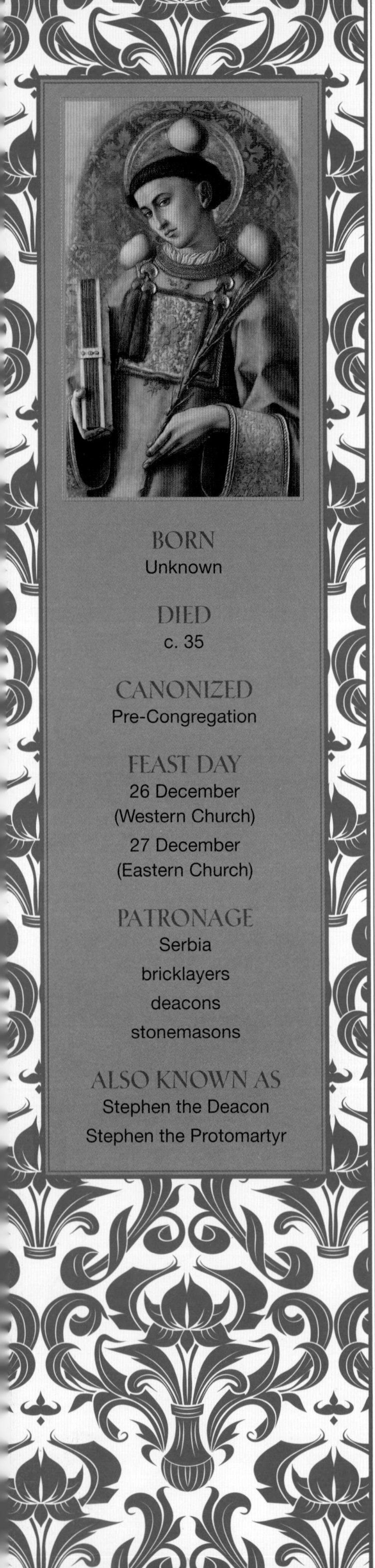

BORN
Unknown

DIED
c. 35

CANONIZED
Pre-Congregation

FEAST DAY
26 December
(Western Church)
27 December
(Eastern Church)

PATRONAGE
Serbia
bricklayers
deacons
stonemasons

ALSO KNOWN AS
Stephen the Deacon
Stephen the Protomartyr

Stephen, foremost among the Church's first seven deacons, became Christianity's first martyr when he died by stoning in Jerusalem, in about the year 35. The Bible describes everything we know about his life and martyrdom in Acts 6:1–8:2. Accused of blasphemy and brought before a hostile Jewish crowd, Stephen pointed to historical precedent: "Ye stiffnecked and uncircumcised in heart and ears, ye do always resist the Holy Ghost: as your fathers did, so do ye. Which of the prophets have not your fathers persecuted?" (Acts 7:51–52). His words angered his audience, and a vision of God and Jesus appearing in the sky to Stephen only enraged them further, so that, in accordance with Hebraic law, they removed him from the city and stoned him to death. Said to be a man "full of faith and power" (Acts 6:8), Stephen forgave his murderers even as he died.

Many artists have depicted the martyrdom of Stephen. In portraits, he usually appears as a young deacon holding a martyr's palm and with three stones to represent how he died.

> *And Stephen, full of faith and power, did great wonders and miracles among the people.*
>
> Acts 6:8

Four centuries after his martyrdom, a priest named Lucian discovered Stephen's tomb and recovered his relics, greatly enhancing Stephen's cult. Initially these resided at a church built in the saint's honour in Jerusalem, near the Damascus Gate; unfortunately, the original building no longer exists. Saint Stephen's Gate in Jerusalem is named after this first martyr but is unlikely to have been the location of his stoning, as some traditions maintain.

Saint Ignatius of Antioch

In a letter he wrote en route to his martyrdom in Rome's Colosseum, Ignatius, bishop of Antioch in Syria, declared, "I shall willingly die for God"; nearly every word he wrote expressed his ardent faith. He was one of Antioch's first bishops and, because he was only 17 or so at the time of his appointment, certainly one of the youngest, yet it is for neither of these accomplishments that Ignatius is chiefly remembered. In a series of letters written to various parties, among them his friend Saint Polycarp, he laid the theological groundwork for crucial elements of later Catholic doctrine. Among other firsts, Ignatius is the earliest-known person to refer to the Church as the "Catholic" Church.

The strength of character Ignatius displayed as he was taken to Rome, a prisoner destined for the Colosseum, made a lasting impression on the Christians who gathered to give him succour along the way. He welcomed martyrdom with open arms, even to the point of pleading with his fellow Christians not to interfere. Today, the Basilica di San Clemente in Rome houses the relics of Ignatius, theologian and most courageous martyr.

An apse mosaic at the Basilica di San Clemente in Rome, which houses the relics of Ignatius.

I am the wheat of God, and let me be ground by the teeth of wild beasts, that I may be found the pure bread of Christ.

The Epistle of Ignatius to the Romans, chapter 4

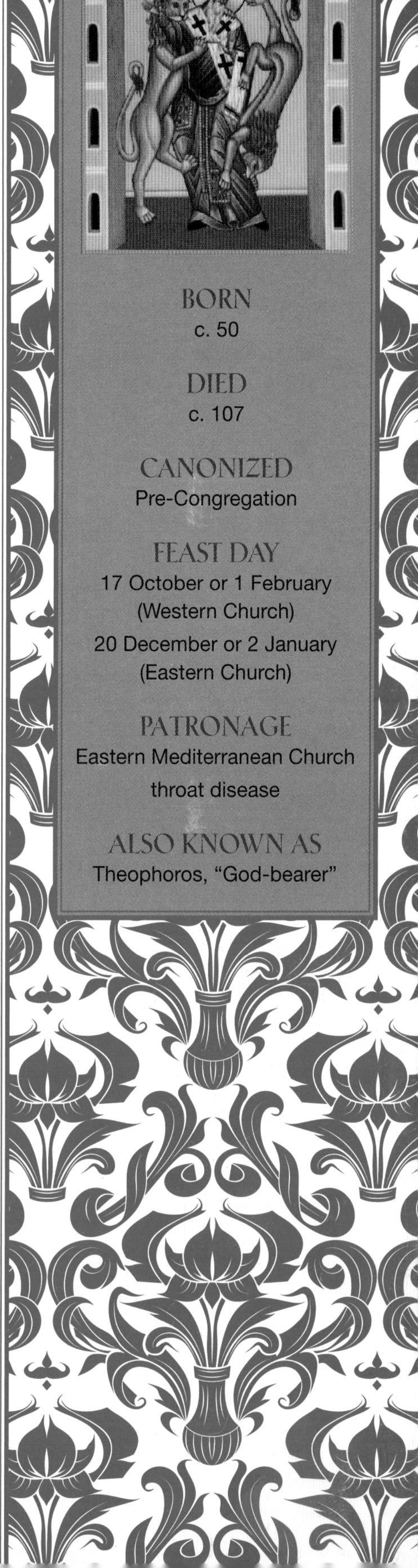

BORN
c. 50

DIED
c. 107

CANONIZED
Pre-Congregation

FEAST DAY
17 October or 1 February (Western Church)
20 December or 2 January (Eastern Church)

PATRONAGE
Eastern Mediterranean Church
throat disease

ALSO KNOWN AS
Theophoros, "God-bearer"

Saint Cecilia

BORN
Unknown

DIED
c. second or third century

CANONIZED
Pre-Congregation

FEAST DAY
22 November

PATRONAGE
composers
music
musicians
organ builders
singers

ALSO KNOWN AS
Cecilia of Rome

One of the most popular saints of the Middle Ages, Cecilia is also one of the most mysterious. Her legend places her squarely in the ranks of other famous virgin martyrs of Late Antiquity: she pledged her virginity to Christ, but was forced to marry Valerian, a pagan patrician. On her wedding day, as the organs were playing, she sang in her heart to Christ (and since the sixteenth century has thus been counted the patron of music). She had a talent for conversion, including her husband on their wedding night, thus protecting her virginity; her brother-in-law; and as many as four hundred others. She was arrested and condemned to suffocation but survived, only to be condemned to beheading. The executioner was unable to decapitate her after three attempts, but after three days Cecilia died.

> *And thou, thou art the flow'r of virgins all.*
>
> Geoffrey Chaucer,
> "The Second Nun's Tale",
> *The Canterbury Tales*

Legend says that Cecilia sang a hymn of praise to God as she lay dying. As patron saint of musicians, Cecilia is usually depicted playing an organ or other musical instrument.

This grisly legend dates to the fifth century. None of the details can be verified; some are flatly contradicted by reliable sources. Cecilia's name does not appear anywhere one might expect – in the martyrologies or works of early Christian authors – so it seems likely that the tale is a complete fabrication. Nevertheless, she remains widely venerated and has inspired many artists and composers over the years.

Saints Perpetua & Felicity

The Carthaginian noblewoman Perpetua and Felicity, her slave, along with four other companions, suffered martyrdom on 7 March, 203. We are fortunate to have contemporary accounts, two of which were purportedly written by Perpetua and one of her slaves. The accounts spell out in detail the trials of these persecuted Christians, which these two women endured even though Perpetua's son was an infant and Felicity was heavily pregnant.

Perpetua's account is written in the first person, the grounds for considering it the earliest surviving text written by a Christian woman.

Brought to trial soon after the Roman Emperor Septimius Severus outlawed conversion to Christianity, neither Perpetua nor any of her four slaves would apostatize. Perpetua's father, a pagan, pleaded with her repeatedly to no avail, even after he brought his infant grandson on a prison visit. The prison was dark and foul, yet none of the five condemned Christians, along with one other Christian who had been arrested with them, would recant. Instead, Perpetua and her fellow prisoner, a man named Saturus, were blessed with visions, while Felicity prayed to be delivered of her child in time to suffer martyrdom with the rest (for the law would not allow a pregnant woman to be killed). Her prayers were answered when she gave birth only two days before the scheduled execution. One of Perpetua's slaves died in prison; the remaining five Christians were led to the arena in Carthage, set upon by wild beasts, and finally put to the sword.

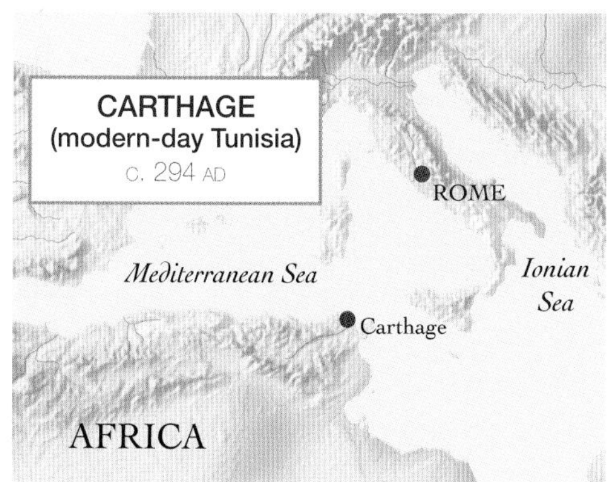

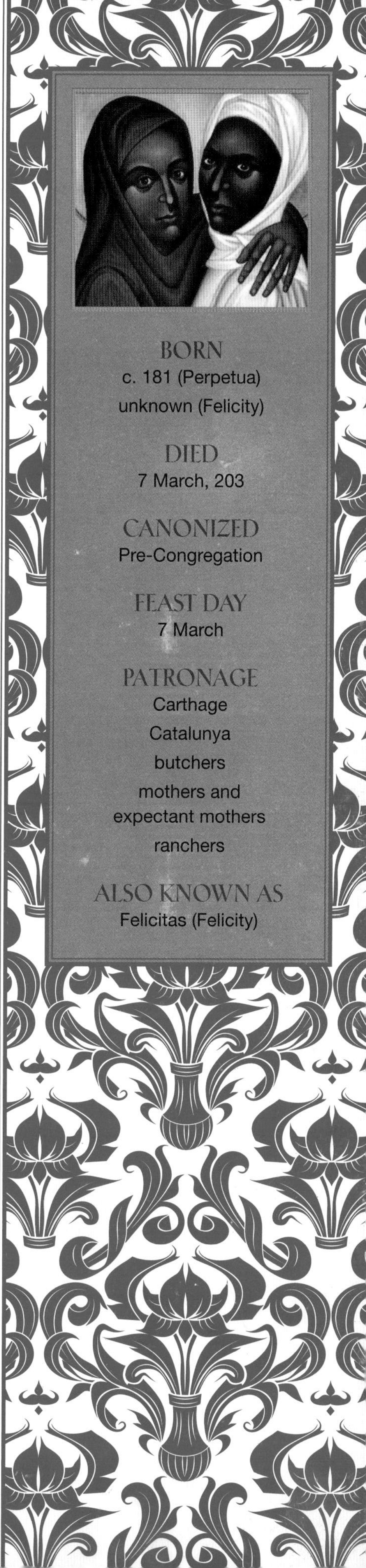

BORN
c. 181 (Perpetua)
unknown (Felicity)

DIED
7 March, 203

CANONIZED
Pre-Congregation

FEAST DAY
7 March

PATRONAGE
Carthage
Catalunya
butchers
mothers and expectant mothers
ranchers

ALSO KNOWN AS
Felicitas (Felicity)

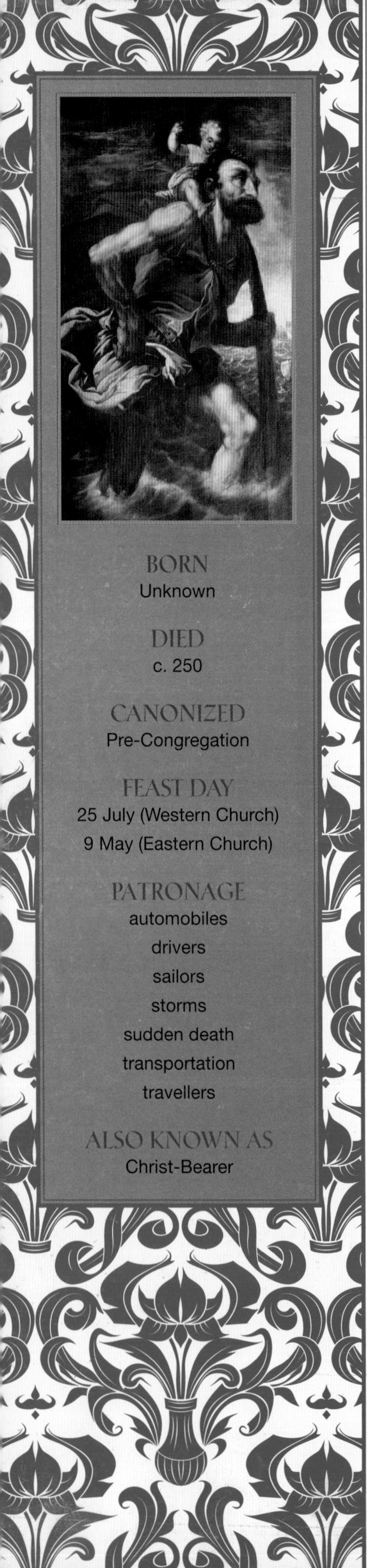

BORN
Unknown

DIED
c. 250

CANONIZED
Pre-Congregation

FEAST DAY
25 July (Western Church)
9 May (Eastern Church)

PATRONAGE
automobiles
drivers
sailors
storms
sudden death
transportation
travellers

ALSO KNOWN AS
Christ-Bearer

Saint CHRISTOPHER

Christopher belongs to legend rather than history. Even his mention in a fifth-century martyrology must be doubted, although a church in Bithynia was dedicated to Saint Christopher as early as 452.

THE CHRIST-BEARER

In all of the versions of his legend, Christopher emerges as a compellingly symbolic figure. Originally called Reprebus, he was a huge cannibalistic brute who lived in the wilderness. In earliest Eastern legends he is described as a cynocephalus, a race of monsters with the bodies of humans and the heads of dogs, who bark but cannot speak.

Proud Reprebus challenged God to demonstrate his power, and an angel granted him speech. Reprebus wandered until he came to a child sitting beside a river. He agreed to carry the child across, but his burden grew progressively heavier until Reprebus feared drowning. The child then revealed himself as Christ, and Christopher – the "Christ-bearer" – converted.

Enormously popular in the Middle Ages, Christopher was counted as one of the Fourteen Holy Helpers. Erected at churches, cities, and bridges, his statues guard against calamity. As Christ-bearer, Christopher today is patron of travellers and transportation devices.

Nearly everyone in Eurasia accepted the fact that there were cynocephali, or dog-headed men, living with other monstrous races. Christopher is often represented as a cynocephalus in Eastern traditions; in the West he is typically a giant.

Saint Denis of Paris

Confusion surrounds the biography of this popular French saint, who is the patron of the entire nation of France.

Legend says Denis travelled to Gaul with six companions and died there, either in the Decian or Valerian persecutions. Gregory of Tours included the story of Denis in his *Historia Francorum*. Written in the sixth century, its details of events three centuries old must be open to question.

In the seventh century, the Frankish king Dagobert I discovered the saint's relics and built the Abbey of Saint-Denis (a cathedral since 1966) to house them. Dagobert himself was the first of many kings to be buried there, beside the legendary first bishop of France.

In the ninth century, the abbot of Saint-Denis, Hilduin, incorrectly conflated Denis with an author known as Pseudo-Dionysius or Pseudo-Denys the Areopagite. Although this person had likely lived not earlier than the fifth century, his works, it was believed, dated to the first, and thus the conflation was compounded with the biblical Denys the Areopagite, described as an Athenian disciple of Saint Paul's. Denis's mission to Paris therefore took on apostolic overtones, and his cult expanded rapidly.

According to legend, after his death by beheading, Denis carried his head to the site of the current Abbey of Saint-Denis in Paris to show where he wanted to be buried. In art, Denis is usually portrayed holding his head.

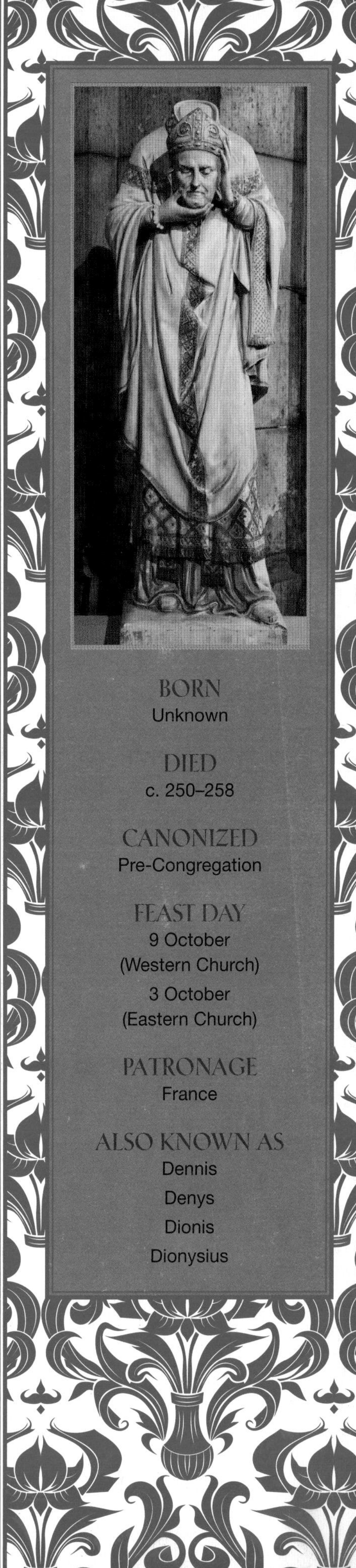

BORN
Unknown

DIED
c. 250–258

CANONIZED
Pre-Congregation

FEAST DAY
9 October (Western Church)
3 October (Eastern Church)

PATRONAGE
France

ALSO KNOWN AS
Dennis
Denys
Dionis
Dionysius

Pope Saint Fabian

BORN
c. 200

DIED
20 January, 250

CANONIZED
Pre-Congregation

FEAST DAY
20 January

PATRONAGE
lead founders
potters

ALSO KNOWN AS
Flavian

Fabian became pope – or bishop of Rome – in 236. His election, according to the historian Eusebius, was decided after a dove (symbolic of the Holy Spirit) landed on his head. The ballots all went to him, although, uniquely, Fabian was a farmer, not a clergyman, and he had not hitherto been known to the electors.

During the reign of Emperor Philip (244–49) Christianity enjoyed a brief respite from the persecutions that intermittently struck the empire. Fabian was able to conduct several important projects, which likely won him the emperor's support. He rebuilt or expanded certain tombs in the Christian catacombs of Rome; translated the relics of his predecessor Pope Saint Pontian (r. 230–35) and Pontian's fellow martyr, Saint Hippolytus; and organized the structure of the Church in Rome, dividing it into seven deaconries. He also collected the acts of the martyrs, whose ranks he was destined to join.

When Decius became emperor in 249 the period of tolerance ended dramatically with one of the worst Christian persecutions in Roman history. Fabian was Decius's first Roman victim in January 250, interred in the Catacomb of Saint Callistus, which he had renovated. His relics were later translated to the church of Saint Sebastian, who died about 300; the two often appear together in artwork.

The Decian Persecution

Decius ruled the Roman Empire from 249 to 251. In January 250 he issued an edict requiring all citizens to sacrifice to the emperor. Although the demanded sacrifice was primarily meant to show allegiance to the state and to its ruler, it was an act that went against the faith of the Christian bishops and their flocks. Many Christians, of both high and low rank, refused, risking torture and death. This edict launched the Empire's first organized persecution of Christians.

Roman silver coin bearing the image of Emperor Decius

Saint Agatha of Sicily

Although inclusion in such sources as Saint Jerome's martyrology and the sixth-century martyrology of Carthage confirms the existence of Agatha's very ancient cult, Agatha's actual life is shrouded in mystery.

Agatha died around the year 250 in Catania, in Sicily, where she is recognized as the city's patron. Her birthplace is said to be either Catania or Palermo. The legend of Agatha, like those of other popular virgin martyrs, is entirely unreliable and shares with them some of its details. According to legend, Agatha refused to marry a pagan, who then sentenced her to suffer shame as a prostitute. Her one-time suitor condemned her as a Christian when she refused to endure the brothel.

In this seventeenth-century painting, Saint Peter heals the wounds of Saint Agatha. In art, Agatha is often pictured holding her own breasts on a platter, for they were crushed and severed in the course of her agonies.

Cathedral of Saint Agatha in Catania, Sicily

Agatha's would-be husband, a Roman consul named Quintinian, turned her over to the magistrate. At first the magistrate merely imprisoned and beat her, but he grew angry when she refused to apostatize. Agatha suffered terrible tortures, including being stretched on the rack and rolled over hot coals. When she prayed the torture would stop so that her soul could join Christ in Heaven, the earth quaked and the walls fell, crushing her torturers and releasing her from her torment.

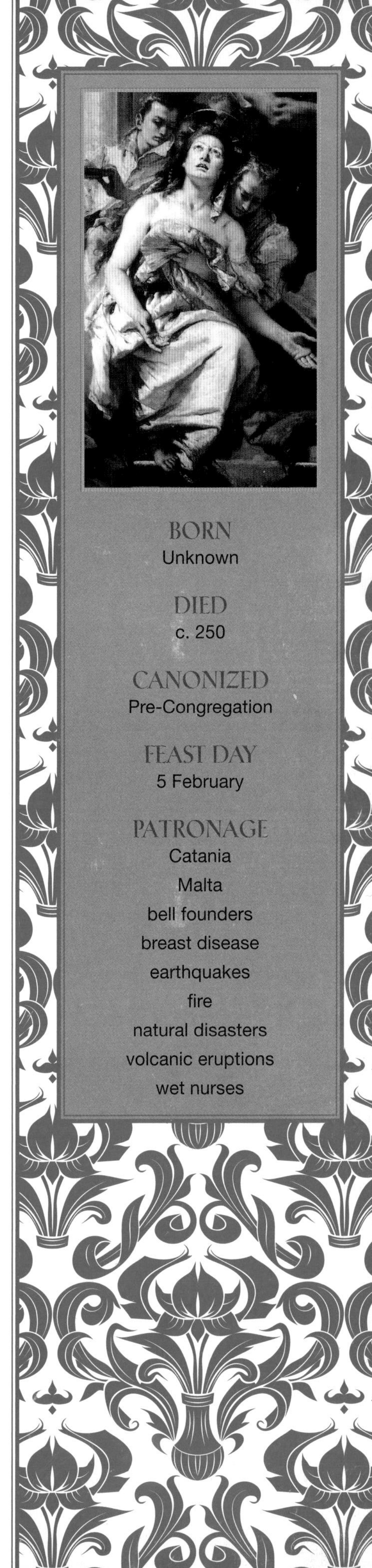

BORN
Unknown

DIED
c. 250

CANONIZED
Pre-Congregation

FEAST DAY
5 February

PATRONAGE
Catania
Malta
bell founders
breast disease
earthquakes
fire
natural disasters
volcanic eruptions
wet nurses

Pope Saint Sixtus II

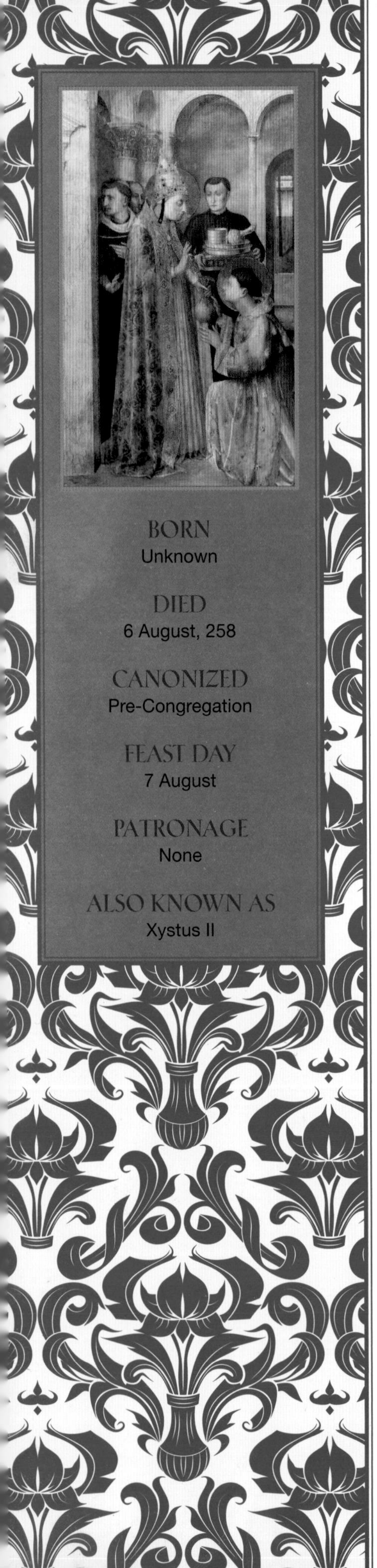

BORN
Unknown

DIED
6 August, 258

CANONIZED
Pre-Congregation

FEAST DAY
7 August

PATRONAGE
None

ALSO KNOWN AS
Xystus II

In 258, Emperor Valerian of Rome decreed the summary execution of all Christian clergymen of a certain rank, including bishops, priests, and deacons. For good measure, he outlawed Christian assembly and cemeteries as well. This was not the first, nor the last, persecution Roman emperors would inflict upon Christians, but it was one of the most restrictive. In Rome the newly elected Pope Sixtus II fell victim to it almost immediately.

Elected as pontiff in 257, Sixtus II had seen the previous persecutions of Christians wax and wane, but on 6 August, 258, he disobeyed Valerian's edict and paid for it with his life. As he spoke to assembled Christians in the Catacomb of Callistus, Roman soldiers marched in, took Sixtus II to a rapid sentencing, and returned him to the cemetery, where they beheaded him and four of his deacons; two other deacons died with them.

Saint Lawrence

According to a popular though likely nonfactual legend, the pope met his chief deacon, Saint Lawrence, on the way to his sentencing. Lawrence had rushed to the scene as soon as he heard of the arrest, hoping to suffer martyrdom alongside the pope; but Sixtus consoled him by prophesying that Lawrence would follow him in three days, which did indeed occur.

The Martyrdom of Saint Lawrence, a relief sculpture *by Juan de León*

The soldiers of Christ, as we know, are not so much killed as crowned.

Saint Cyprian, in a letter about Sixtus II's death

Saint Cyprian of Carthage

Saint Cyprian was a wealthy Carthaginian who converted when middle-aged. He escaped the Decian persecution of Christians (249–251) only to become the first martyred bishop of Carthage during the Valerian persecution (256–260).

Carthage commanded a primary place among Roman cities, and the bishop of Carthage thus enjoyed a loud voice among Christian leaders. When Emperor Decius commanded all Christian bishops be put to death in 249 (barely a year after Carthage had elected Cyprian), Cyprian went into hiding, because his position made him an obvious target. Some thought this cowardly, yet Cyprian concluded that he was more help to his followers alive, and from his place of hiding he sent financial aid to persecuted Christians and wrote much-needed letters and panegyrics to provide guidance and moral support.

He cannot have God for his Father who has not the Church for his mother.

Saint Cyprian

Ruins of Roman villas in Tunis, Tunisia. By the early centuries after Christ, the once mighty Carthaginian empire had become the centre of the Roman province of Africa. The city of Carthage, now a suburb of Tunis, was a major centre of early Christianity.

Nevertheless, when Emperor Valerian again called for the death of bishops (as well as other ecclesiastics), Cyprian did not resist arrest. In August 257, the Romans sent him into exile; one month later, Cyprian dreamed that he had been sentenced to death. At first petrified by this vision, the following morning he accepted the prophecy calmly. Its fulfilment came exactly one year after he had the dream, on September 14, 258. For his refusal to apostatize, the Roman proconsul sentenced him to beheading.

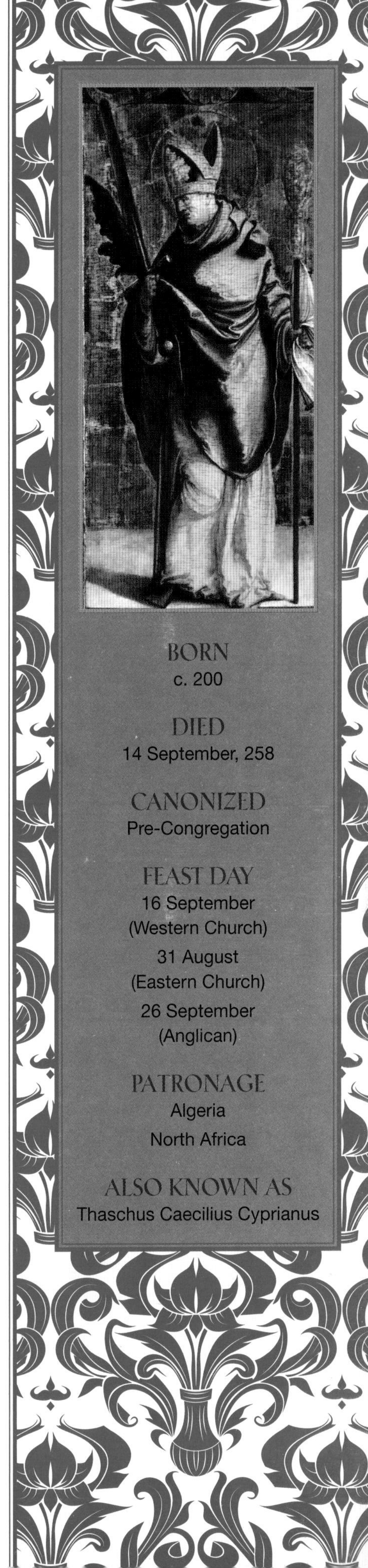

BORN
c. 200

DIED
14 September, 258

CANONIZED
Pre-Congregation

FEAST DAY
16 September
(Western Church)
31 August
(Eastern Church)
26 September
(Anglican)

PATRONAGE
Algeria
North Africa

ALSO KNOWN AS
Thaschus Caecilius Cyprianus

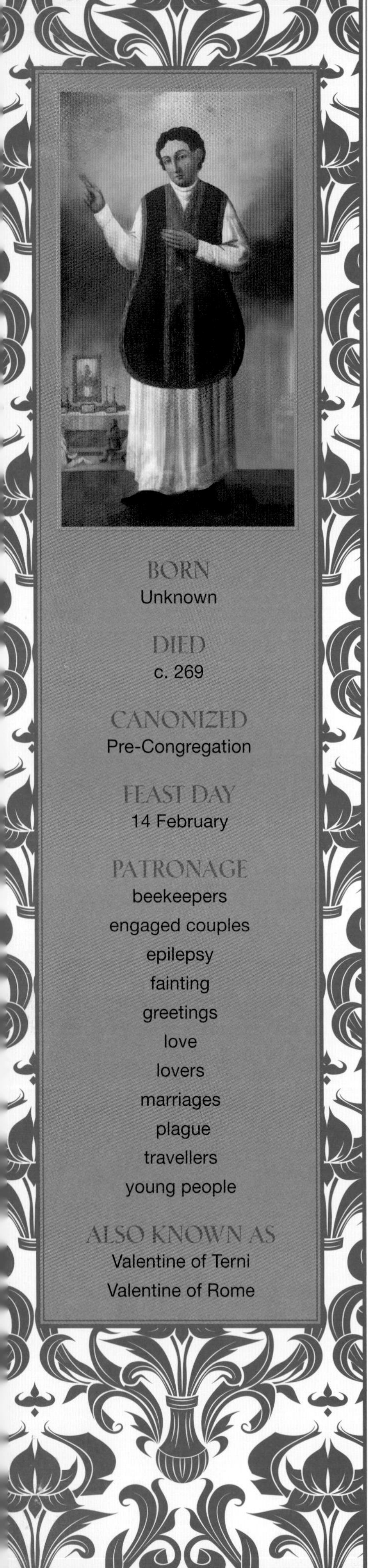

BORN
Unknown

DIED
c. 269

CANONIZED
Pre-Congregation

FEAST DAY
14 February

PATRONAGE
beekeepers
engaged couples
epilepsy
fainting
greetings
love
lovers
marriages
plague
travellers
young people

ALSO KNOWN AS
Valentine of Terni
Valentine of Rome

Saint VALENTINE

Unlike other early saints, who are known to history from a few scant mentions in the oldest martyrologies, Valentine appears too often. Of the three Valentines mentioned, it is not clear which is the martyr whose feast day is still celebrated throughout the West, although many scholars agree that it is possible – even likely – that the three separate Valentines are actually one and the same person.

ABOVE: *Valentine baptizing Saint Lucilla. Most depictions of the saint show him dressed in the robes of a bishop.*

Despite the relative profligacy of his name and the popularity of his eponymous holiday, Valentine remains a shadowy figure. Even Valentine's association with love probably stems from later legendary accounts, concocted after the association had been developed. One such legend depicts Valentine as a sympathetic figure, marrying couples from his prison cell after the emperor had outlawed marriage among his soldiers. Another claims that Valentine miraculously restored vision to his jailor's blind daughter, later sending her a note signed, "from your Valentine".

Such accounts cannot be allowed much historical credence, but it is certainly true that since at least medieval times Valentine has been recognized as the saint of love and lovers.

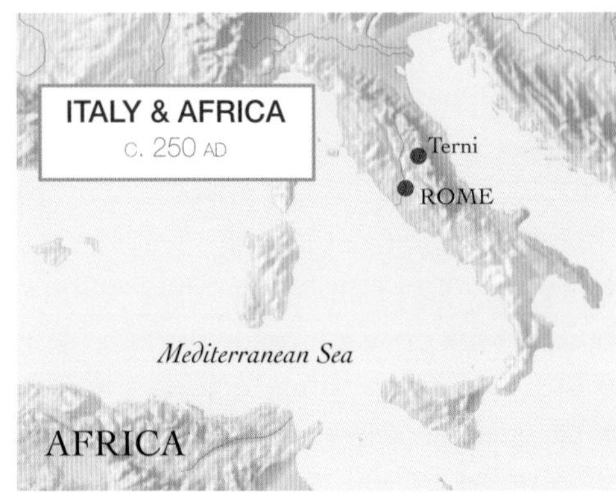

RIGHT: *Sources identify a Valentine from Terni, a Valentine from Rome, and a Valentine from Africa. All three, however, may be the same person, who simply travelled in those regions.*

Saint Barbara

One of the four principal virgin martyrs venerated in the Middle Ages (the others are Saints Catherine of Alexandria, Margaret of Antioch, and Dorothea), Barbara is probably fictional, yet her cult spread widely in both the West and the East during the early Middle Ages. The best-known version of her tale is recounted in *The Golden Legend*, the highly popular thirteenth-century compilation of saints' lives by Jacobus de Voragine.

The daughter of a wealthy pagan, Dioscorus, the beautiful Barbara spent much of her life locked in a tower built by her protective father. Dioscorus ordered that a bathhouse be built for her use while he went away on a long trip; when he returned, he was enraged to discover a cross carved into the wall and three windows instead of the two he had specified. Barbara explained that the windows represented the Holy Trinity and that she had miraculously carved the cross using only her finger. After a chase, in which angels aided Barbara, her infuriated father finally captured her and turned her in.

The Roman prefect repeatedly tortured Barbara, yet her wounds healed each night, and she would not renounce her faith. Dioscorus himself finally executed his own daughter only to be struck by lightning for his misdeed as he left the place of execution. A Christian named Valentinus buried Barbara, and many miracles occurred afterwards at her tomb.

This painting shows Saint Barbara crushing her pagan father while a donor kneels before her. Artists most often show Barbara standing by a tower or holding a miniature one. She often also clutches a palm branch and a chalice.

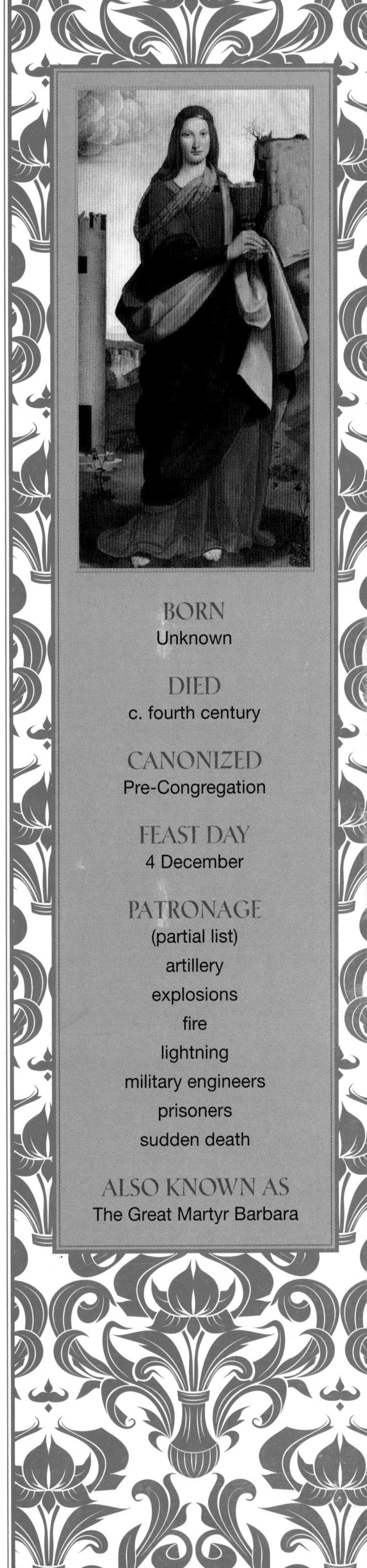

BORN
Unknown

DIED
c. fourth century

CANONIZED
Pre-Congregation

FEAST DAY
4 December

PATRONAGE
(partial list)
artillery
explosions
fire
lightning
military engineers
prisoners
sudden death

ALSO KNOWN AS
The Great Martyr Barbara

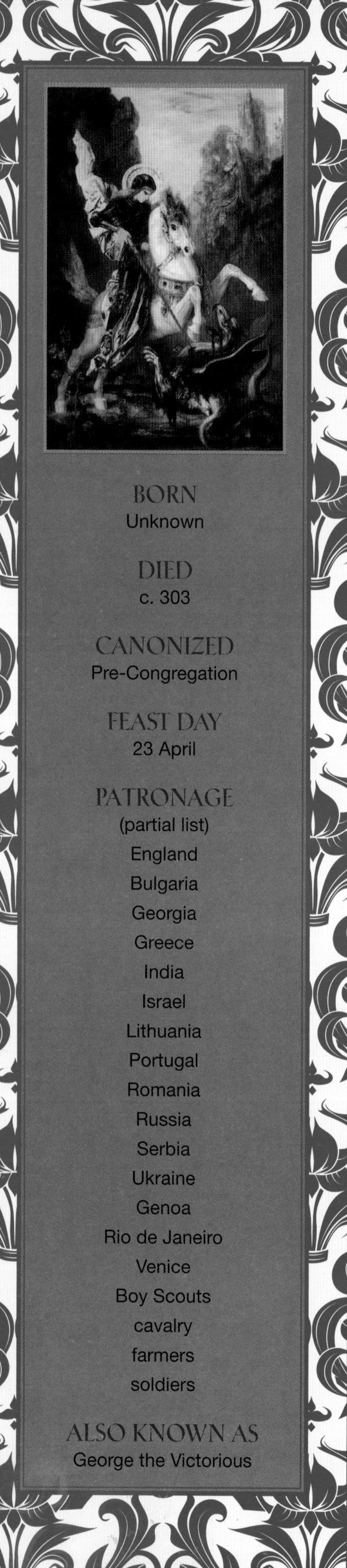

BORN
Unknown

DIED
c. 303

CANONIZED
Pre-Congregation

FEAST DAY
23 April

PATRONAGE
(partial list)
England
Bulgaria
Georgia
Greece
India
Israel
Lithuania
Portugal
Romania
Russia
Serbia
Ukraine
Genoa
Rio de Janeiro
Venice
Boy Scouts
cavalry
farmers
soldiers

ALSO KNOWN AS
George the Victorious

Saint GEORGE

While travelling one day, George passed a swamp near a village plagued by a dragon. The villagers had to bring sheep to the dragon every day, and when they ran out of sheep they started to draw lots and send the unlucky winner instead. The day George came to the swamp he discovered that the villagers had sent the princess to the dragon. George made the sign of the cross over the dragon and stabbed it with his lance. He then took the princess's garter, threw it around the dragon's neck, and led the beast to the village, where he killed it. The relieved king offered George many riches, but the saint refused and went on his way.

George's famous legend dates from the eleventh or twelfth century and is surely not historical truth. In reality, George was a soldier and officer in Emperor Diocletian's guard and seems to have been held in high regard. Nevertheless, he publicly protested the emperor's persecution of Christians at the beginning of the fourth century and as a result was tortured and martyred. He became a very popular saint in both Eastern and Western Christianity during the Middle Ages, and Crusaders bore his arms – a red cross on a white background – into battle. Eventually, England adopted George's cross as the nation's flag; it appears also in the Union flag representing the United Kingdom.

Many cities and nations claim George as their patron, including Russia, which shows an image of the saint at the centre of its coat of arms.

Saint Agnes of Rome

One of several popular virgin martyrs, Agnes is said to have died in the Diocletian persecution in Rome at the age of 13 or even 12. Her legend, which dates to the fifth century, resembles the legends of several other virgin martyrs: having consecrated her virginity to Jesus Christ, she refused to marry a pagan suitor, who first tried to place her in a brothel (one source relates that he was struck blind when he tried to touch her, but Agnes restored his sight through prayer), then denounced her to the authorities. The specifics of her martyrdom are unclear; various sources say she died by burning, decapitation, or the sword (slitting her throat).

Agnes appears frequently in medieval artwork, usually appearing as a young girl accompanied by her emblem, a lamb – symbol of Christ and purity and whose Latin name (agnus) *inspired the association.*

Although her legend cannot be trusted in its details, early veneration of Agnes is shown from her inclusion in a martyrology of 354, while Saint Ambrose, Saint Jerome, and Pope Damasus I all included her in their writings on martyrs.

Agnes was buried in Rome, and during the reign of Constantine a basilica was erected over the catacombs that contained her grave. Basilica di Sant'Agnese Fuori le Mura (Basilica of St Agnes Outside the Walls), rebuilt in the seventh century, still houses her tomb.

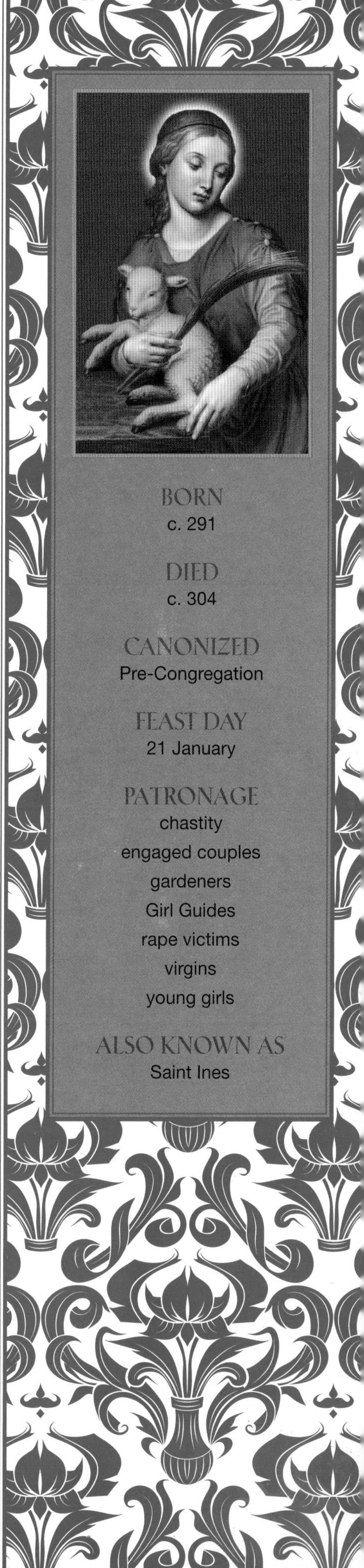

BORN
c. 291

DIED
c. 304

CANONIZED
Pre-Congregation

FEAST DAY
21 January

PATRONAGE
chastity
engaged couples
gardeners
Girl Guides
rape victims
virgins
young girls

ALSO KNOWN AS
Saint Ines

A Closer Look: *Hagiography*

Hagiography is the study of saints. These works attempt to record the lives and, especially, the miracles associated with these holy women and men.

THE ART OF HAGIOGRAPHY

The art of writing a saint's life, or hagiography, flourished in the Middle Ages, especially in the stone houses of God – monasteries, churches, and cathedrals – that sheltered the literature and learning of an age. These hagiographies are an extraordinary font of knowledge, not only about the saints but also, more subtly, about those who wrote about them. Sometimes hagiographers wrote with political motives, to lionize one saint – and the church that held his relics – and thus encourage pilgrimages, donations, and the slow assumption of power. Mostly, however, hagiographers wrote to glorify their subject; some of the best hagiographers, like Bede the Venerable or Gregory of Tours, became saints in their own right. Although these hagiographies, which encouraged conversion, were a vital source of history, especially in the Middle Ages, they are still valuable today. They constitute a record of the most significant Christian holy men and women, and their value cannot be overstated.

An illustration from a copy of Bede the Venerable's The Life and Miracles of St Cuthbert, Bishop of Lindesfarne, *shows King Athelstan presenting the work to the saint.*

The martyrdom of Saints Primus and Felician, from a fourteenth-century manuscript of The Golden Legend

The Bollandists

Perhaps the most famous hagiographers and hagiolaters (those who study hagiology) are the Bollandists, named after their founder, Jean Bolland (1596–1665).

Bolland, a Jesuit priest, became interested in compiling and examining the lives of the saints. The first two volumes of the work, *Acta Sanctorum (Acts of the Saints)*, were published in 1643. The sixty-eighth and final volume was published in 1940, but the Bollandists still research and publish today.

MARIÆ
MAGDALENÆ
REGIÆ PRINCIPI HUNGARIÆ, BOHEMIÆ ET SERENISSIMÆ
ARCHIDUCI
DUCI BURGUNDIÆ, BRABANTIÆ, LUXEMBURGI, LIMBURGI, GELDRIÆ, STYRIÆ, CARINTHIÆ, CARNIOLIÆ: COMITI FLANDRIÆ, NAMURCI TYROLIS, GORITIÆ &c.

Mmenſa prope operis noſtri de Actis Sanctorum moles ut nova acceſſione continuo accreſcit, ita poſt ſeptem menſis Junii & quatuor Julii tomos, hic ordine duodecimus eſt Auſtriacis auſpiciis editus, Tuo autem nomini, ARCHIDUX SERENISSIMA,
*
ex

The dedication page of the Bollandists' Acta Sanctorum, *July volume 5 (1727), to Maria Magdalena, of Austria, sister of Emperor Charles VI.*

THE LIVES OF THE SAINTS

Dating from 996 to 997, this important work, written by Abbot Ælfric of Eynsham, covers the lives of 39 saints, including some of the earliest saints of the Roman Catholic Church.

THE GOLDEN LEGEND

First appearing near the year 1260, *The Golden Legend* by Jacobus de Voragine was one of Europe's most popular and widely disseminated books into the sixteenth century. De Voragine, Archbishop of Genoa, wrote in Latin, but over the centuries translators made his work widely available to vernacular audiences. *The Golden Legend* outlines the biographies of some two hundred saints, and to compile this impressive collection, the archbishop likely drew on more than one hundred different sources. Filled with miracles and fantastic tales (even de Voragine found some of them unlikely), *The Golden Legend* still delights today and provides important insight into the worship of saints in the Late Medieval period.

The Crucifixion *by Ottaviano Nelli, which adorns the Chapel of the Trinci Palace, in Foligno, Italy, shows (at far left) the Archbishop Jacobus de Voragine present at the event with his book* The Golden Legend *in his hands.*

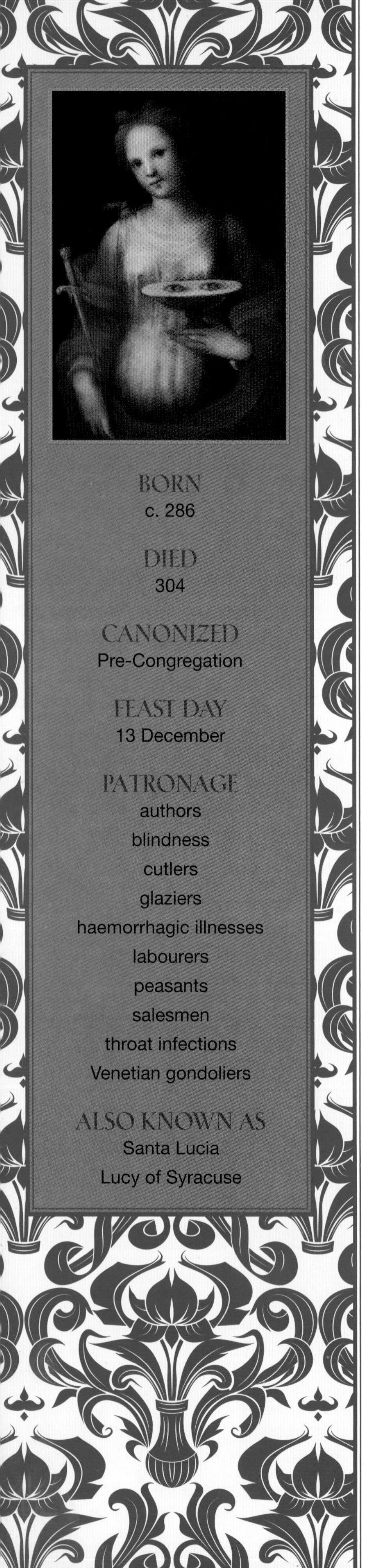

BORN
c. 286

DIED
304

CANONIZED
Pre-Congregation

FEAST DAY
13 December

PATRONAGE
authors
blindness
cutlers
glaziers
haemorrhagic illnesses
labourers
peasants
salesmen
throat infections
Venetian gondoliers

ALSO KNOWN AS
Santa Lucia
Lucy of Syracuse

Saint Lucy

According to legend, Lucy was born in Syracuse to wealthy parents. Raised by her mother, a woman of dubious piety named Eutychia, Lucy consecrated her virginity to God while still a girl. Despite Lucy's objections, Eutychia betrothed her to a pagan, Paschasius.

Demonstrating the power of true Christian faith, Lucy took her mother on a pilgrimage to the tomb of Saint Agatha, where Eutychia was miraculously cured of a haemorrhagic disease. Eutychia spared her daughter a pagan marriage, allowing Lucy to distribute their wealth among the poor.

All might have been well but for the greed of Paschasius, who betrayed Lucy to the Roman authorities, who were then engaged in Rome's most brutal Christian persecution. Brought before the governor and commanded to worship Roman gods, Lucy refused.

The governor ordered Lucy to prostitute herself, but she proclaimed, "The greater my defilement against my will, the surer is my maidenhood." She avoided debasement, for though many men attempted to carry her to a brothel the Holy Spirit rendered her immovable. Fire was brought against her, but she would not burn; they blinded her, but her vision returned. Lucy was finally executed by the sword, but not before prophesying the downfall of Emperors Diocletian and Maximian.

Saint Lucy's Day

Lucy's cult became enormously popular in Scandinavia, where even today largely Protestant or even secular communities still celebrate Saint Lucy's Day on 13 December.

It is still traditional for one girl in each family to dress up as Lucy in a long white dress and red sash. She wears a crown of evergreens topped with lit candles and walks through the darkened house bearing a tray of buns and coffee.

In Sweden, it is typically the youngest daughter who serves her family lussekatter, *or "Lucy's cats", on the morning of Saint Lucy's Day.*

Saint Anastasia

Although Anastasia was one of the most venerated saints of the Christian Church in the fourth and fifth centuries, very little is known about her life. Late legends call her a Roman noblewoman educated by Saint Chrysogonus, but she was martyred in Sirmium, a major Roman city whose ruins are now in Serbia. It is certain that both she and Saint Chrysogonus died during Emperor Diocletian's persecution of Christians.

According to one late tradition Anastasia inadvertently revealed her religion to court officials when she learned of Chrysogonus's death by beheading, weeping for her teacher as she did so. She refused repeated efforts to force her to renounce Christianity, miraculously surviving attempts to drown her and starve her to death before dying a martyr in the flames.

Although today Saint Anastasia is relatively obscure, one trace of her former glory remains: she is the only saint given a special commemoration in the second Mass of the Roman liturgy on 25 December, which was celebrated in her honour for many years before the day was adopted for Jesus Christ.

The Diocletian Persecution

Christianity had been illegal in the Roman Empire since the late first century, but major persecutions instigated by Roman emperors did not begin until 249, when Emperor Decius declared that everyone in the Empire had to make a pagan sacrifice before empire officials. Persecutions waxed and waned for the next 50 years, until Emperor Diocletian undertook the final and most extensive attempt to eradicate Christianity in 303.

Until then, Christians had enjoyed relative peace under his reign; but the emperor now tried to force the old pagan religion of Rome onto his subjects. The Great Persecution would last a full ten years, even after Diocletian abdicated in 305. Many Christians suffered martyrdom during this period, often enduring torture in addition to painful deaths, but ultimately the persecution failed. Far from being stamped out, Christianity became the official religion of Rome when Constantine marched his victorious troops into the city in 312.

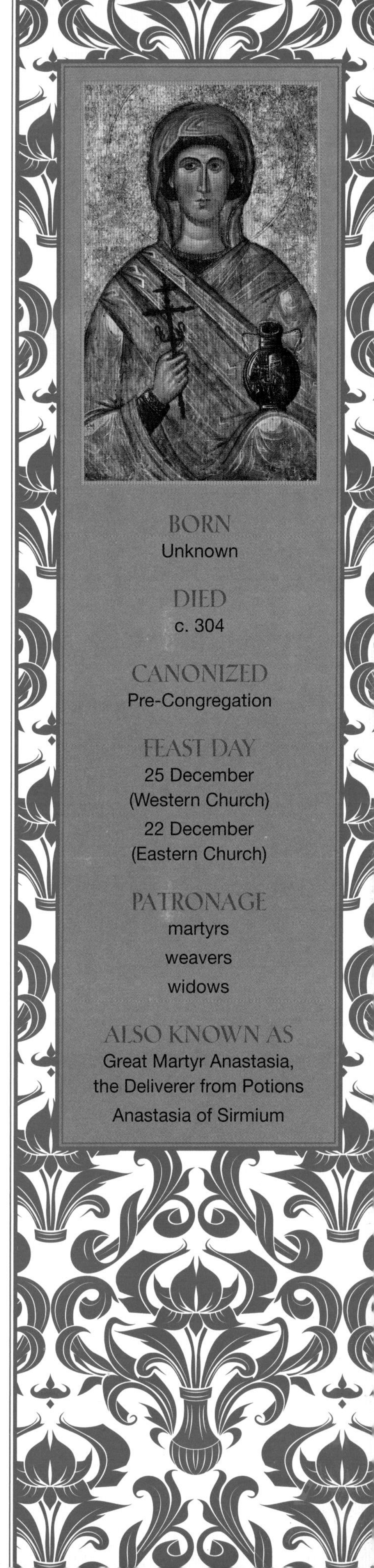

BORN
Unknown

DIED
c. 304

CANONIZED
Pre-Congregation

FEAST DAY
25 December
(Western Church)
22 December
(Eastern Church)

PATRONAGE
martyrs
weavers
widows

ALSO KNOWN AS
Great Martyr Anastasia,
the Deliverer from Potions
Anastasia of Sirmium

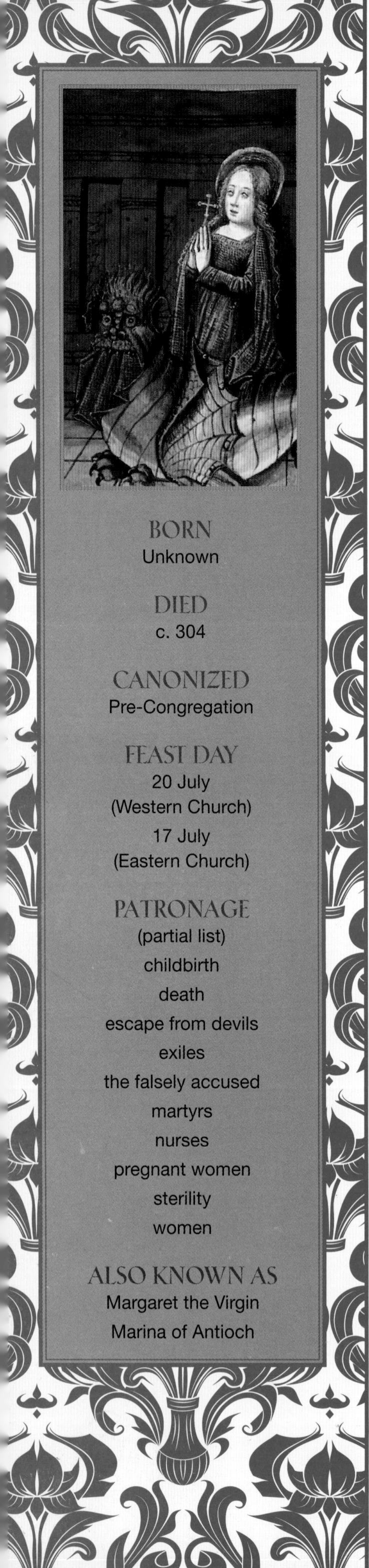

BORN
Unknown

DIED
c. 304

CANONIZED
Pre-Congregation

FEAST DAY
20 July
(Western Church)
17 July
(Eastern Church)

PATRONAGE
(partial list)
childbirth
death
escape from devils
exiles
the falsely accused
martyrs
nurses
pregnant women
sterility
women

ALSO KNOWN AS
Margaret the Virgin
Marina of Antioch

Saint Margaret *of Antioch*

Although she was one of the most popular medieval saints, nothing of historical value is known about Margaret; no one can even say with certainty when she lived. The untrustworthiness of sources led Pope Paul VI to suppress her cult and remove her feast day from the Roman calendar in 1969. Yet her popularity in former times was immense, and even now some researchers suspect she may have both lived and been martyred even if nothing else can be stated with confidence.

Her legend, known in several versions from the Middle Ages, states that she was born in Antioch to a pagan priest, but that she was raised by a Christian foster mother, her own mother having died soon after Margaret's birth. Though very beautiful, she was chaste and holy, and when her beauty attracted the attentions of a pagan prefect she rejected his advances. Scorned, the prefect turned Margaret over to the authorities, denouncing her as a Christian. Miraculously saved from fire and boiling water, Margaret wrestled with the Devil himself while in prison. Satan appeared as a dragon and swallowed her, but the young woman made the sign of the cross, and the demon disgorged her and vanished. Her piety and grace at her place of execution caused the watching multitude to convert, whereupon they were all martyred before Margaret herself was beheaded.

The Fourteen Holy Helpers

During the Middle Ages, faithful Catholics in the Rhineland, Hungary, and parts of Scandinavia venerated a group of 14 saints whose intercession was thought to be particularly effective against earthly trials. They became especially popular in the fourteenth century, when the bubonic plague first struck Europe's cities. All save Saint Giles are martyrs. The specific saints in the grouping changed somewhat depending on time and place, but the usual list includes Saints Acacius, Barbara, Blaise, Catherine of Alexandria, Christopher, Cyricus, Denis of Paris, Erasmus, Eustace, George, Giles, Margaret of Antioch, Pantaleon and Vitus.

Saint CATHERINE of Alexandria

Catherine, according to her legend, was born to a noble family and was evidently a determined, brave young woman. Not content to wait out the persecution of Christians under the Roman emperors of the first decade of the fourth century, Catherine travelled to Emperor Maximian and remonstrated with him stubbornly. Irritated, the emperor called forth his pagan philosophers, but these learned men were no match for the educated young Christian, and she managed to convert some of the philosophers, a host of soldiers, and even the empress – all of whom the furious Maximian executed. He sent Catherine to die an agonizing death on the spiked wheel, but the instrument was broken through the intercession of an angel. Catherine was beheaded instead, whereupon angels flew her body to Mount Sinai.

Catherine of Alexandria is usually depicted with a large wheel. According to tradition, she was sentenced to execution on one of these devices. It miraculously broke before it could kill her, so she was instead beheaded. The wheel, also called the breaking wheel, then became known as the Catherine wheel.

The fabulous nature of Catherine's story led the Vatican to suppress her cult in 1969, but Pope John Paul II restored her to the Catholic calendar in 2002. Today her cult is fairly modest, but during the Middle Ages she maintained a large following, in some cases rivalling devotion to the apostles. Along with her fellow virgin martyrs Barbara and Margaret of Antioch, Catherine was one of the most valued of the Fourteen Holy Helpers.

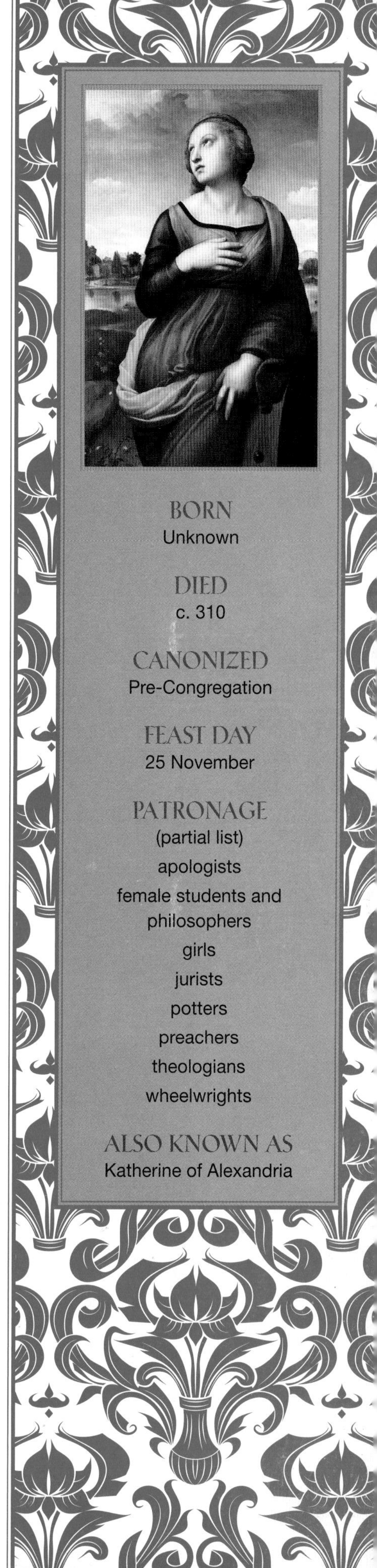

BORN
Unknown

DIED
c. 310

CANONIZED
Pre-Congregation

FEAST DAY
25 November

PATRONAGE
(partial list)
apologists
female students and philosophers
girls
jurists
potters
preachers
theologians
wheelwrights

ALSO KNOWN AS
Katherine of Alexandria

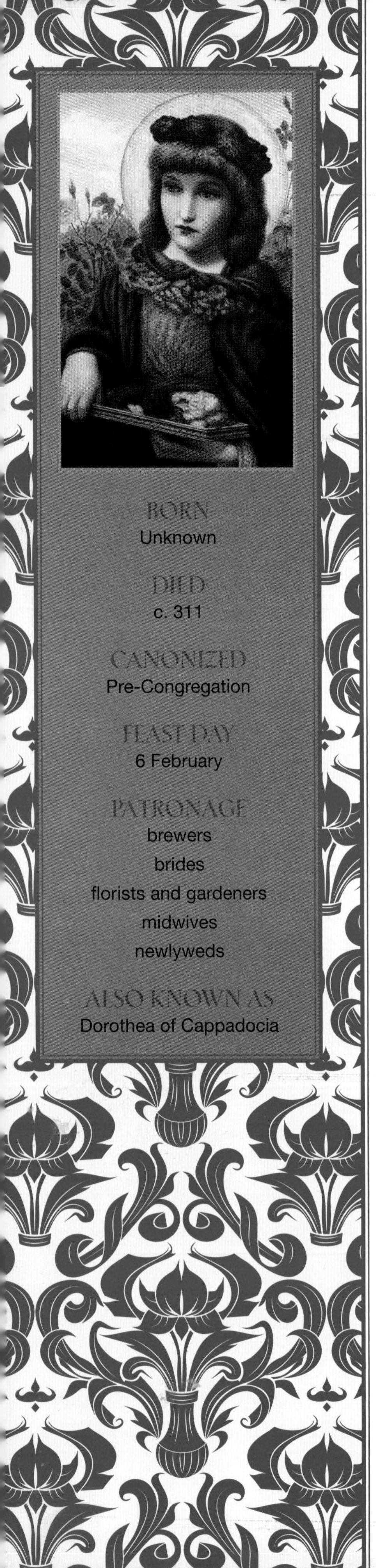

BORN
Unknown

DIED
c. 311

CANONIZED
Pre-Congregation

FEAST DAY
6 February

PATRONAGE
brewers
brides
florists and gardeners
midwives
newlyweds

ALSO KNOWN AS
Dorothea of Cappadocia

Saint Dorothea of Caesarea

Sometime during the Diocletian persecution, Roman officials placed Dorothea of Caesarea on trial for the crime of practising Christianity. In an effort to force her to apostatize, they tortured her and even sent her two sisters to her prison cell. Fearing torture, her sisters had renounced Christ, but though the Roman governor expected Dorothea to follow their example, Dorothea instead persuaded them to return to their faith. She watched as they suffered martyrdom together, supporting them all the while with visions of Heaven and God's mercy.

On the way to her own execution she encountered Theophilus, a pagan lawyer, among the gathering crowd. "Bride of Christ", he mocked her as she passed, "send me some fruits from your bridegroom's garden." Gravely, Dorothea nodded her head, and Theophilus and his companions cruelly laughed. Yet just before her execution, Dorothea prayed, and an angelic child appeared. Dorothea gave the child her headdress and sent it to Theophilus who, stunned, smelled roses and fruits on the blessed garment. Converting on the spot, he earned the crown of martyrdom alongside Saint Dorothea.

Dorothea is often depicted with an angel. In late medieval Sweden, she was counted as a fifteenth Holy Helper. She, along with Saints Barbara, Catherine of Alexandria, and Margaret of Antioch, is known as one of the "Main Virgins".

Little of Dorothea's legend can be substantiated and, in 1969, the Vatican removed her feast day from the Roman Catholic calendar. Although of fairly minor status today, Dorothea enjoyed a widespread cult in the Middle Ages, and her legend inspired her patronage of flowers, trees and gardeners.

Saint Blaise

The decade-long Diocletian persecution ended in the West when Emperor Constantine converted to Christianity. In the East, however, where Roman Emperor Licinius governed, the persecution continued until 324. During this time Blaise, Bishop of Sebaste in Cappadocia, retired to a cave (traditionally on Mount Erciyes) in the arid, pockmarked Cappadocian landscape. According to legend, wild birds found and succoured him there, and he performed many miracles.

Despite his seclusion, soldiers of the local governor, Agricolaus, found Blaise. During his torture with iron wool combs, several Christian women were forced to collect the saint's blood; the governor then told them to sacrifice to pagan idols, but instead the women tossed the idols into a lake. Infuriated, the governor not only executed the women but also their children. Blaise underwent further torture before his own execution by beheading.

A physician before he became a bishop, Blaise became a highly venerated saint during the Middle Ages and is listed as one of the Fourteen Holy Helpers. His intercession was sought against all manner of illness.

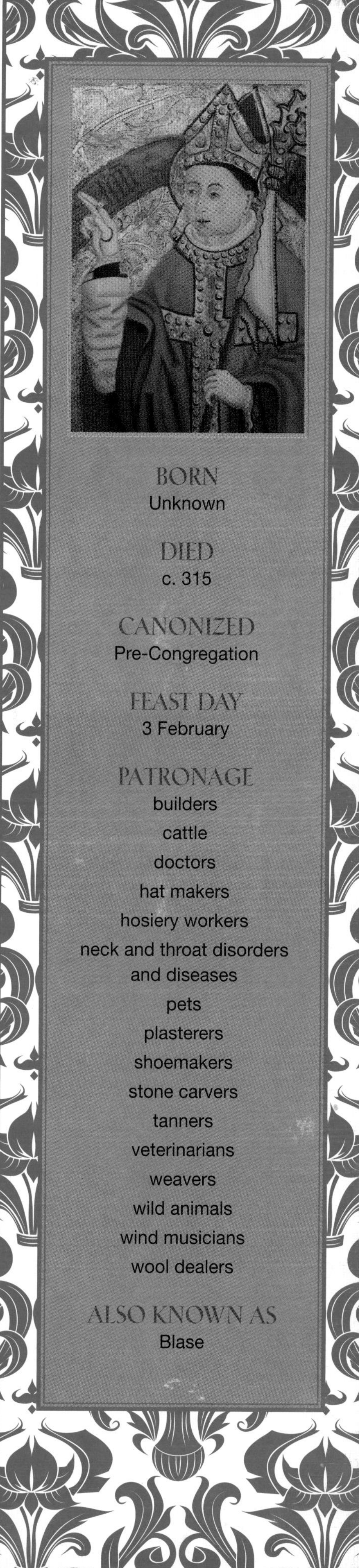

BORN
Unknown

DIED
c. 315

CANONIZED
Pre-Congregation

FEAST DAY
3 February

PATRONAGE
builders
cattle
doctors
hat makers
hosiery workers
neck and throat disorders and diseases
pets
plasterers
shoemakers
stone carvers
tanners
veterinarians
weavers
wild animals
wind musicians
wool dealers

ALSO KNOWN AS
Blase

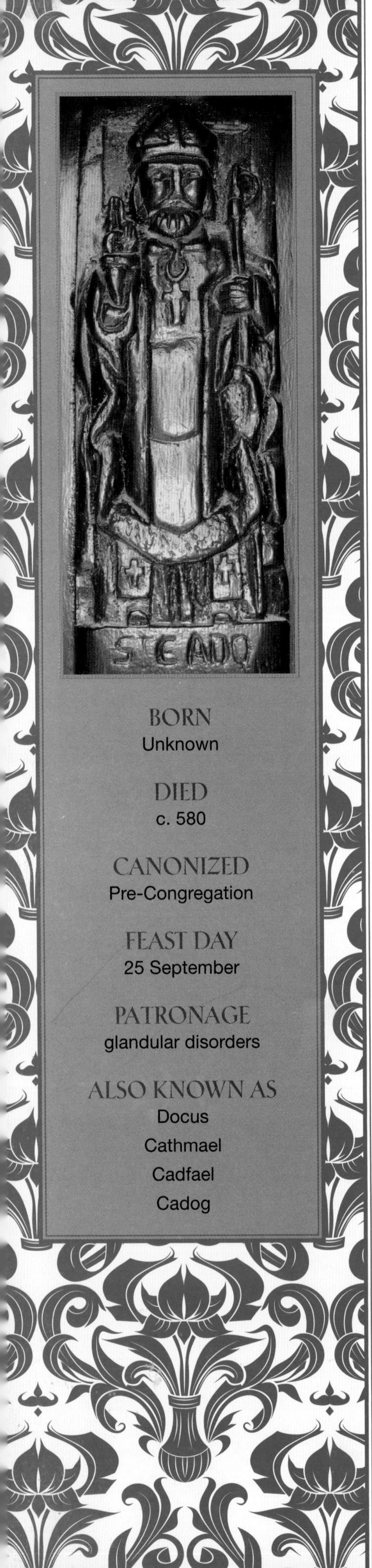

BORN
Unknown

DIED
c. 580

CANONIZED
Pre-Congregation

FEAST DAY
25 September

PATRONAGE
glandular disorders

ALSO KNOWN AS
Docus
Cathmael
Cadfael
Cadog

Saint Cadoc

Born the son of a king, Cadoc, one of the main saints of Wales, renounced his heritage, became a monk, and converted his royal parents to Christianity. The monastery he founded at Llancarfan became a major centre of learning and is associated with several other British saints, among them Gildas the Wise and Illtyd, a supposed kinsman of King Arthur.

With a foundation dating from around 1200, Saint Cadoc's Church in Llancarfan stands on the site of Cadoc's sixth-century abbey.

After founding his monastery, Cadoc roamed the world, establishing a second monastery in Scotland, travelling to Rome and Greece, and returning from Jerusalem with water from the River Jordan, with which he created a well at Llancarfan whose healing powers earned it centuries of renown. Despite this fame, the monastery did not survive the Norman invasions of the eleventh and twelfth centuries. A church was rebuilt on the location, however, and still stands today. Cadoc himself, a consummate traveller and tireless missionary, met his own end among the still-pagan Saxons of Britain, who martyred him somewhere near Weedon, England, around the year 580.

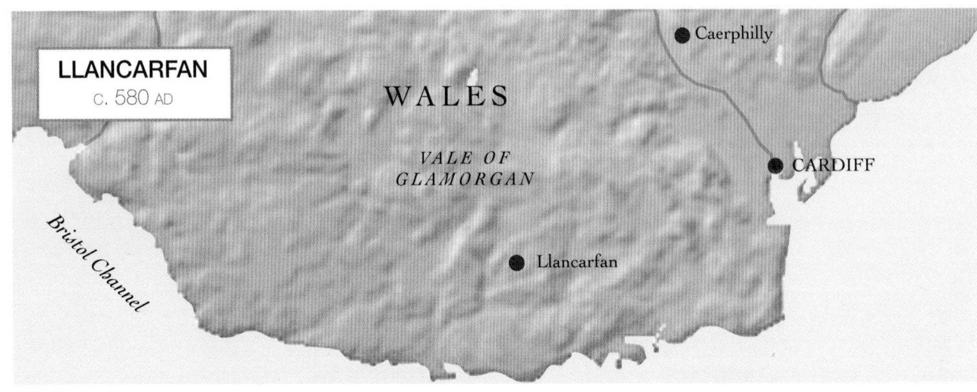

Saint Stanislaus of Szczepanów

Born into nobility on July 26, 1030, Stanislaus rose to pre-eminence at a troubled time in the young nation of Poland. Having chosen to adopt Roman Catholicism less than a hundred years earlier, in 966, Poland sat on what was still a developing frontier, facing both Eastern Orthodox Christianity on one side and the still mostly pagan peoples of the eastern Baltic on the other.

Stanislaus's famous oratorical skills converted many undecided and lapsed Catholics within Poland's own borders, but it was his relationship with tyrannical King Boleslaus II that ultimately led to his sainthood and martyrdom. Boleslaus II enjoyed resounding military success, but his bullying personality alienated him from the Church as well as the Polish nobility. When a nobleman's wife refused to commit adultery he outraged the nobles by abducting and imprisoning her, but his absolute power kept them silent.

By now the bishop of Cracow, Stanislaus would not keep his peace in the face of such effrontery and he excommunicated the wilful king. Even this did not lead to repentance; instead, the king ordered the bishop executed, and when his soldiers refused, Boleslaus himself entered the chapel where Stanislaus was holding the Holy Host during Mass, slaughtering him on 8 May, 1079.

The fourteenth-century Anjou legendarium of the Kings of Hungary illustrates the martyrdom of Saint Stanislaus. The panel on the top left shows his ordination as bishop of Cracow. The top right shows him resurrecting Peter. The bottom left shows King Bolesłaus murdering Stanislaus, and the bottom right shows the king directing his body being cut in pieces.

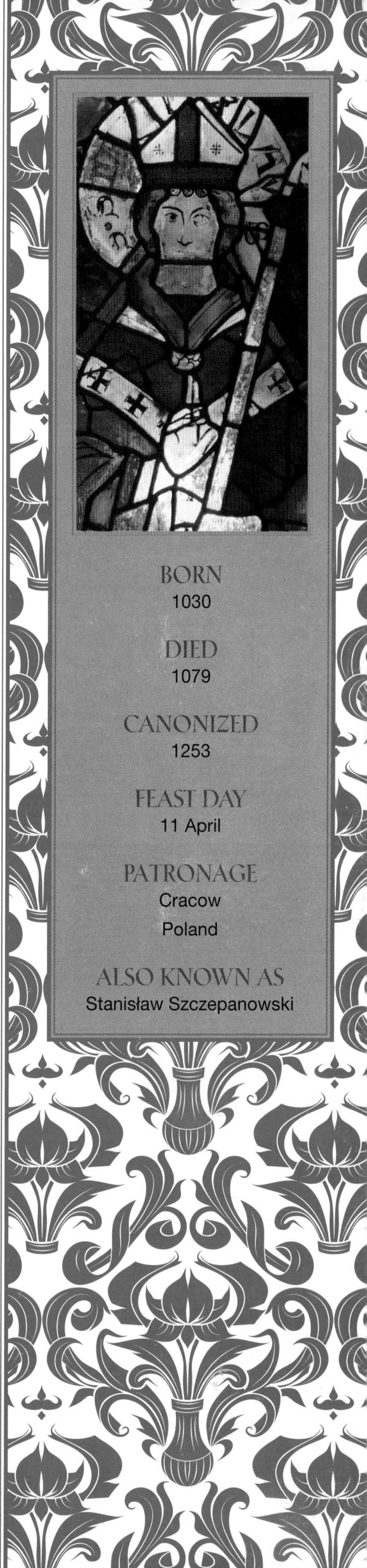

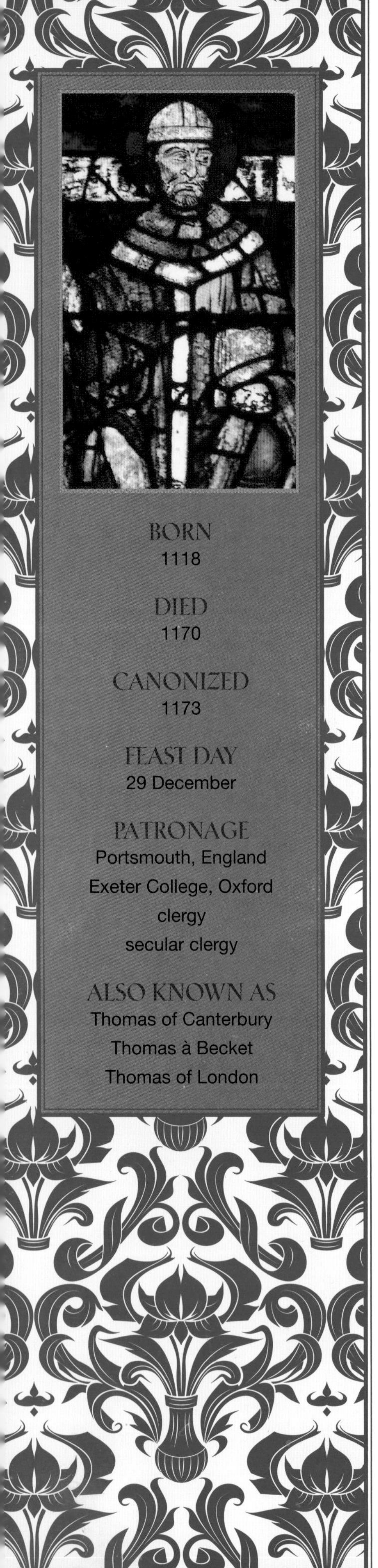

BORN
1118

DIED
1170

CANONIZED
1173

FEAST DAY
29 December

PATRONAGE
Portsmouth, England
Exeter College, Oxford
clergy
secular clergy

ALSO KNOWN AS
Thomas of Canterbury
Thomas à Becket
Thomas of London

Saint THOMAS Becket

"We will triumph over the enemy,", said Saint Thomas Becket on the day of his murder, "through suffering rather than by fighting," and it can hardly be denied that the sainted archbishop of Canterbury suffered, died and triumphed on that cold December day.

As a young man, the London-born Thomas entered the household of the archbishop of Canterbury, the head of all bishops in England. Recognizing Thomas's diverse talents, Archbishop Theobald promoted him several times until Thomas attained the position of archdeacon of Canterbury. Theobald then recommended him to the young Henry II: soon the monarch and the archdeacon were fast friends. In 1155, Henry named Thomas Lord Chancellor, a position second in influence and power only to the king himself.

THE CROWN AND THE MITRE

In 1161 Theobald died, and Henry immediately pressed the vacated post upon his friend. Thomas accepted with reluctance: as archbishop he would have to oppose the king's position towards the Church.

Still Thomas threw himself into his duties as archbishop with all of the considerable acumen and willpower he possessed. Although he had enjoyed a courtly lifestyle, he now gave up fine clothes, walked barefoot, and restricted his diet to the simple meals of a godly man. He disposed of his riches, read and reread the Bible, and practised self-flagellation.

Almost at once, as Thomas predicted, his role as archbishop brought him into conflict with the king. Powerful, overbearing and exceedingly ambitious,

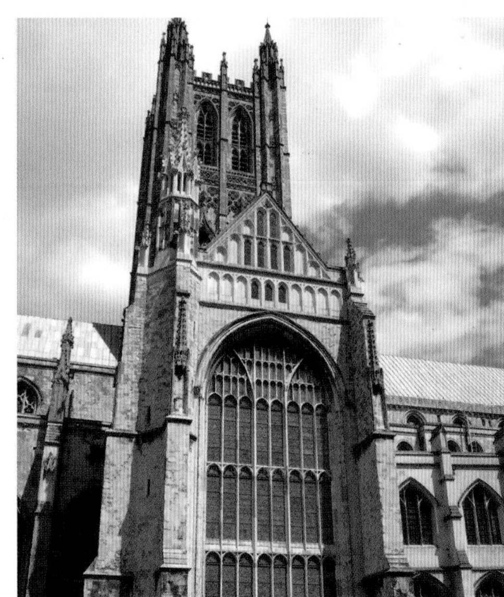

Canterbury Cathedral

Henry resented the Church's considerable power and wealth and, in the autumn of 1163, he put forth a demand that clergy charged with civil crimes be tried not by the Church but by secular authorities.

Thomas flatly refused, prompting Henry to then mount attacks not only on the Church but also on Thomas personally. Sued for an incredible 30,000 pounds and faced with the mighty king's wrath, Thomas fled England. It took several years for the pair to arrive at a partial reconciliation, and Thomas eventually returned to England on 1 December, 1170.

This Meddlesome Priest

The most troublesome issue that remained involved the archbishop of York and the bishops of London and Salisbury. These three had obeyed Henry's wish in crowning his son heir-apparent, a power that had traditionally been Canterbury's alone. Thomas excommunicated the insubordinate bishops and suspended the archbishop. The three then visited Henry while he sojourned in Normandy with his knights and members of court. Henry listened with mounting anger as they recounted Thomas's intractable stance. Finally he shouted, "Will no one rid me of this meddlesome priest?"

No one knows precisely what Henry intended with this remark, but four of his knights took it upon themselves to answer what they understood to be a royal command. Sailing across the channel, the four travelled directly to Canterbury, reaching the cathedral on 29 December, 1170. At first they left their weapons outside and demanded that the excommunicated bishops be restored to the church; when Thomas refused, they left.

Henry may not have issued the order to kill Thomas, but his words stirred his knights to act.

Later that day as Thomas led the gathered monks into the cloister, the armoured knights reappeared, weapons in hand. Frightened, the monks scattered, leaving Thomas alone with his stalwart friend, Edward Grim. Even the sight of the archbishop standing robed in his cloister and the sound of distant monks singing vespers did not stay the knights. Again they demanded that Thomas receive the bishops, and again Thomas refused. "Then you will now die," warned the knights. Brave Thomas lifted his eyes and thoughts to Heaven and replied: "And I am prepared to die for my Lord." Swords rose and fell in the shadows of Canterbury's cathedral, spilling on holy ground the blood of the archbishop, a man once loved by the king and now murdered by his men.

King Henry II of England: both friend and enemy of the martyred saint.

Saint THOMAS More

BORN
7 February, 1477 or 1478

DIED
6 July, 1535

CANONIZED
1935

FEAST DAY
22 June

PATRONAGE
adopted children
civil servants
large families
lawyers
politicians
statesmen
step-parents
troubled marriages
widowers

Until his final years, Thomas More seemed to lead a blessed life. A pious man, witty and intelligent, he flirted with joining a monastic order but instead married and entered public life, receiving an excellent education at Oxford and becoming a brilliant lawyer.

Sir Thomas's career soared until 1529 when he became Lord Chancellor of England, in which capacity he served a scant three years. That year the English king, Henry VIII, determined to divorce his wife, Catherine of Aragon, in order to marry Anne Boleyn. The pope's refusal to allow the divorce led to increasingly bad relations between Henry and the Roman Catholic Church, and eventually led Henry to break away from the Church entirely, taking his nation with him.

> *More is a man of an angel's wit and singular learning. . . . A man for all seasons.*
>
> Robert Whittington, 1520

Sir Thomas entered the Tower of London, where he was executed, through the Traitor's Gate.

Sir Thomas had maintained a close relationship with Henry, but he could no longer bear the king's behaviour. Resigning his post as Lord Chancellor, he refused to acknowledge the legitimacy of Anne Boleyn and ultimately refused to accept either the Act of Succession, which disinherited Catherine's daughter, or the Oath of Supremacy, which placed the monarch at the head of the Church of England. The irate Henry imprisoned Thomas in the Tower of London and had him executed there, on 6 July, 1535. More's legendary final words were, "I die the King's good servant – but God's first."

Saint ANDREW Kim Taegon

It was not until the late nineteenth century that Korea began to open its borders to Westerners and Western influences. Before then, Korea had strictly prohibited the influx of foreign cultures, so that even though the first Christians arrived in the late sixteenth century, Christianity was not widely practised there for many years.

Nevertheless, many Koreans converted to Catholicism despite the shortage of priests. Among the converts were Andrew Kim Taegon's parents, who baptized him at 15 and sent him to a seminary in Portuguese Macau. Ordained as a priest in 1845, he became the first native Korean priest, returning in secret to his country to minister to Christians there. The nineteenth century saw repeated persecutions of Korean Christians under the isolationist Joseon Dynasty. Andrew Kim Taegon's own father had fallen victim to a persecution in 1821; in 1846, his son followed in his footsteps, suffering first torture and then beheading.

> *How can persecution be considered as anything other than the command of God?*
>
> SAINT ANDREW KIM TAEGON

Korean Catholics suffered particularly severe persecutions in 1839, 1846 and 1866, with at least eight thousand of the faithful killed. In 1984, 103 of these martyrs were canonized.

Andrew Kim Taegon was one of 103 Korean martyrs canonized by Pope John Paul II on May 6, 1984. Among the others were 13-year-old Peter Yu Taechoi and Paul Chong Hasang, who was martyred in 1839 and was considered a founder of the Korean Catholic Church for his tireless efforts to unite Korean Christians and win religious tolerance for them.

BORN
10 December, 1855

DIED
11 June, 1900

CANONIZED
2000
(Eastern Orthodox Church)

FEAST DAY
11 June
(Eastern Church)

PATRONAGE
None

ALSO KNOWN AS
The Priest Mitrophan
Metrophanes Chi Sung

Saint MITROPHAN Tsi-Chung

In 1900, a wave of violence swept through China. The Boxer Rebellion, named for the secret society behind it, aimed to kill or drive out all non-Chinese in China. Among those targeted were Christians, Chinese converts, Europeans and Russians.

Hundreds of Christians died during the Rebellion, including the 222 Holy Chinese Martyrs of the Eastern Orthodox Church. Of these, the most famous is Mitrophan Tsi-Chung. Raised a Christian and educated at a Beijing (then called Peking) mission, Tsi-Chung seemed destined for the priesthood but at first refused ordination, feeling that a man of his humble origins did not deserve such an elevated state. Only after much persuasion did he at last relent.

> *How can a man of such low capability and such feeble virtue dare raise to such a high station?*
>
> Saint Mitrophan Tsi-Chung

An icon of the Holy Chinese Martyrs

Many Christians took refuge with Father Mitrophan during the terrible days of rebellion, when Boxers threatened Christians with violence and burned their homes and shops. The storm broke at ten o'clock on the night of 10 June, when soldiers came to Mitrophan's home. They killed him first, stabbing him repeatedly as he knelt in the garden, massacring all who had remained with him – mostly, according to one account, women and children. Elsewhere in the city they tortured and killed members of his family, including his wife, Tatiana, and his sons, Isaac, 23, and Jean, 7. His executioners horrifically

Saint MAXIMILIAN Kolbe

Maximilian Kolbe travelled widely from his native Poland, founding a monastery in Japan and the Knights of the Immaculata (now the Militia of the Immaculata) in Rome. His father fought for Polish independence from Russia and for his troubles was hanged in 1914. Maximilian, an active and pious man even in the turbulent political era in which he was born, lived through World War I, only to contract tuberculosis in 1920.

Maximilian's real troubles, however, did not begin until 1939. Having returned to Poland from Japan in 1936, he was arrested and then released by the Gestapo. For the next two years he harboured refugees and Jews escaping the Nazis and published anti-Nazi material from his friary.

Arrested again in 1941, the Nazis sent Maximilian to Auschwitz, the infamous concentration camp, where he not only endured the trials suffered by all imprisoned there but also comforted and inspired his fellow prisoners. When the guards selected ten victims to suffer death by starvation, Maximilian performed his final act of charity; knowing one of the chosen had a wife and children, he offered to take the man's place. Maximilian and three others survived for two weeks before the impatient guards killed them with injections of carbolic acid. Having led the others in prayer through their starvation, Maximilian now serenely offered his arm for the injection.

For his act of volunteering to die in place of a stranger in the Nazi German concentration camp of Auschwitz (above), Pope Paul VI named Maximilian Kolbe (below) a confessor and an unofficial "martyr of charity".

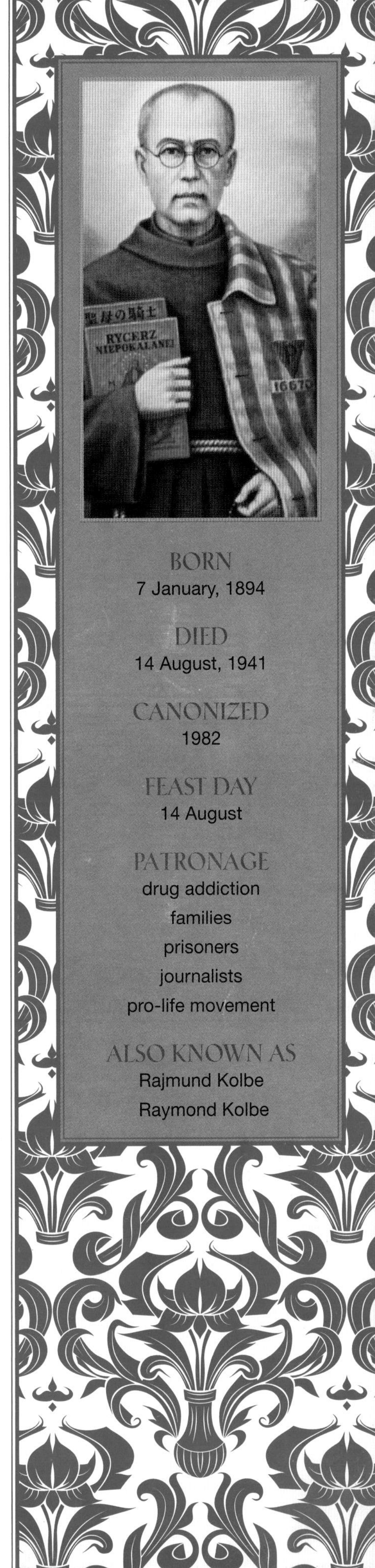

BORN
7 January, 1894

DIED
14 August, 1941

CANONIZED
1982

FEAST DAY
14 August

PATRONAGE
drug addiction
families
prisoners
journalists
pro-life movement

ALSO KNOWN AS
Rajmund Kolbe
Raymond Kolbe

Saints of the Word & the Book

Early Christian theologians laid the groundwork for later contemplation; the most influential are known as Fathers of the Church. These include Athanasius, Basil the Great, Augustine of Hippo, and Hilary of Poitiers, called Greek or Latin Fathers after their primary language and generally from the earliest centuries of the Church. Saint Isidore of Seville, dying in 636, is known as the "last of the Latin Fathers".

Later theologian saints were orthodox scholars, who devoted their intellectual resources to defending the Church and dedicated their lives to God. Saint Jerome retreated to an eremitic existence in the desert; others, like Saints Bonaventure, Francis de Sales and Thérèse of Lisieux, joined monastic orders.

Historians such as Bede the Venerable and Gregory of Tours and brilliant preachers like Anthony of Padua also had a lasting impact on Church doctrine. The greatest Church scholars are called Doctors of the Church, and the influence of some of the most brilliant intellects in this category – such as Augustine of Hippo and Thomas Aquinas – penetrated well beyond the Church. The saints included here not only lived for the Church, but through their words and writings also helped to shape and guide it.

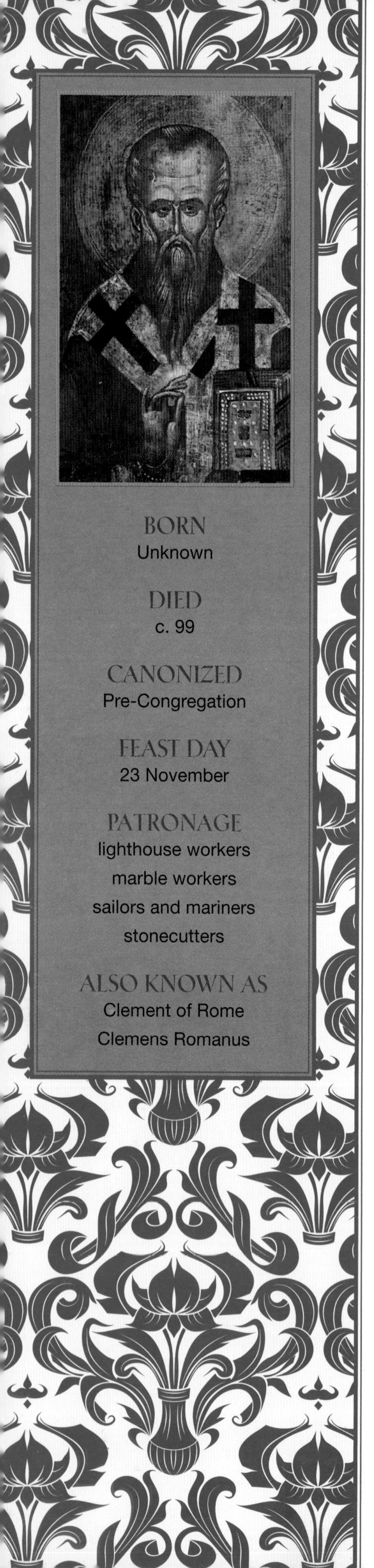

BORN
Unknown

DIED
c. 99

CANONIZED
Pre-Congregation

FEAST DAY
23 November

PATRONAGE
lighthouse workers
marble workers
sailors and mariners
stonecutters

ALSO KNOWN AS
Clement of Rome
Clemens Romanus

Pope Saint Clement I

A student of the Apostles, particularly Peter (who likely ordained Clement as a priest), Clement was one of the first bishops of Rome, a position not yet recognized as the papacy. History says nothing about his life or death, and though Saint Jerome, among others, equates Clement with the Clement mentioned in the Bible (Philippians 4:3) it is unlikely that they are one and the same.

Only one of Clement's writings survives, but it enjoys some prominence among the earliest Christian tracts and establishes him among the Apostolic Fathers – those theologians who led the early Church and knew the Apostles. Writing to admonish the Corinthians, who had deposed their bishops, Clement argued in his letter, known as 1 Clement, that bishops derive their authority from the Apostles (who themselves derived it from Jesus Christ). This would help establish a fundamental church hierarchy. In addition, the very fact of Clement's letter suggests that even at that early date (1 Clement dates as early as year 70), the bishop of Rome occupied a primary place among bishops and other Church leaders.

Around 868, Saint Cyril discovered what he believed to be the relics of Clement, buried with an anchor in a Crimean tomb. Cyril took them to Rome, where they were deposited in the Basilica of Saint Clement along with the relics of Saint Ignatius of Antioch. This basilica, which dates to the fourth century and was known to Jerome, still keeps Clement's relics today.

According to tradition, Pope Saint Clement was martyred by being tied to an anchor and thrown from a boat into the Black Sea.

Saint IRENAEUS

A missionary, bishop, and first of the great theologians, Irenaeus was born in Asia Minor (modern Turkey), but served as a missionary in southern Gaul (France) and became bishop of Lugdunum (Lyons) around 178. As a young man, he was a student of Bishop Saint Polycarp who, together with Pope Saint Clement I and Saint Ignatius of Antioch, is one of the three most significant Apostolic Fathers.

Irenaeus's most important arguments concerned the legitimacy of the Gospel of Saint John, the nature and significance of the Holy Eucharist, and the primacy of the bishop of Rome (not called "pope" nor recognized as the head of the Catholic Church until centuries later). Because Irenaeus was such an early figure and knew Polycarp – who had known John the Evangelist – these arguments carried enormous weight and helped establish Catholic doctrine.

Yet his unremitting position against heretics, particularly Gnostics, gives Irenaeus his fame. Gnostics maintained a dualistic philosophy, which, because it tended to deny that God solely created the material world, was inimical to the Church. Irenaeus's most famous work, *Adversus Haereses* (*Against Heretics*) outlines the Gnostic position in detail before addressing its errors. In the 1940s, an unearthed trove of Gnostic writings vindicated Irenaeus as a fair-minded, accurate writer: he had neither embellished nor altered any Gnostic position to the betterment of his own.

> *The glory of God is a human being fully alive; and to be alive consists in beholding God.*
>
> SAINT IRENAEUS

A statue of Irenaeus from a Copenhagen church.

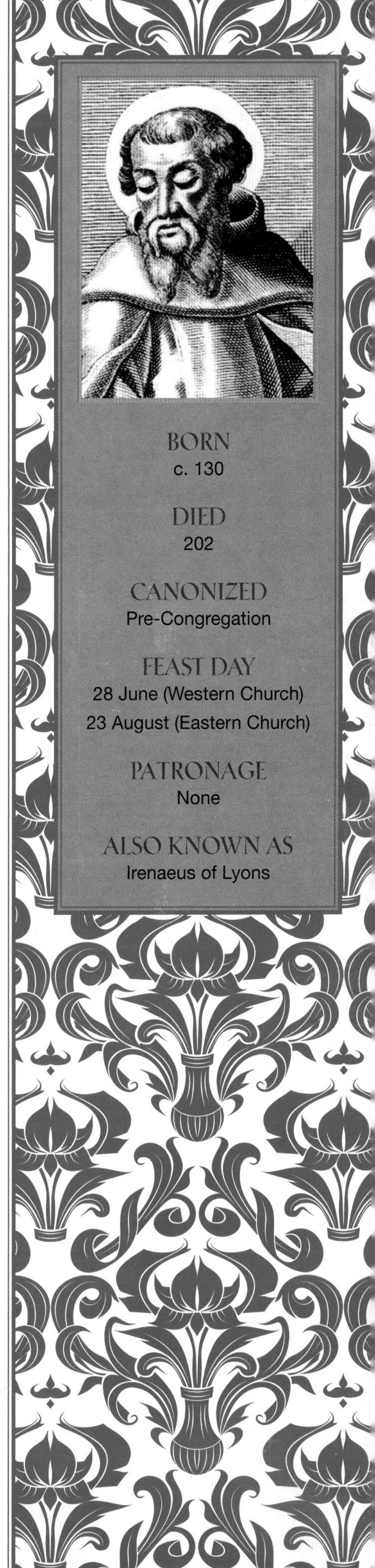

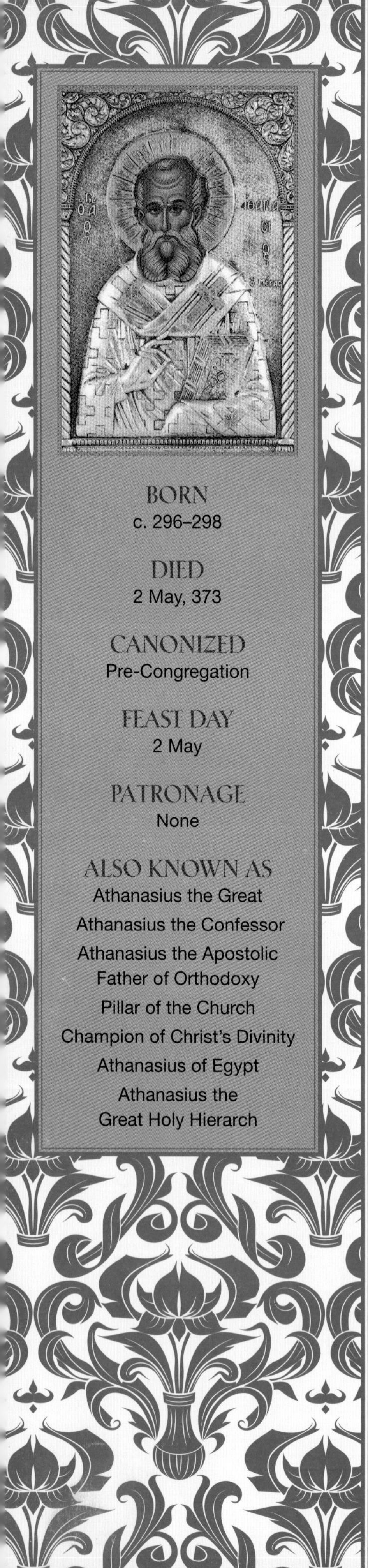

BORN
c. 296–298

DIED
2 May, 373

CANONIZED
Pre-Congregation

FEAST DAY
2 May

PATRONAGE
None

ALSO KNOWN AS
Athanasius the Great
Athanasius the Confessor
Athanasius the Apostolic Father of Orthodoxy
Pillar of the Church
Champion of Christ's Divinity
Athanasius of Egypt
Athanasius the Great Holy Hierarch

Saint ATHANASIUS of Alexandria

By the time Athanasius reached adulthood, Gnosticism, which Saint Irenaeus so successfully railed against, had declined, but a new heresy had risen in the East: Arianism. Arians denied the divinity of Christ, instead proclaiming that God and Jesus Christ were separate, the one having created the other. This made Christ a kind of inferior god. Because the nature of Christ and his relationship to God were central to the Christian faith, this heresy struck at the core of the Church, threatening to overthrow it from within.

> *The Son of God became man so that we might become God.*
>
> Saint Athanasius of Alexandria

THE NICENE CREED

Emperor Constantine himself took an interest in the debate, convening a council to address the subject. The First Council of Nicaea gathered in spring 325 and proceeded to hammer out the Nicene Creed, intending to settle the issue and reunite the orthodox with the heretics. As deacon to Bishop Alexander of Alexandria, Athanasius attended the council and there displayed his theological acumen and unremitting defence of orthodox belief.

The Nicene Creed, later a major tenet of both the Eastern and Western Churches, and indeed many Protestant denominations, stated that God, Christ, and the Holy Spirit were of the same divine substance and manifestations of the one God. The orthodox bishops, however, were too weak to enforce this view, and Arianism neither failed nor flagged. In fact, Constantine's son and heir, Constantius, dedicated himself to the Arian cause.

BISHOP IN EXILE

Bishop of Alexandria since 326, Saint Athanasius mounted a lifelong attack on Arianism. His numerous opponents included his fellow Eastern bishops, along with the emperors of Rome.

The First Council of Nicaea. Although Athanasius was only a deacon and personal secretary to the bishop of Alexandria, he is well remembered for his forceful stand against the Arians in the council.

When he refused Constantine's order to let Arians take communion, false charges were brought against him; when he refused to address the charges at an Arian-staffed synod, the emperor exiled him. It was the first exile of five that this Pillar of the Church (a title bestowed on him by Gregory of Nazianzus) would suffer.

Athanasius wrote constantly during the 17 years he spent in intermittent exile in Rome, Gaul, Asia Minor, and the Egyptian desert. It is possible that he even spent some months hiding in his father's tomb in Alexandria. No fewer than four emperors exiled him, always in sympathy to the Arians for either philosophical or political reasons. Yet despite imperial displeasure, hostile bishops, and the occasional violent crowd, Athanasius never wavered in his faith or his determination to unseat the heresy.

Athanasius finally returned to his bishopric seat in 365. His exiles over, he spent his remaining years still writing until his death on 2 May , 373. The efforts of this stalwart defender of the faith were rewarded when Constantinople hosted the Second General Council in 381, where Gregory of Nyssa put forward an orthodox creed in line with the Nicene. The tireless Athanasius had simply worn out the Arian heresy, and when Constantinople – previously an Arian stronghold – fell, the heretic

Athanasius is buried in Chiesa di San Zaccaria *in Venice, Italy.*

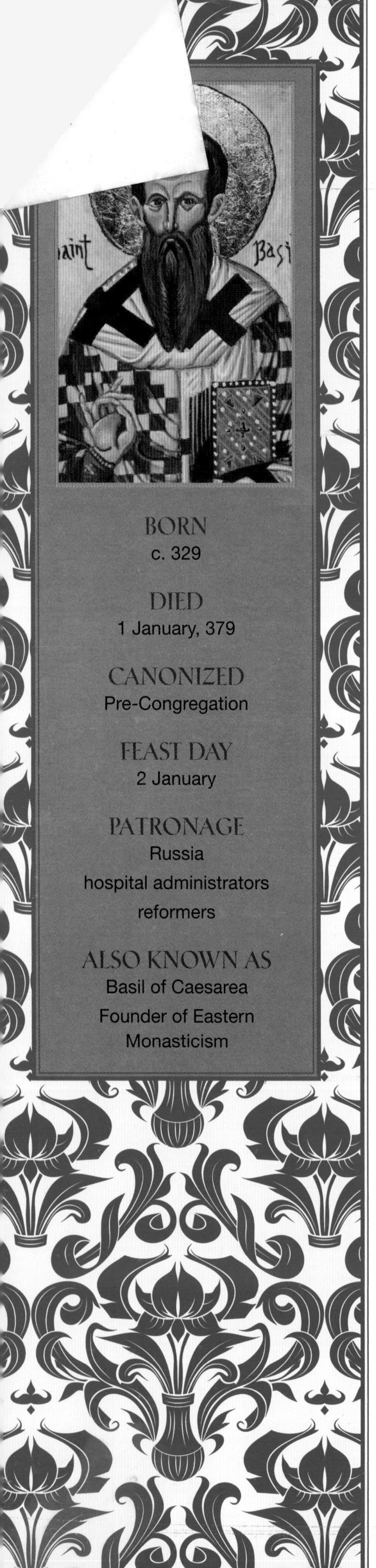

Saint Basil the Great

Born into a veritable dynasty of saints and surrounded by such men as Saints Athanasius, Hilary of Poitiers and Gregory of Nazianzus, Basil the Great nevertheless stands in an exalted position. Recognized as the best among the "Three Cappadocians" – a group that includes Basil's brother, Gregory of Nyssa, and his friend Gregory of Nazianzus – Basil excelled at everything he set his mind to.

An eighteenth-century depiction of Basil celebrating mass with the Arian Emperor Valens in attendance (at foreground right), who is so struck by the angelic occasion that he swoons.

A FAMILY OF SAINTS

In addition to Basil and Gregory of Nyssa, Basil's father, grandmother, brother and sister were all canonized. At first educated by his grandmother, Basil went on to receive an excellent education in Caesarea, Constantinople and Athens, three of the wealthiest cities in the Roman Empire and each home to long traditions of superb pedagogy. In Caesarea he met Gregory of Nazianzus. The two became fast friends in Athens, and despite a falling-out late in life Gregory wrote florid panegyrics in Basil's honour.

Basil might have drifted away from the Church after his exposure to such metropolises, where he had enjoyed considerable successes, but for the example of his sister, Macrina. Macrina had established a sort of protomonastery on the family estate in Pontus, located in Asia Minor. Inspired, Basil travelled widely to monasteries from Egypt to Mesopotamia before returning to Pontus and founding one of his

The Three Holy Hierarchs

Saint Basil the Great ranks high among the saints. The Eastern Orthodox Church and Eastern Catholic Churches have given Basil, Gregory of Nazianzus, and John Chrysostom the title of Three Holy Hierarchs. Basil, Gregory of Nazianzus and Gregory of Nyssa are collectively referred to as the Cappadocian Fathers. The Eastern Orthodox Church and the Roman Catholic Church have also named Basil a Doctor of the Church. He is also referred to as "the revealer of heavenly mysteries".

own. This was the first cenobitic, or communal, monastery in Asia Minor, and Basil dedicated himself to writing a firm and vaunted Rule by which the monks should live and worship. For this feat Basil is called the Founder of Eastern Monasticism.

A Standard of Virtue

While in his early thirties Basil became embroiled in the dispute that threatened to sunder the Church, namely, the issue of Arianism. Second only to Athanasius in combating this heresy, Basil stood firm against the rising heretic tide in Caesarea, so that with Athanasius in Egypt and Hilary of Poitiers in Gaul the three formed a kind of unifying triangle of orthodoxy, one which would eventually win the day – though not, sadly, within any of their lifetimes.

Having founded a monastery (and indeed an entire monastic system) and staked his ground as an orthodox in the face of an extreme but popular heresy, Basil moved now into the episcopal and administrative sphere, where he again excelled.

He took a post under Bishop Eusebius of Caesarea, elected in 362, and proved so effective at his administrative duties that he affronted the bishop. The two men managed to come to an arrangement, however, especially in light of the Arian heresy, and the enormously influential bishopric of Caesarea thus came under Basil's aegis. In 370 he succeeded Eusebius, and in the nine years he served as bishop he turned the church of Caesarea into a model of Christian behaviour. When he died, the entire city, including Jews and pagans, came out to mourn him, for as Gregory of Nazianzus commented in his eulogy, "he was a standard of virtue to us all".

An early map of Asia Minor. Saint Basil the Great, also known as Basil of Caesarea, was the bishop of Caesarea Mazaca in Cappadocia, Asia Minor, which is in modern-day Turkey.

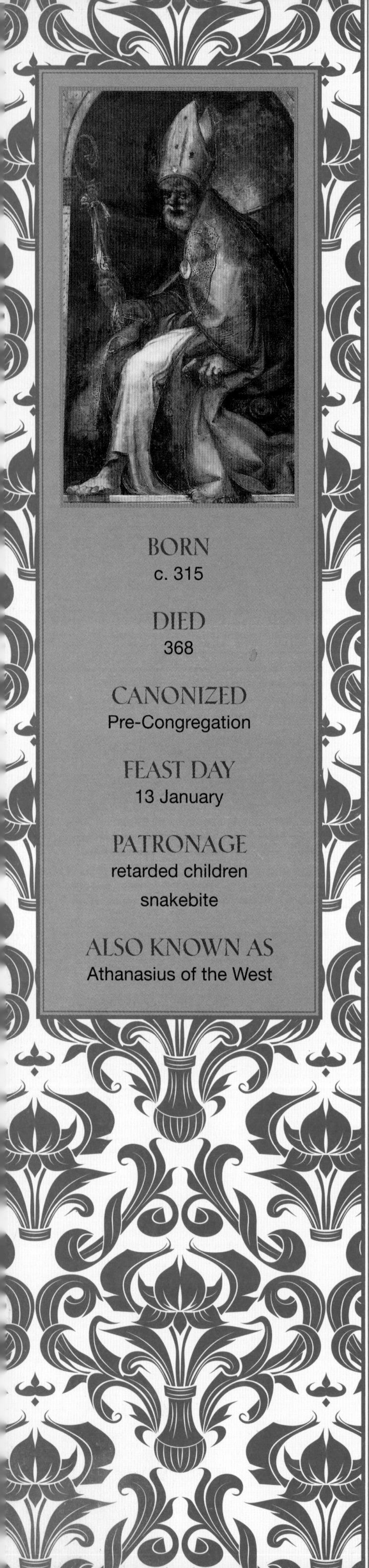

Saint HILARY *of Poitiers*

Hilary was an accomplished scholar by the time he read the Bible and became convinced of its truths. A late convert and former Neoplatonist, Hilary had studied classical rhetoric and philosophy, and as a Christian put these disciplines to work converting his fellow inhabitants of Poitiers and leading the local community there.

He was so successful an orator that, even though he was only a recent convert, the Christians of Poitiers elected him bishop in 350. At the time, the Arian heresy had risen to great heights in the East and now threatened to spread west. The Arians had a powerful adherent in Constantius, emperor of the East, to whom Hilary, valiantly repelling the heresy, appealed personally.

Here, however, his vaunted rhetoric failed him. The emperor exiled the bishop to Phrygia in Asia Minor. Now in the heartland of Arianism, Hilary argued so persuasively for Catholic doctrine that local Arian bishops asked the emperor to send him home. Returning to Poitiers, Hilary continued to combat Arianism in the West even as his contemporary Saint Athanasius did in the East. Sadly, Hilary did not live to see the victory of orthodoxy at the Second General Council in Constantinople in 381, but he certainly deserves credit for halting Arianism's spread into Gaul and helping to turn the tide against the heresy.

For one to attempt to speak of God in terms more precise than He Himself has used: to undertake such a thing is to embark upon the boundless, to dare the incomprehensible.

Saint Hilary of Poitiers

Saint Monica

Saint Monica, chiefly famous as the mother of Saint Augustine, owes her status as patron of mothers to her long and patient suffering on her son's behalf. She struggled with alcoholism and an unhappy marriage, both compounded by difficulties with her mother-in-law, who lived with her and her husband, Patricius. But in the end her quiet patience and faith converted both her mother-in-law and Patricius, a disreputable pagan. Patricius received baptism in the last year of his life, 370, but Monica's efforts to convert her family were not yet over.

Augustine's siblings converted early, but Augustine himself – the eldest – sorely tried his mother's patience. She resorted to prayer after arguing with him ceaselessly for several years, eventually following him to Milan where he had his remarkable conversion experience. After this, she told him, "All my hopes for the world have been fulfilled." She had been praying for his conversion for 17 years. Monica died in Ostia, Italy, a port town, which was a stopping place on their way to Africa. There she was buried and all but forgotten until the thirteenth century, when her cult began in earnest. In the fifteenth century, her relics were moved to Rome and deposited in a chapel to the left of the high altar in the Basilica di Sant'Agostino, which was built in honour of her son.

Monica never gave up on her wayward son, following Augustine across the continent and constantly fasting and praying for him. Her dogged patience and faith converted even her husband and mother-in-law.

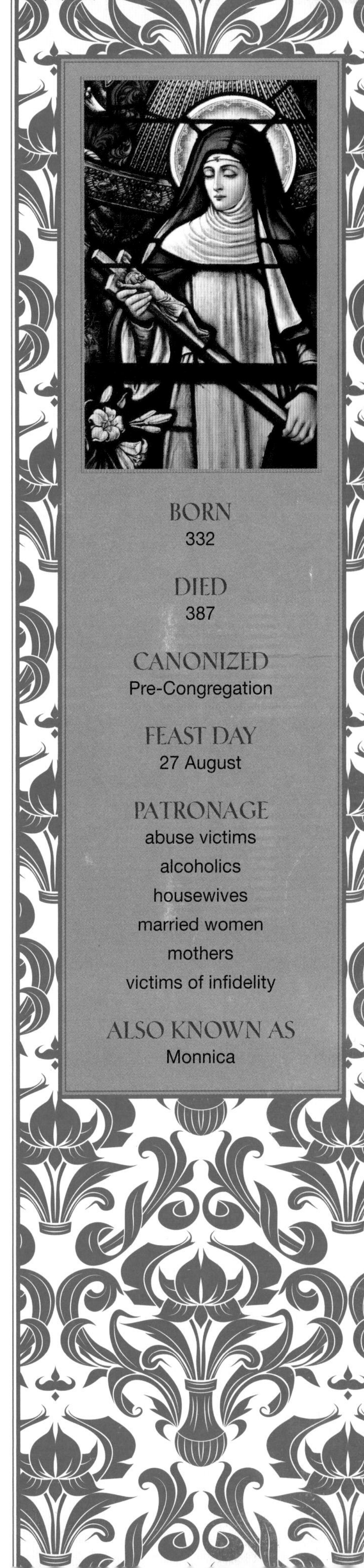

BORN
332

DIED
387

CANONIZED
Pre-Congregation

FEAST DAY
27 August

PATRONAGE
abuse victims
alcoholics
housewives
married women
mothers
victims of infidelity

ALSO KNOWN AS
Monnica

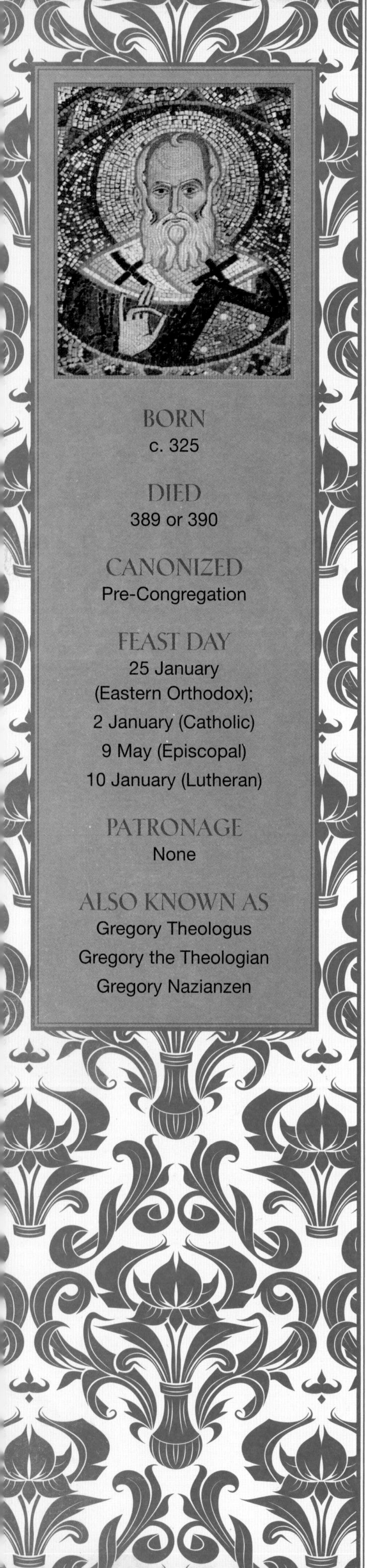

BORN
c. 325

DIED
389 or 390

CANONIZED
Pre-Congregation

FEAST DAY
25 January
(Eastern Orthodox);
2 January (Catholic)
9 May (Episcopal)
10 January (Lutheran)

PATRONAGE
None

ALSO KNOWN AS
Gregory Theologus
Gregory the Theologian
Gregory Nazianzen

Saint GREGORY *of Nazianzus*

A student of Saint Athanasius and teacher to Saint Jerome, Gregory's beautiful and precise theology won him the title "the Divine", an honour shared only by the Apostle Saint John.

Like his friend Basil the Great, Gregory of Nazianzus was born into a family of saints: his father, mother and sister were all canonized. Also like Basil, Gregory received an excellent education in some of the Roman Empire's finest schools and displayed an astounding genius for oratory. Yet unlike Basil, Gregory only entered into the priesthood and episcopal administration with great reluctance. Indeed, the happiest times of his life were likely those he spent with Basil at the latter's new monastic community in Pontus and the last six years of his life, which he spent in secluded retirement, writing.

The Cappadocian Fathers: Basil the Great; his brother, Gregory of Nyssa; and Gregory of Nazianzus. They are also known as the Cappadocian philosophers.

The times did not allow for the life of monastic contemplation that Gregory might have led, however; again and again, he found himself elected to positions he did not seek. His father forced him into the priesthood; Basil forced him to become bishop of Sasima; Theodosius, emperor of the East and a devout Catholic, forced him to lead the charge against Arianism as bishop of Constantinople. There is no doubt that, reluctant administrator though he may have been, Gregory's long history of soaring oratory in defence of orthodoxy produced the devastating effect

Saint Ambrose

Celebrated nearly as much for his statecraft as his clear, practical theology, Ambrose navigated the Catholics of Milan through the trials of the Arian heresy, as well as the politically fraught relationships with the headstrong but devout Emperor Theodosius and the heretical but powerful Empress Justina.

There is no time of life past learning something.

Saint Ambrose

As consular governor of Liguria and Aemilia, Ambrose was sent to Milan's cathedral in 374 when the Arian bishop Auxentius died. He intended to promote peace and unity among the fractious Catholics and Arians, but much to his dismay he found himself elected bishop instead. Although a Christian, he had not yet been baptized, and he hurriedly went through this ceremony as well as a crash course on theology and Greek philosophers, Origen and Saint Basil chief among them.

Bishop of Milan from 7 December, 374, until his death, Ambrose proved a wise choice. Competent and pious, he deftly navigated both political intrigues and dangerous heresies, and today is recognized as a guiding light of the Early church and one of the Church's most distinguished theologians.

Saint Ambrose and Emperor Theodosius

BORN
c. 339

DIED
397

CANONIZED
Pre-Congregation

FEAST DAY
7 December

PATRONAGE
(partial list)
Bologna, Italy
Milan, Italy
bees
beekeepers
bakers
bishops
candle makers
chandlers
domestic animals
geese
gingerbread makers
learning
stonemasons
students
wax refiners

ALSO KNOWN AS
Ambrose of Milan
Ambrogio

Saint Jerome

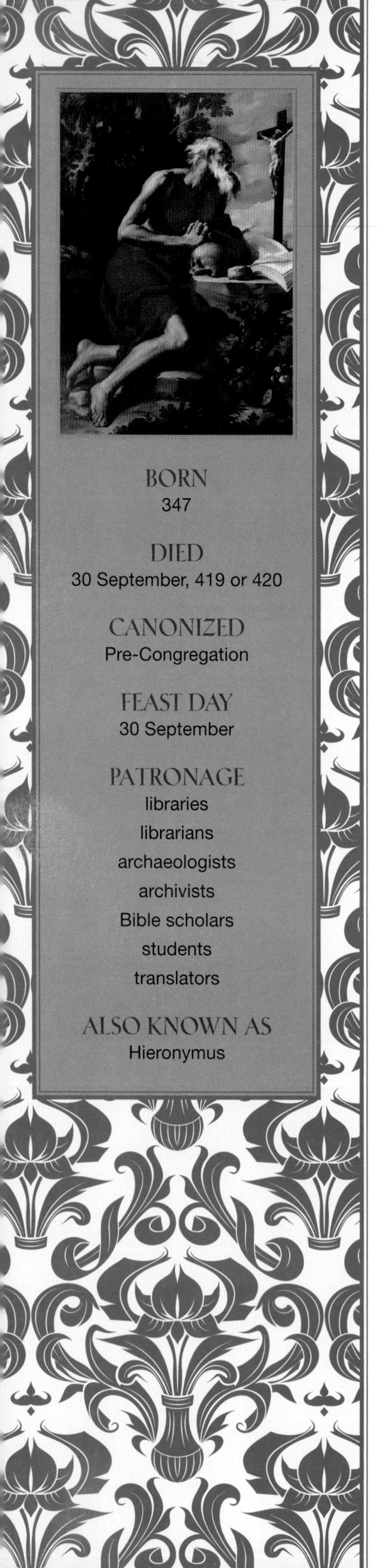

BORN
347

DIED
30 September, 419 or 420

CANONIZED
Pre-Congregation

FEAST DAY
30 September

PATRONAGE
libraries
librarians
archaeologists
archivists
Bible scholars
students
translators

ALSO KNOWN AS
Hieronymus

A controversial figure, both in his own time and today, Jerome was nevertheless one of the most famous and influential Doctors of the Church.

Born near Aquileia, Italy, Jerome learned Greek and Latin and studied the pagan classics in Rome. After his studies in Rome he travelled through Italy and Gaul to Trier, where he became interested in theology.

Jerome's devotion to biblical exegesis and Christian doctrine did not fully form, however, until he reached Antioch in 374. There he dreamed that he was called by God himself, whom he encountered as a judge, to account for his love of pagan literature and philosophers. Beaten for his transgressions, he cried out for mercy and swore that he would never again take pleasure in such "worldly books", and upon awakening, he dedicated himself to a monkish life.

After his student days in Rome, Jerome retreated to the desert of Chalcis, southwest of Antioch, to live the hermetic life. Even there, the industrious Jerome found time to write.

Jerome in the Desert

Jerome lived as a hermit in the desert for several years. He suffered greatly, wrestling with temptations. Jerome described his trials in a letter to Saint Eustochium, saying, "In my cold body, and in my parched-up flesh, which seemed dead before its death, concupiscence was able to live; and though I vigorously repressed all its sallies, it strove always to rise again. Finding myself abandoned, as it were, to the power of this enemy, I threw myself in spirit at the feet of Jesus, watering them with my tears, and I tamed my flesh by fasting whole weeks."

Jerome eventually emerged from the desert an ardent Catholic. By nature a scholar, he had by now added Hebrew to his list of languages and he travelled to

The Vulgate

Jerome's translation of the Bible, called the Vulgate (from *versio vulgate*, or "common translation") became the standard Catholic Bible for the next 1,550 years. Translated directly from Hebrew and Chaldean, it replaced earlier Latin translations from the Greek, and despite the polyglot character of medieval Europe and the linguistic evolution of Latin, it served as the standard biblical text in the West until the Protestant Reformation.

Constantinople to resume his studies, this time under Gregory of Nazianzus.

LATER YEARS

After Constantinople, Jerome returned to Rome in 382, where he stayed for three years. It was here that he first started his career as a biblical translator. But Rome proved unfriendly, especially after the death of Pope Damasus in 383. Jerome's acerbic derision of people and practices he found distasteful earned him many enemies, and the new pope disliked him. Taking himself to Bethlehem, he and Saint Paula established monastic communities for both women and men and various charitable institutions.

Yet Jerome's fierce defence of Orthodoxy did not abate, nor did he cease to publish pointed criticisms, quarrelling even with Saint Augustine. Ever prolific, Jerome continued also to work on his masterpiece, a translation into Latin of the entire Bible. Fire, barbarian invasions – even violent attacks on his person would not stay his hand, and Jerome died peacefully in 420, a veteran theologian and true Doctor of the Church.

Be at peace with your own soul, then heaven and earth will be at peace with you.

SAINT JEROME

ABOVE AND LEFT: *Jerome is often shown with a lion. Jacobus de Voragine in* The Golden Legend *first told the tale of Saint Jerome removing a thorn from a lion's paw. The grateful beast then became his devoted companion.*

Saint AUGUSTINE *of Hippo*

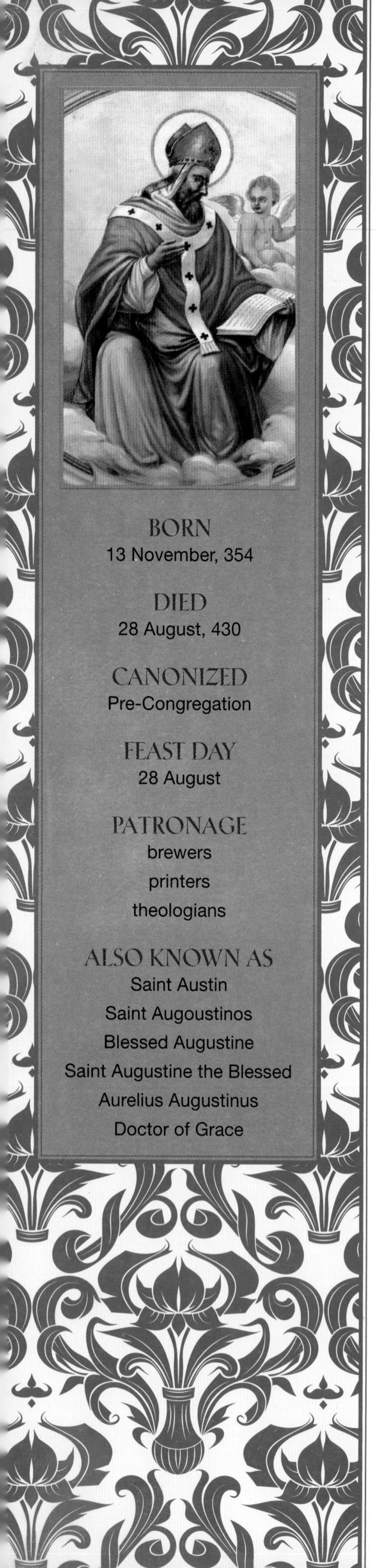

BORN
13 November, 354

DIED
28 August, 430

CANONIZED
Pre-Congregation

FEAST DAY
28 August

PATRONAGE
brewers
printers
theologians

ALSO KNOWN AS
Saint Austin
Saint Augoustinos
Blessed Augustine
Saint Augustine the Blessed
Aurelius Augustinus
Doctor of Grace

Saint Augustine remains one of the most compelling figures in the Catholic Church, a renowned philosopher not only in Christian history but also in all of Western civilization.

Augustine was born to a pagan father who converted late in life at the relentless urging of Augustine's mother, Monica, who is canonized in her own right. The first thirty years of his life were, in his own words, spent "inflamed with desire for a surfeit of hell's pleasures". He was lustful, vain and mischievous, and he lived, unmarried, with a woman who bore him a son.

Yet during this ill-spent youth he studied Latin, Greek, and rhetoric; his calibre as a philosopher and writer was soon evident. For a period of more than nine years he argued vehemently in favour of his Manichaean faith, then popular throughout the Roman Empire.

IN THE GARDENS OF MILAN

Saint Augustine gradually became disenchanted with Manichaeism, yet believing the Bible to be contradictory and senseless, he turned to Neoplatonist and Academic philosophers before finally consenting to read Scripture.

One important turning point came in Milan, where Saint Ambrose gently inspired Augustine to come and hear him preach. He reached Milan in 384; in August 386, Saint Augustine experienced a revelation.

> *He who created us without our help will not save us without our consent.*
>
> 
>
> SAINT AUGUSTINE OF HIPPO

In great distress one day, feeling utterly unable to lead a pure, sinless life, he collapsed under a fig tree in a garden. All at once the voice of a child came to him, seemingly from a nearby house, singing, "Take it and read, take it and read." Recalling that Saint Anthony of Egypt had heard a personal commandment in the Gospels, Augustine took up his Bible and read the first passage he saw: "Not in revelling and drunkenness,

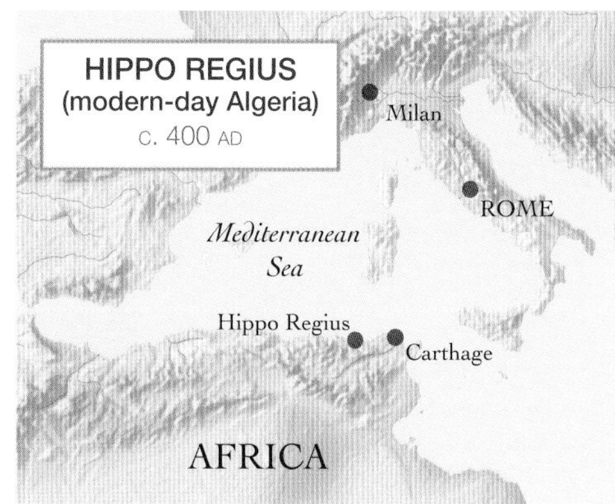

not in lust and wantonness, not in quarrels and rivalries. Rather, arm yourselves with the Lord Jesus Christ; spend no more thought on nature and nature's appetites" (Romans 13:13–14).

On 24 April of the following year, during Eastertide, Saint Ambrose baptized Augustine.

THE DOCTOR OF GRACE

Augustine became a champion of the Church. Devoting all of his considerable intellect to its causes, he campaigned against Manichees and heretics with such fervour and brilliance that his arguments remain fundamental Catholic doctrine today. He even succeeded in converting a Manichaean doctor after defeating him in public debate.

In the course of his struggles with Donatist heretics, Augustine decisively settled the issue of clerics who had renounced their faith during the Diocletian persecutions but had returned to their positions under Constantine I. Donatists held the rigorous view that sacraments celebrated by these apostates were invalid. Augustine advanced the doctrine that the Sacrament of Penance worked to absolve the sinners within its ranks, and most important, it was not the character of the individual priest that validated the sacraments, it was the office of priest itself. In arguing with Pelagian heretics, Augustine established the position that salvation stems ultimately from the grace of God, not firstly from free will. This still informs the Catholic Church's – and most Protestant churches' – philosophy of free will and grace, so that Augustine is known as the Doctor of Grace.

A reluctant convert, Augustine went on to become the foremost scholar of the ancient Western Church. His works still prove influential in the modern Church.

BORN
c. 360

DIED
14 September, 407

CANONIZED
Pre-Congregation

FEAST DAY
13 September
(Western Church)
13 November
(Eastern Church)

PATRONAGE
Constantinople
education
epilepsy
lecturers
orators
preachers

Saint John Chrysostom

In 553, Pope Vigilius first bestowed upon John the name *Chrysostom*, which means "golden-mouthed". Although sadly persecuted to the end of his life by the hostile parties in Constantinople, the brilliance of his oration and his most famous work, *On the Priesthood,* ensured Saint John Chrysostom a place among the most revered Doctors of the Church.

Drawn at first to extreme asceticism, John suffered severe damage to his health during his two years as a hermit. He returned then to Antioch, where he served the bishopric as lector and priest. One of the finest preachers ever to grace the Christian church, John was famous throughout the Byzantine Empire when suddenly, in 398, he was elevated to bishop of Constantinople, the empire's capital.

This seemingly congenial advancement cast John into a world of trouble. Although he remained wildly popular among the common folk and the poor, his efforts to reform the impious clergy and negotiate palace politics made him many enemies, especially Empress Eudoxia. Exiled twice, badly mistreated during his second exile, John died in Comana, a city in Asia Minor.

John suffered much, but he left an astonishing theological legacy; his homilies are still considered brilliant today.

Soon after John returned from his first exile, the people of Constantinople erected a silver statue of Eudoxia at the Church of the Holy Wisdom (now the Hagia Sophia). John objected publicly to the licentious celebrations that accompanied the raising of the statue, and the offended empress banished him.

Saint Cyril of Alexandria

Cyril of Alexandria, Patriarch of Alexandria, is one of the more controversial theologians of the early Church, most famous for his opposition to the Nestorian heresy, fomented by Nestorius, Patriarch of Constantinople. The theological dispute centred on the nature of Christ: to what extent was he human, and to what extent God? Nestorius held the Gnostic view that because Christ was divine, Mary could not be his mother and thus should be called Theotokos ("God-bearer").

Cyril had Rome on his side, but Nestorius was a powerful adversary. Their rivalry was possibly enhanced by episcopal politics; before 381, the See of Alexandria held primacy over the East, but since that time Constantinople had dominated. Councils were called and letters flew between Rome, Constantinople, and Alexandria. Eventually, the two patriarchs excommunicated each other and were both arrested.

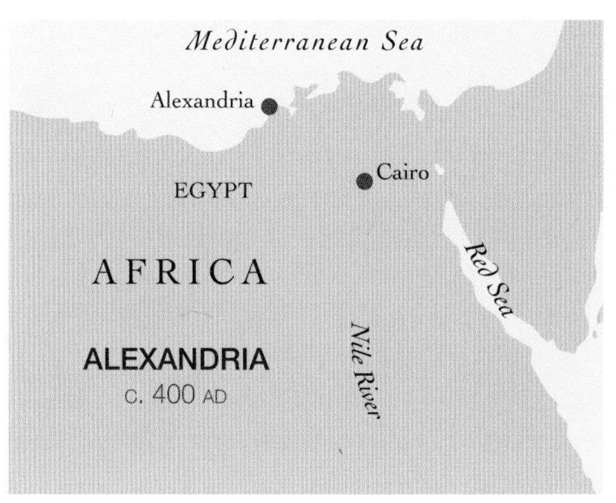

Cyril is known for his ruminations on the nature of Christ and of the Holy Trinity.

In the end, however, Cyril was vindicated and restored. He remains controversial, however, especially for his repression of Novatian heretics, some of his behaviour during the Nestorian dispute, and his expulsion of Jews from Alexandria. Nevertheless, writing in the tradition of Athanasius, Cyril left a valuable theological legacy, particularly regarding the nature of the Incarnation (that is, Christ as the incarnated God) and the Holy Trinity.

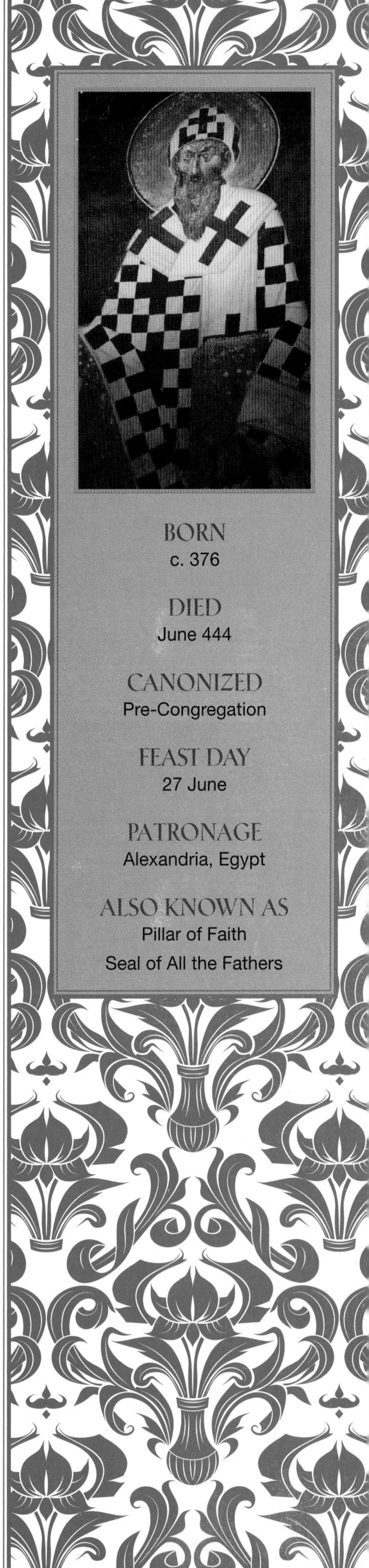

BORN
c. 376

DIED
June 444

CANONIZED
Pre-Congregation

FEAST DAY
27 June

PATRONAGE
Alexandria, Egypt

ALSO KNOWN AS
Pillar of Faith
Seal of All the Fathers

Pope Saint Leo I

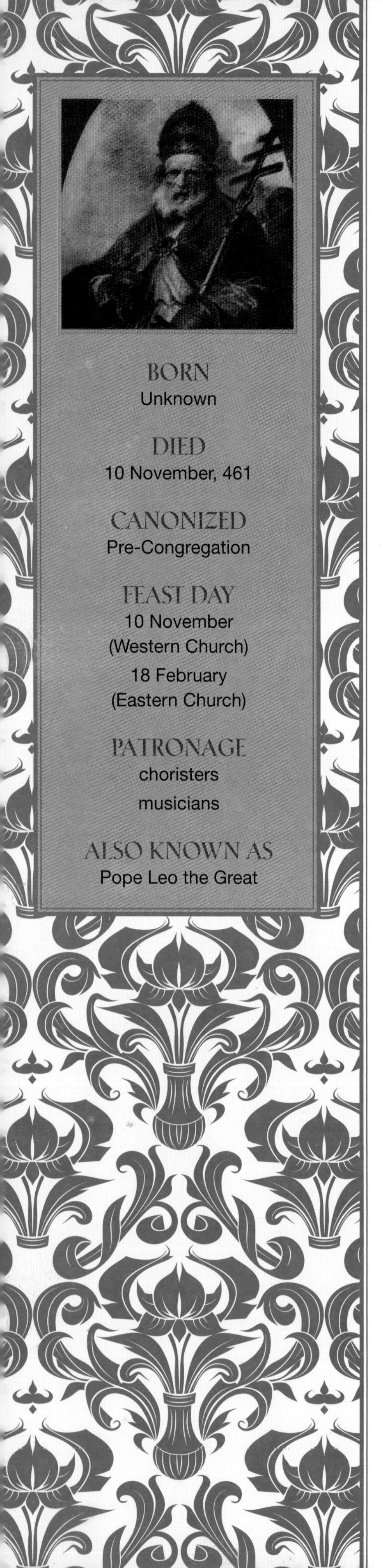

BORN
Unknown

DIED
10 November, 461

CANONIZED
Pre-Congregation

FEAST DAY
10 November
(Western Church)
18 February
(Eastern Church)

PATRONAGE
choristers
musicians

ALSO KNOWN AS
Pope Leo the Great

Pope Leo I, first pope to be called "the Great", proved himself an able administrator, clearheaded theologian and superb diplomat at one of the Church's most difficult and crucial times. With the Eastern patriarchs riven by theological disputes and heresies, and the Western Empire crumbling under the weight of failed institutions and invasions, the stability of the Catholic Church was precarious indeed.

Upon Leo's assumption of the papacy, he set to work reforming and standardizing practices throughout the Church, firmly establishing the jurisdiction of the bishop of Rome over the whole Church in the process. He was firm but conciliatory with heretics, stating several fundamental orthodox doctrines with lucid simplicity.

Despite his theological and administrative abilities, however, Leo I is best known for his meeting with Attila the Hun in 452. Having savaged his way through Europe, Attila had entered Italy itself. Leo, still only a deacon at the time, went to meet Attila and, amazingly, persuaded him to withdraw from Italy. Later, during Leo's pontificate in 455, African Vandals attacked and looted Rome, and Leo managed to prevent them from killing and burning at will.

Pope Leo rides to the city gates to meet with Attila the Hun, feared enemy of the Roman Empire.

Saint GREGORY of Tours

Gregory of Tours was born in Clermont-Ferrand and raised by an uncle, who was bishop of that city. He received a religious education but felt no particular calling to the Church until he nearly died from a serious illness. He ascended to bishop of Tours in 573, a perilous time of civil war among the perpetually quarrelsome Merovingian rulers.

Though an indifferent theologian, Gregory proved himself an able leader, managing to provide for his flock despite near-constant unrest. He built churches, upheld justice, and generally provided an authoritative presence. He laboured under no fewer than four kings, and only the last of them, Childebert II, established an era of some peace and prosperity.

Yet it is as a historian that Gregory is best known. Gregory became a hagiographer, particularly of Saint Martin of Tours, whose tomb drew many pilgrims to Gregory's city. He wrote also on Church Fathers and martyrs, especially those of his native Gaul, but his major contribution was a ten-volume work, *Historia Francorum (History of the Franks)*. This started with Adam and ended in Gregory's own day, and if some of its suppositions are suspect to modern readers, it is nevertheless an invaluable source of early medieval history and an impressive accomplishment for a bishop with so much else to trouble him.

Tell me now, when was the Father without wisdom? When was He without light, without life, without truth, without justice?

Saint Gregory of Tours

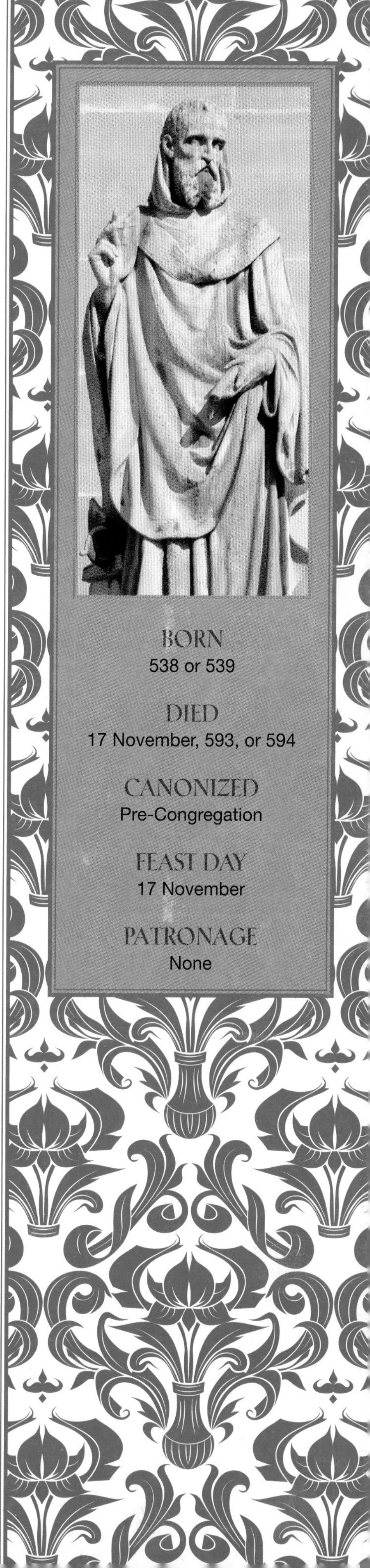

BORN
538 or 539

DIED
17 November, 593, or 594

CANONIZED
Pre-Congregation

FEAST DAY
17 November

PATRONAGE
None

Saint Isidore of Seville

BORN
c. 560

DIED
4 April, 636

CANONIZED
1595

FEAST DAY
4 April

PATRONAGE
computers
the internet
savants
students

ALSO KNOWN AS
Isidore the Bishop

Ascending to bishop of Seville immediately following the death of his brother Leander, Isidore almost single-handedly forged a union between the remnants of classical culture and the ruling Gothic tribes. He was dedicated to education, having received his own at the first cathedral school in Spain. At the Fourth National Council of Toledo, in 633, he persuaded his fellow bishops to enact an edict requiring them to build similar schools in their own cities.

Isidore's greatest and most famous accomplishment is his *Etymologies*, a compendium of knowledge and the most respected encyclopedia for more than a thousand years. Its twenty volumes covered an astounding array of subjects, from medicine to zoology, from law to architecture, from theology to agriculture. Relying on more than 150 authors for its information, the *Etymologies* formed a much-needed bridge between classical learning and the Middle Ages.

Isidore is sometimes called the last of the great Latin Fathers, and certainly he was one of the most influential. As the Church came to take over altogether the social duty of education in the course of the Middle Ages, Isidore's early insistence on this function is especially noteworthy. Nor was this the sum of his accomplishments: he wrote several volumes beyond *Etymologies*, stressed the role of monasteries, and stamped out the Arian heresy in Spain, which had taken root among the Gothic tribes centuries earlier.

A statue of Isidore sits outside the Biblioteca Nacional de España, in Madrid.

Saint Bede the Venerable

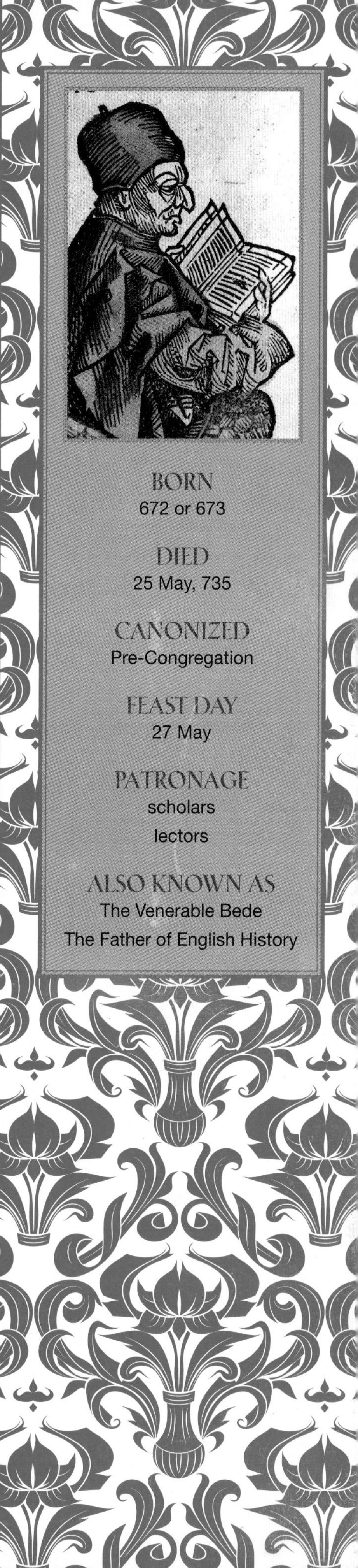

BORN
672 or 673

DIED
25 May, 735

CANONIZED
Pre-Congregation

FEAST DAY
27 May

PATRONAGE
scholars
lectors

ALSO KNOWN AS
The Venerable Bede
The Father of English History

Born in 672 or 673, Bede lived in what at the time was the very frontier of Christendom. Although the Celtic peoples living in the British Isles – particularly in Ireland and Wales – had converted to Christianity some 200 years previously, the Anglo-Saxon peoples of England, including Northumbria, had come only lately to the Christian fold. Bede's prolific commentary, exegesis and translation of parts of the Bible were important for his fellow Northumbrians.

The oldest part of St Paul's Church at Jarrow is the only extant structure from the monastery where Bede lived and worked.

By the ninth century, other English churchmen were referring to Bede, an outstanding scholar, as "Venerable", and today Bede is recognized for his most famous work, *Historia Ecclesiastica Gentis Anglorum (An Ecclesiastical History of the English People)*.

Bede's history begins with the Roman occupation of Britain and traces the long and sometimes violently opposed history of conversion to Christianity among the Anglo-Saxon kingdoms of England. His account provides the only insight of its kind on Anglo-Saxon history to the eighth century.

Saint Bede was fortunate in his placement at Wearmouth and Jarrow, which had been blessed with a wonderful library by their founder, Benedict Biscop. Bede was familiar with many classical authors and could read Greek and probably some Hebrew as well as Latin, of course. As an adult he never ceased to write. Education, whether receiving or bestowing, genuinely delighted him, as he says in his own words, so it is hardly surprising that he obeyed his scholarly impulse literally to the day of his death, when he finished translating the Gospel of Saint John.

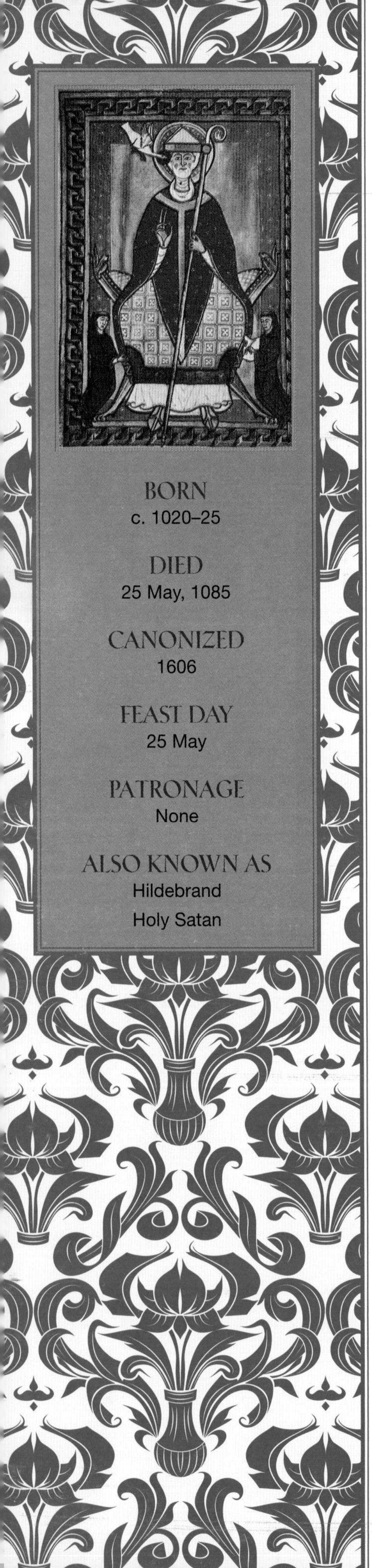

BORN
c. 1020–25

DIED
25 May, 1085

CANONIZED
1606

FEAST DAY
25 May

PATRONAGE
None

ALSO KNOWN AS
Hildebrand
Holy Satan

Pope Saint GREGORY VII

The entire ecclesiastical reform movement of the eleventh century is called the Gregorian Reform after Gregory VII, the most successful and energetic of a series of reforming popes. He was born into the lower classes, the son of a peasant or carpenter, but rose to become one of the most powerful men in Europe.

Growing concern about lax adherence to monastic rule, lowered moral standards in the clergy and excessive interference by secular powers led to a hotly contested but much-needed Church reform. From 1049 to 1099, every pope in succession carried out reforms, but it is Gregory VII who stands at the head of the charge. Even before he was elected pope, Gregory – then called Hildebrand – had started the process of reformation. As cardinal-subdeacon, he completely rejuvenated Saint Paul Outside-the-Walls, an ancient monastery in Rome that was crumbling from neglect and mismanagement, while its monks received women and allowed livestock to wander freely through the abandoned halls.

ABOVE: *Gregory VII emerged victorious in the struggle between pope and king over the issue of investiture, the appointing of bishops and other clergymen. In 1077, Henry IV travelled to northern Italy to make peace with the pope. As penance for his sins, he donned a hair shirt and stood barefoot in the snow at the gate of the fortress at Canossa in the middle of winter.*

LEFT: *Ruins of the castle at Canossa. Henry's dramatic bid for repentance became known as the "Walk to Canossa".*

The Trouble with Investiture

Among other reforms, Gregory abolished the practice of lay investiture, by which a secular authority appointed bishops or abbots and handed the appointee his symbol of office (either a ring or a staff). Passed in 1075, the decree caught the attention of Henry IV, emperor in name but constantly faced with fractious, rebellious barons. A large portion of the emperor's support came from abbots, bishops and other high churchmen, whom the crown had invested and who controlled more than a third of the territory claimed by Henry.

Although merely symbolic, the ceremony of investiture was fraught with political, economic and spiritual meanings, and Henry and Gregory fought nearly to the death over it. Nor did the issue end there: not until 1122 did the Holy Roman Empire and the papacy finally agree on a lasting compromise, by which the emperors relinquished the right to hand over the symbols of office but retained the right to point at the chosen appointee with the royal sceptre before the pope could begin the performance of the ceremony.

POPE AND EMPEROR

As pope, Gregory imposed similar reforms throughout the Church with the goal of restoring its spiritual purity and establishing the primacy of Rome. To that end, Gregory disentangled the powers of secular rulers from the Church (Gregory himself was the last pope whose election was ratified by an emperor), reformed the rules of papal election within the Church, and put forth strong decrees against married clergy, simony, and the selling of Church property.

I loved justice,

and I hated iniquity,

so I die in exile.

Pope Saint Gregory VII

Wax funeral effigy of Gregory VII in Salerno Cathedral. After Gregory excommunicated Henry IV a second time, the Holy Roman Emperor exiled the pope, who spent his final days in a castle by the sea in Salerno.

He was so successful in these reforms that his detractors began referring to him as "Holy Satan". Among his worst enemies was Holy Roman Emperor Henry IV. Affronted by some of Saint Gregory's reforms, Henry kidnapped the pope, attacked Rome, and even crowned his own choice for pope, the antipope Clement III. Still Gregory refused to back down before the emperor's anger, even when obliged to escape Rome and continue his papacy from Salerno. Gregory excommunicated both emperor and antipope.

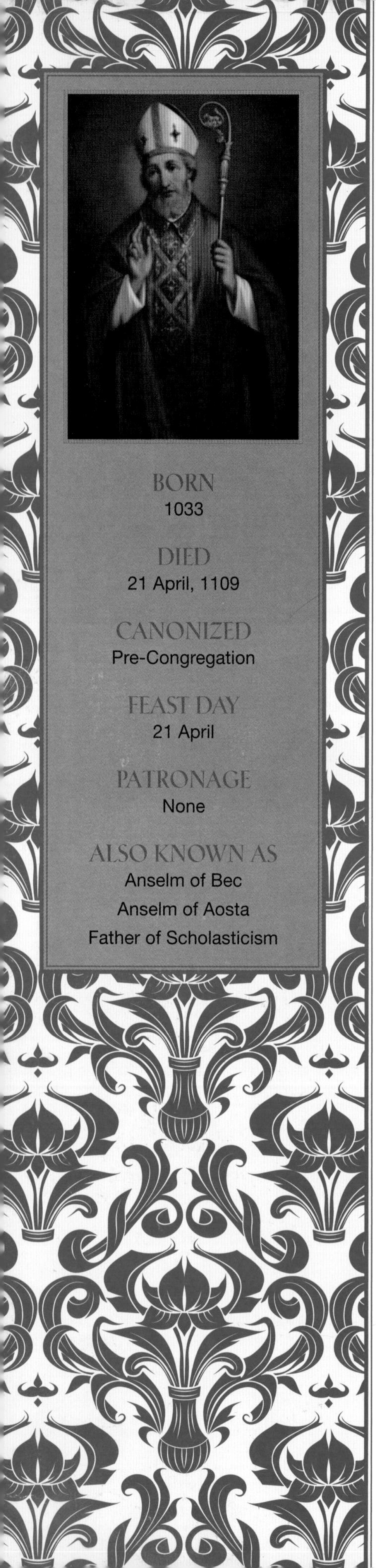

BORN
1033

DIED
21 April, 1109

CANONIZED
Pre-Congregation

FEAST DAY
21 April

PATRONAGE
None

ALSO KNOWN AS
Anselm of Bec
Anselm of Aosta
Father of Scholasticism

Saint Anselm *of Canterbury*

Born in Aosta, Italy, Anselm travelled through Burgundy, France and Normandy as a young man, joining the Benedictine order at Bec Abbey in Normandy in 1060. Intelligent and gentle, he became prior at Bec only three years later and abbot in 1078.

William Rufus became king of England in 1087 and immediately asserted his authority over the Church. When Lanfranc of Lombardy, archbishop of Canterbury and Anselm's former mentor, died in 1089, William refused to appoint a new archbishop for four years, robbing the see of its income and tossing the English clergy into confusion.

Finally, the king appointed Anselm as archbishop, despite the latter's extreme reluctance. The two men immediately began to quarrel over the king's interference in church matters and specifically over the problem of investiture. The quarrel outlasted William himself; his brother and successor, Henry I, inherited the issue. Finally, in 1107, after two exiles and many trips to Rome, Anselm won the day and spent his remaining time writing.

Always drawn more to philosophy and quiet contemplation than to politics, Anselm is renowned today for his theological work, much of which he completed before becoming archbishop. Saint Thomas Aquinas and the later philosophers Hegel, Kant and Descartes engaged his famous ontological argument for the existence of God.

Anselm, at left, meeting Queen Matilda. As well as having an official connection, the two were also friends, and he was her spiritual adviser. During his exile, Matilda wrote to him regularly and also staunchly pleaded his case to her husband, Henry I. Many of the letters the queen wrote the archbishop still survive.

Saint ANTHONY of Padua

Only 36 when he died, Saint Anthony of Padua rapidly became one of Catholicism's most revered saints, canonized just a year after his death. Born in Lisbon, Portugal, Anthony entered a religious community when he was 15 years old; he was so dedicated to the Church that when he was 17 he moved to a more distant convent in Coimbra in order to avoid the distractions of friends and family.

In 1220, when the relics of the first Franciscan martyrs arrived in Coimbra, Anthony was inflamed with the desire to follow in their footsteps. He set out for Morocco to convert the Muslims there, but an illness and then a shipwreck intervened, and he eventually arrived at Montepaolo, Italy. He went unrecognized until he attended a gathering of Dominicans and Franciscans at Forli. No one had been asked to give the sermon – the result of an oversight – and in desperation Anthony's superior told the young monk to speak.

That was the beginning of Anthony's fame, for his genius lay in preaching, and he so deftly expounded on the mysteries that Saint Francis himself in 1224 asked Anthony to teach theology. As a professor, Anthony spoke at Bologna, Montpellier and Toulouse, devoting himself particularly to countering heresy but also continuing to preach. Many miracles accompanied his legendary oratory, and 30 years after his death Saint Bonaventure opened Anthony's tomb to discover that the blessed tongue remained uncorrupted.

In art, Anthony of Padua is often shown with the Christ Child appearing from an open book. In some, such as this, he also holds a lily stalk.

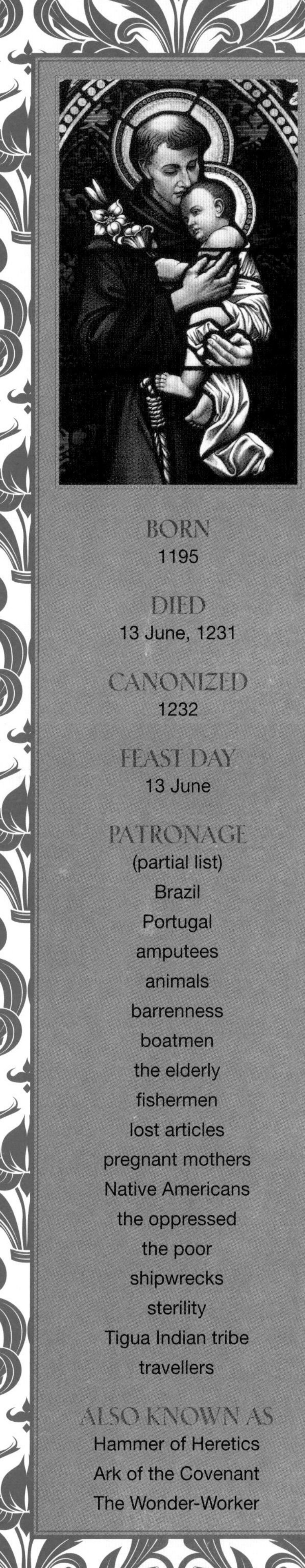

BORN
1195

DIED
13 June, 1231

CANONIZED
1232

FEAST DAY
13 June

PATRONAGE
(partial list)
Brazil
Portugal
amputees
animals
barrenness
boatmen
the elderly
fishermen
lost articles
pregnant mothers
Native Americans
the oppressed
the poor
shipwrecks
sterility
Tigua Indian tribe
travellers

ALSO KNOWN AS
Hammer of Heretics
Ark of the Covenant
The Wonder-Worker

A Closer Look: Canonization

All Saints *by Albrecht Dürer*

The earliest of all the many saints were martyrs, declared through a disorganized process of loud local acclaim. By the fourth century, individual churches had compiled martyrologies, and congregations started to venerate non-martyred saints, but the process remained local and organic – as it still does in the Eastern Orthodox Church. In the West, the urge to have a deceased Christian canonized by the pope (that is, declared a saint) gradually grew over the course of the early Middle Ages. Starting with Church reforms, centralization, and homogenization in the twelfth century, the process of canonization became ever more structured and fell increasingly under the pope's jurisdiction.

The First Saints

Christians started venerating saints at least by the second century; by the start of the third century, Christians celebrated the feast of Saints Peter and Paul on June 29 – a date still maintained today. The veneration of human beings now in Heaven as capable intercessors for humans still on earth was originally a Judaic practice begun in biblical times. As their Christian counterparts would later do, Jews erected shrines to the select among their fallen, venerating them at their graves, and both Jews and early Christians shared a special reverence for martyrs.

Saints Peter and Paul

Path to Sainthood

Since 1983, the Roman Catholic Church has followed the Congregation for the Causes of Saints, which designates a lengthy five-step path to sainthood for non-martyrs.

- **Servant of God.** The first step begins when a local bishop gives permission to open an investigation into the virtues of an individual.
- **Declaration "Non Cultus".** The second step entails exhumation and examination of the body of the Servant of God, and relics are taken.
- **Venerable/Heroic in Virtue.** The third step comes when enough information has been gathered, and a recommendation is made to the pope that he proclaims the Servant of God's heroic virtue. The individual is now referred to by the title "Venerable".
- **Blessed.** The fourth step includes the Church's statement that the Venerable is "worthy of belief". A feast day is assigned, but its celebration is restricted, and no church may be built to honour the Blessed. This step is known as "beatification".
- **Saint.** At least two miracles must have been performed after death for canonization. A canonized saint is assigned a feast day that may be celebrated anywhere within the Church. The faithful may freely celebrate the saint and build churches to honour him or her.

During his short reign as pope, Sixtus V (r. 1585–90) implemented several far-reaching Church reforms, including the organization of the canonization process.

In the eighteenth century, Pope Benedict XIV wrote De servorum Dei beatificatione et beatorum canonizatione, *the definitive work on canonization.*

THE CONGREGATION OF RITES

Finally, in 1588, Pope Sixtus V organized the Sacred Congregation of Rites to oversee the canonization process. By now, local acclaim was insufficient: canonization required meticulous examination of the worthiness of the person under review and the veracity of miracles attributed to the candidate. By the time Pope Benedict XIV wrote his definitive work in the 1730s on canonization in the Roman Catholic Church, the distinction between venerable, blessed, and saint had become standard. In the West this careful, often lengthy process is still followed today, although the Congregation of Rites is now called the Congregation for the Causes of Saints.

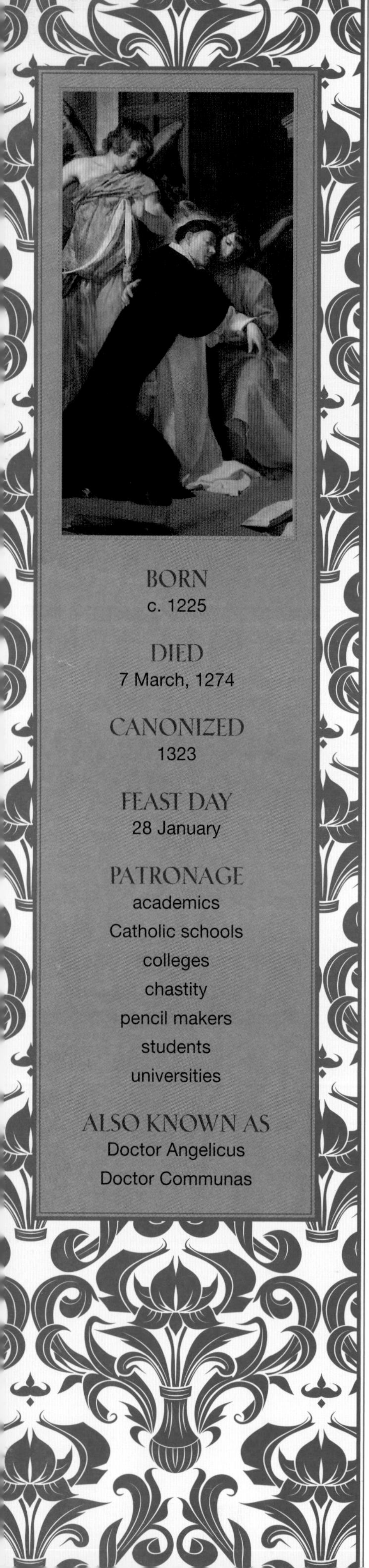

BORN
c. 1225

DIED
7 March, 1274

CANONIZED
1323

FEAST DAY
28 January

PATRONAGE
academics
Catholic schools
colleges
chastity
pencil makers
students
universities

ALSO KNOWN AS
Doctor Angelicus
Doctor Communas

Saint THOMAS Aquinas

One of Western civilization's greatest minds, Thomas Aquinas is, even today, a philosopher of worldwide renown. His greatest work, *Summa Theologica,* is an exhaustive report on Christian theology, written with unwavering clarity and precision of thought and logic. Tragically, Thomas died before its completion, but its five existing volumes still define Catholic doctrine and mark an important milestone in the history of Western philosophy.

THE DUMB OX

Born about 1225 to an upper-class family near Aquino, Italy, Thomas fought with his parents to join the Dominican order, whose emphasis on study and pedagogy appealed to him even as a teenager. In Paris and Cologne he studied under Albertus Magnus. This scholar-saint once predicted that although the physically large but quiet Thomas might be mocked as a "dumb ox", Thomas would "one day produce such a bellowing that it will be heard throughout the world".

Thomas's career as a scholar and lecturer took him from Paris to Cologne and all over central Italy. A prolific writer, he published, in addition to his major works, many brilliant arguments, treatises and commentaries, seemingly with preternatural speed. He completed one of his most famous works, *Summa Contra Gentiles,* around 1264, after about five years of work. This engaged Jews, Muslims, heretics, and pagans with Aristotelian reasoning and represents a triumph of Scholastic thought.

Thomas shown vanquishing a heretic with the power of his words. The quiet student developed into one of the most influential and rational voices in the Catholic Church.

A Rational Faith

Scholasticism arose in the West in the thirteenth century, largely in response to the reintroduction of classical philosophers like Aristotle, preserved in Arabic but lost to Latin scholars for many centuries. Scholastics aimed to integrate reason with Christian faith. Thomas felt that reason could be applied to buttress all aspects of Catholicism but that faith stemmed first from divine revelation. Brilliantly and methodically, Thomas laid out his arguments with such sagacity that philosophers and theologians today are still referring to *Summa Theologica*. In this masterpiece he laid out his arguments for considering Christianity wholly rational, including his famous "Five Ways" – five arguments for reasoning the existence of God from the experience of the world.

Three things are necessary for the salvation of man: to know what he ought to believe; to know what he ought to desire; and to know what he ought to do.

Saint Thomas Aquinas

In the painting The Apotheosis of Saint Thomas Aquinas *by Francisco de Zurbarán, Thomas is shown flanked by apostles, prophets, popes, and other church leaders, in a pose that suggests that he is the definer of orthodoxy.*

Thomas had nearly completed the *Summa Theologica* when he died, quite young, at age 49. He apparently suffered a kind of breakdown three months before his death, and given the weighty amount and impressive quality of the work he produced – at his height he could dictate to four scribes at once on separate subjects – it seems likely that overwork contributed to his rapid decline. Yet his legacy remains immense, his "bellowing" indeed still resonating throughout the world.

Saint Bonaventure

BORN
1217

DIED
15 July, 1274

CANONIZED
1482

FEAST DAY
15 July

PATRONAGE
Lyons, France

ALSO KNOWN AS
The Seraphic Doctor

Ranked with other great minds of the thirteenth century like Saint Thomas Aquinas and Roger Bacon, Bonaventure is one of only 35 saints declared a Doctor of the Church. He joined the Franciscan order in 1243 or 1244, just after receiving his master of arts degree from the University of Paris. He was awarded a master of theology in 1254.

For the next three years, Bonaventure taught theology and published his own work, but his purely intellectual life as a scholar did not last long: in 1257, having just reached the minimum age of 40, he was named minister general of the Friars Minor – leader of the Franciscans. Now obliged to perform both administrative and scholarly duties, Bonaventure showed that he possessed grace and political skill in addition to a commanding intellect.

Bonaventure guided his Franciscan friars, then riven by two hostile factions, through the troubles of the mid-thirteenth century while managing to produce his most famous work, *Itinerarium mentis in Deum (Journey to the Mind of God),* which discussed Saint Francis's vision of Christ as a six-winged seraph and expounded on its mystical significance. Bonaventure, who also produced the definitive life of Saint Francis, exhibited a decidedly mystical strain in many of his works, which are still referred to by theologians today.

The suddenness of Bonaventure's death while advising Pope Gregory X at the Ecumenical Council of Lyon led his secretary to suspect poisoning, though this was never confirmed.

Saint Albertus *Magnus*

One of the greatest scientists and philosophers of his day, Albertus Magnus read widely and performed his own experiments. In one, he suspended himself on a rope over a cliff to investigate the nesting habits of eagles. He also experimented with silver nitrate and discovered that he could separate silver from gold by using nitric acid.

Albertus pioneered the reintroduction in Western scholarship of Aristotle and other Greek philosophers. Western scholars had rediscovered their works, preserved in Arabic but not in Latin, since the disintegration of the Roman Empire in Late Antiquity, in the twelfth century. These works demanded the attention of Catholic theologians, and Albertus became one of the first to delve into them. His interest in virtually everything led him to acquire the title "Universal Doctor", owing to the breadth of his knowledge.

Albertus outlived his star pupil, Thomas Aquinas, whose passing he mourned deeply. Born in Swabia, Albertus died in Cologne six years after Thomas. He had been a professor at Paris and Cologne for decades, and a Dominican monk since 1222.

The aim of natural science is not simply to accept the statements of others, but to investigate the causes that are at work in nature.

Saint Albertus Magnus

A statue on the campus of the University of Cologne honours Saint Albertus Magnus, considered the finest of German medieval scholars and theologians.

BORN
c. 1206

DIED
15 November, 1280

CANONIZED
1931

FEAST DAY
15 November

PATRONAGE
Cologne University
medical technicians
miners
naturalists
schoolchildren
students
theology students

ALSO KNOWN AS
Albert the Great
Doctor Universalis
Doctor Expertus
Albert the German
Universal Doctor

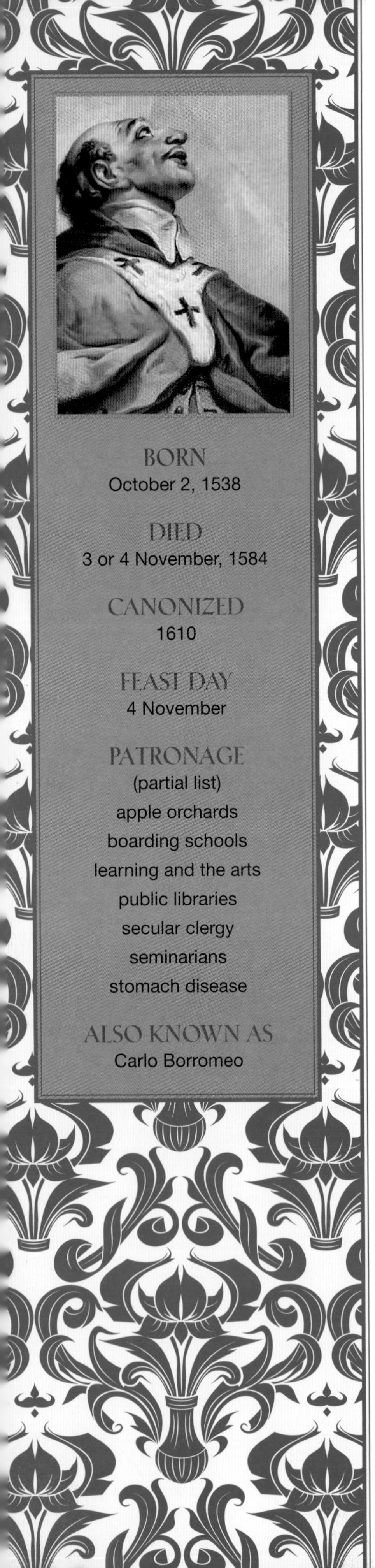

BORN
October 2, 1538

DIED
3 or 4 November, 1584

CANONIZED
1610

FEAST DAY
4 November

PATRONAGE
(partial list)
apple orchards
boarding schools
learning and the arts
public libraries
secular clergy
seminarians
stomach disease

ALSO KNOWN AS
Carlo Borromeo

Saint Charles Borromeo

For a cardinal known as a great reformer during an age of excess and abuses, Charles Borromeo had an unlikely pedigree. Born to a noble father and a mother of the infamous Medici family, Charles was nephew to the pope – another Medici. His privileged upbringing and his advantageous connections could have produced just the sort of deplorable behaviour that sparked Martin Luther to lead the Protestant Reformation in 1517.

Instead, Charles became a leading figure in the Catholic Reformation. He opened seminaries, held councils and synods, and organized efforts to aid the poor during a great plague in 1576, spending so much of his own money on relief efforts that he went into debt. He made improving the morality of the clergy and restoring the purity of the Church his life's work.

His most lasting accomplishment, perhaps, began when he persuaded his uncle Pope Pius V to reconvene the Council of Trent. At his urging the council met nine times between 1559 and 1563 until it finished its work. Perhaps one of the most important events in Church history, the council codified the reform efforts in the Church, affirmed and detailed Catholic doctrine, and rebuffed Protestantism. It was so successful at realigning Church morals and beliefs that another ecumenical council would not be held again until 1868.

Saint Aloysius Gonzaga

In 1580 Charles Borromeo met a promising young aristocrat named Aloysius Gonzaga, who had not yet received Holy Communion. The cardinal then gave this to Aloysius. Aloysius later went on to join a Jesuit order against his family's wishes; they had raised him to be a soldier and disinherited him when he chose religious orders instead. Aloysius, like his mentor and confessor, went on to canonization.

Saint Robert Bellarmine

Born in 1542 at Montepulciano, Robert Bellarmine became the first Jesuit professor at the University of Leuven in 1570. A graduate of the Jesuit Roman College and the University of Padua, Robert was noble by birth and a grandnephew of Pope Marcellus II; he was to spend his adult life circulating in the highest echelons of Catholic rank.

He wrote his most famous work, *On Controversies and Heresy*, while serving the Roman College as chair of controversial theology. Pope Sixtus V took affront to the restrictions on papal authority Robert proposed in *Controversies of the Christian Faith against the Heretics of This Time*, intending to ban it, but he died before he could do so. Robert retained his position, and his fame as a theologian and preacher continued to spread.

Pope Clement VIII named Robert his personal theologian in 1597, promoting him to cardinal two years later. He served under three more popes – five in total – as a chief member of the Holy Office, continuing to write and living with saintly austerity. Several of his works are still popular today.

> *Since death is nothing more than the end of life, it is certain that all who live well to the end, die well.*

Saint Robert Bellarmine

Castle Arenberg, part of the Katholieke Universiteit Leuven, Belgium. Founded in 1425 by Pope Martin V, the old University of Leuven now exists as two entities: Katholieke Universiteit Leuven, Dutch-speaking, in Leuven; and Université catholique de Louvain, French-speaking, in Louvain-la-Neuve.

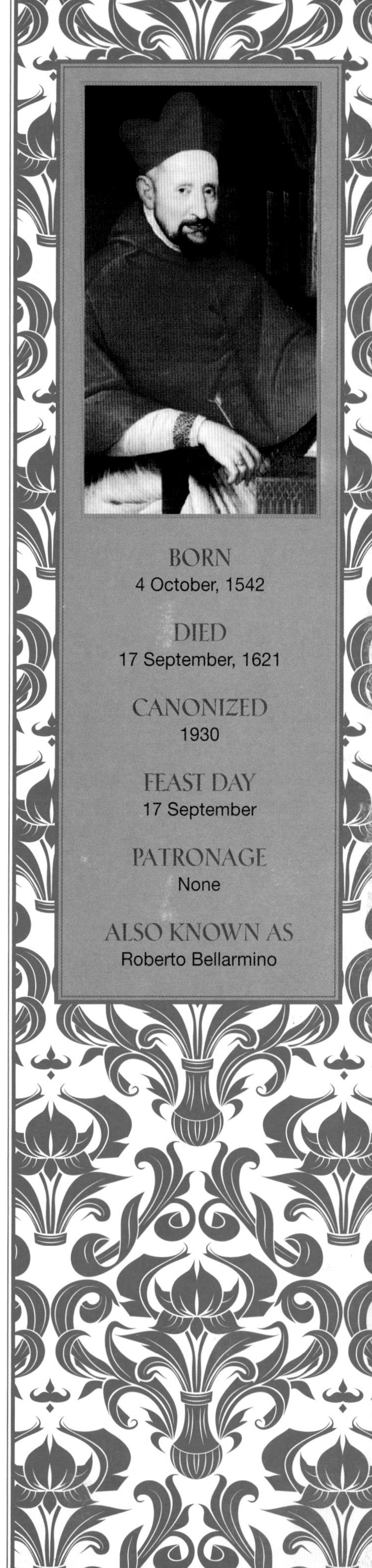

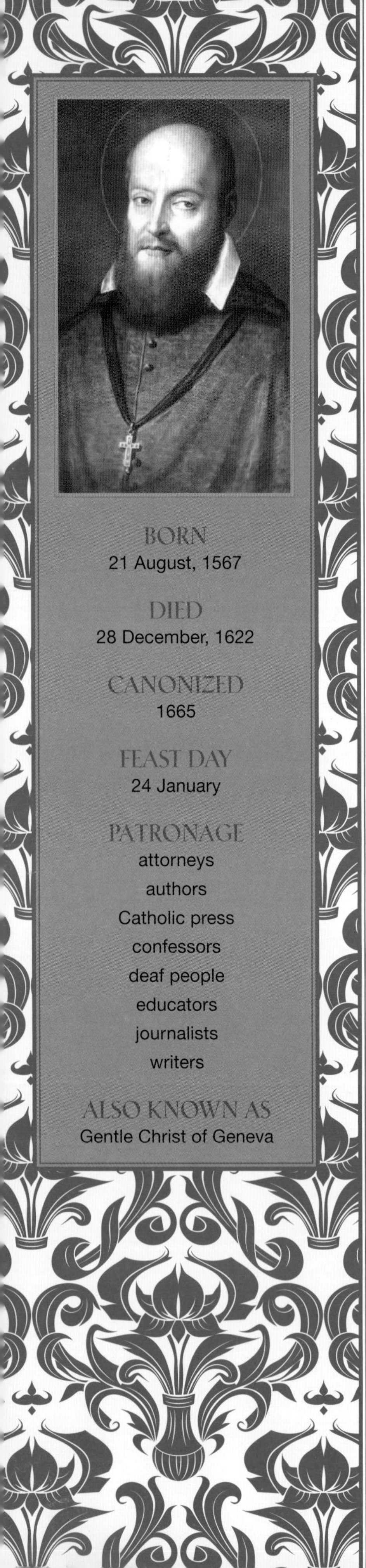

BORN
21 August, 1567

DIED
28 December, 1622

CANONIZED
1665

FEAST DAY
24 January

PATRONAGE
attorneys
authors
Catholic press
confessors
deaf people
educators
journalists
writers

ALSO KNOWN AS
Gentle Christ of Geneva

Saint FRANCIS de Sales

He was a remarkable man in a remarkable age, eschewing a life of privilege and wealth for one of trial and service. The eldest son of a noble family in Savoy, Francis de Sales was born at the height of the religious wars that tormented Europe for more than a century. Yet at birth he seemed destined for a comfortable existence: his father, intending to see him a magistrate at the upper levels of government, sent him to fine schools and arranged a marriage with an aristocratic heiress.

In 1923, Pope Pius XI proclaimed Francis de Sales a patron of writers and journalists because he often used religion-themed flyers and books to convert the Calvinists.

Francis, however, who took courses in theology while studying for a law degree, felt a different calling. He made a vow of chastity, rejected his fiancée, and enraged his father by refusing an appointment to the Senate of Savoy. Fortunately, the bishop of Geneva mollified Francis's irate parents by making Francis provost of the Chapter of Geneva, a suitably high-ranking ecclesiastical office.

Francis threw himself into his new duties. Geneva, where John Calvin had lived, preached, and eventually died, was a veritable Calvinist fortress, and the whole region had proven inimical to Catholics for many years. Calvinism had so triumphed, in fact, that the bishop of Geneva had been forced to flee, ministering to the See of Geneva from Annecy. Nevertheless, Francis travelled recklessly through Protestant territory, preaching so successfully that he converted many Calvinists.

A BRILLIANT PREACHER

Against Francis's wishes, his bishop promoted him to coadjutor and sent him to Rome in 1599. There he met Pope Clement VIII, who issued his famous prophecy about Francis's salutary effects on those to whom he preached. From Rome Francis travelled to Paris, where he met and befriended King Henry IV and Henry's secretary Cardinal de Bérulle. He would return to France several times, drawing large crowds and delivering brilliant sermons, and it was on a trip to Lyons in 1622 that he died, crying "God's will be done! Jesus, my God and my all!"

In addition to his work as an administrator and evangelist, Francis was a prolific writer, distributing pamphlets to Protestants, reflecting in treatises on such aspects of Catholic theology as love and piety, and publishing a great many sermons and letters. His overarching theme was divine love, and as he wrote with simple grace and obvious humility, many of his writings are as popular today as they were when first published. For this outstanding work, Pope Pius IX declared Francis a Doctor of the Church in 1877.

Francis de Sales was a compelling speaker, with a natural understanding of his audience. Despite his privileged background, he also had a natural rapport with his poorer parishioners.

Calvinism

John Calvin, born in France in 1509, became one of the greatest leaders of the Protestant Reformation. Brilliant and ruthlessly logical, Calvin argued relentlessly against a Catholic Church he saw as hopelessly corrupt. Geneva was, perhaps, where he met with the most success: converted wholly to Calvinism by 1535, in 1552 the ruling council declared Calvin's *Institutes* a "holy doctrine" and tried to stamp out – sometimes violently – any hint of Catholicism within its walls.

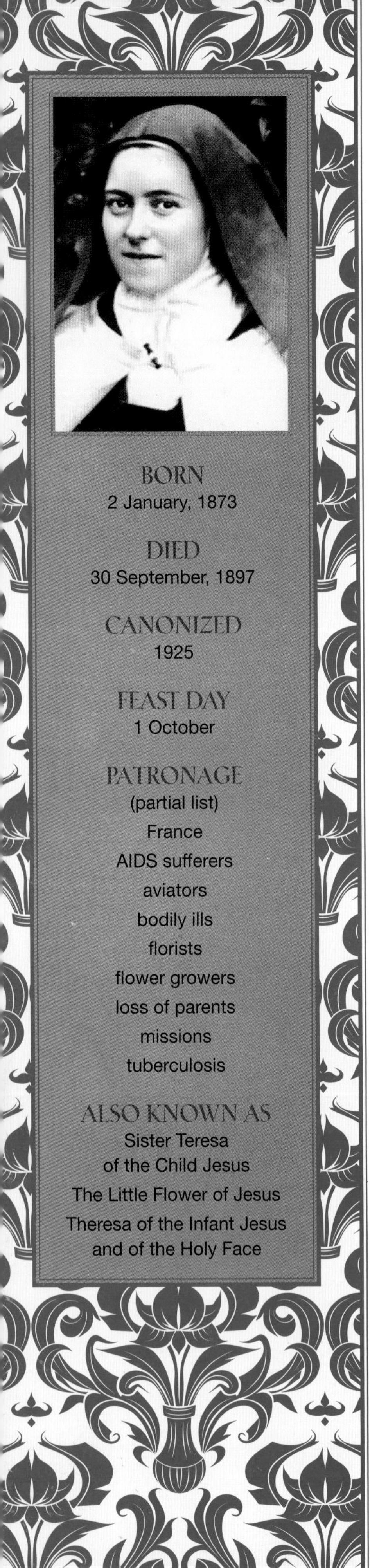

BORN
2 January, 1873

DIED
30 September, 1897

CANONIZED
1925

FEAST DAY
1 October

PATRONAGE
(partial list)
France
AIDS sufferers
aviators
bodily ills
florists
flower growers
loss of parents
missions
tuberculosis

ALSO KNOWN AS
Sister Teresa of the Child Jesus
The Little Flower of Jesus
Theresa of the Infant Jesus and of the Holy Face

Saint THÉRÈSE *of Lisieux*

Thérèse of Lisieux was born at Alençon, France, and christened Marie-Françoise Thérèse Martin by her devout parents. Even as a young child she displayed an unusual predilection for religious devotion; at the age of nine she tried to follow her sister Pauline into the convent of the Discalced Carmelites at Lisieux. Dreadfully ill at age ten, she was blessed with a vision of Mary, mother of Christ, who healed her.

Basilica of St Thérèse of Lisieux in Normandy, completed in 1954, receives more than two million visitors a year, making it the second-largest pilgrimage site in France, after Lourdes.

> *Without love, deeds, even the most brilliant, count as nothing.*
>
> 
>
> Saint Thérèse of Lisieux

Thérèse redoubled her efforts to enter the convent, which was reluctant to accept such a young woman and insisted she wait until she turned 21. So determined was Thérèse, however, that she made a personal appeal to Pope Leo XIII, who granted her an audience when she travelled to Rome. She was then 15 years old.

Although the pope referred the matter to the mother superior, Thérèse was finally accepted and admitted to the convent in 1888. She devoted herself to spiritual fulfilment, but her life was not without suffering: her father died in 1894, leaving her parentless (her mother died during Thérèse's childhood), and in 1896 she again fell ill, dying of tuberculosis on 30 September, 1897, just 24 years old.

THE LITTLE WAY

Obeying a request from the prioress (who was also her older sister, Pauline), Thérèse began to write her autobiography in 1895. She continued her efforts during her sickness, and it is largely on this work that Thérèse's fame and popularity rests.

Thérèse's intuitions about God and her penetrating insights on living a spiritual life astonished her fellow religious when she published them in her book, *The Story of a Soul*. In contrast to the nineteenth-century monastic norm of ritualized severity, Thérèse called her religious practice "the little way", and advocated a childlike love of and trust in God – a "spiritual childhood".

Although she had a limited education and lived only a short time, Pope John Paul II, recognizing the clarity and profundity of Thérèse's spiritual understanding, declared her a Doctor of the Church – one of only three women to be so honoured. One of his predecessors, Pope Pius X, who reigned from 1903 to 1914, had already called her "the greatest saint of modern times", her holiness so apparent that Pope Pius XI waived the 50-year waiting period, then canon law, canonizing her a mere 28 years after her death.

LEFT: *A reproduction of the drawing of the Holy Face of Jesus by Thérèse's sister Céline, known as Sister Genevieve of the Holy Face. Thérèse wore an image of the Holy Face over her heart.*

BELOW: *In her short years on earth, Saint Thérèse of Lisieux had a lasting impact on the faithful, and devotion to the Little Flower spread quickly after her death. One of the most popular saints of the modern day, her story continues to inspire countless people with its emphasis on seeking perfection in the small things of every day.*

Thérèse and all four of her older sisters became nuns. Her eldest sisters, Marie and Pauline, were already at Lisieux Carmel when Thérèse entered the order. Céline followed after the death of their father. The fifth Martin sister, Léonie, entered the Visitandine convent at Caen.

Saints of the Bible

The saints in the following pages appear in and, in some cases, wrote parts of the Holy Bible. The Bible, whose canonical form was settled by the Church Fathers by the start of the fifth century, includes writings that are recognized as divinely inspired. Decisions about which texts to include in the Bible and which to eschew have not always been easy and have been revisited more than once in the history of Christianity. Moreover, even when the choice of texts has been made, authorities have, historically, differed on the order in which they should occur.

Nevertheless, at the time of Saint Irenaeus, roughly from 130 to 202, the veracity of the four gospels of Saints Matthew, Mark, Luke and John had been established, and shortly after that the Acts of the Apostles and the Pauline letters were added to the orthodox list. Because these texts focus on Jesus Christ and his Apostles, the Saints of the Bible include some of the most influential and revered Christian saints of all, such as the Blessed Virgin Mary, Mary Magdalene, Peter and Paul.

Saint John the Baptist

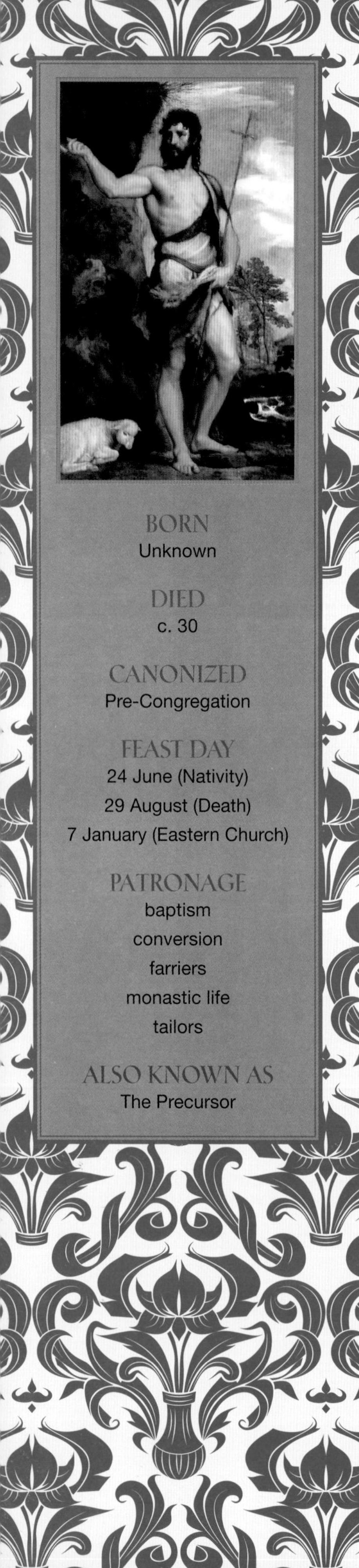

BORN
Unknown

DIED
c. 30

CANONIZED
Pre-Congregation

FEAST DAY
24 June (Nativity)
29 August (Death)
7 January (Eastern Church)

PATRONAGE
baptism
conversion
farriers
monastic life
tailors

ALSO KNOWN AS
The Precursor

Born to Zacharias, a priest of the temple of Jerusalem, and Elisabeth, a relative of Mary, John the Baptist was uniquely cleansed of original sin in his mother's womb. His story appears in all four Gospels, but Saint Luke gives the fullest account.

In spite of their many prayers, Zacharias and Elisabeth had given up on having children, for they had grown old and Elisabeth was barren. One day Zacharias went to fill the incense in the temple; there he encountered the Archangel Gabriel standing beside the altar. Though filled with awe, Zacharias doubted the archangel's prophecy that his wife would bear a child. Enraged at his doubt, Gabriel struck Zacharias dumb.

Saint Elisabeth

Elisabeth achieved sainthood not only for giving birth to John the Baptist, but also for being one of the first to know that Mary would become the mother of Jesus.

Both Elisabeth and Zacharias are recognized as saints, East and West; Eastern churches venerate Zacharias as a martyr, killed at Herod's command in Jerusalem's temple. The only information about the couple is found in the Gospel of Luke. Elisabeth passes out of history with John's circumcision and naming (Luke 1: 59–63), but it was Elisabeth who, over her family's protests, insisted that he be called John. When Zacharias agreed, the dumbness with which Gabriel had struck him for disbelief vanished.

Despite his ministry's remote site in the wilderness in Judea, John drew crowds of followers.

In art, John the Baptist is often included in childhood scenes of the life of Jesus. Even in paintings that depict John and Jesus as infants or children, John is often clothed in the camel-hair cloak of a hermit, bannered staff in hand, and accompanied by a lamb.

Yet the prophecy came true: Elisabeth did conceive and gave birth to John. While she was pregnant, Mary came to see her, for she, too, had received a prophecy from Gabriel and had conceived a child. John, still in the womb, sensed the presence of Christ and leaped with joy – much to his mother's amazement.

BAPTISM BY FIRE

The Bible is silent on the matter of John's childhood, and the chronology is uncertain. John lived as an anchorite in the desert for many years, subsisting on locusts and honey and wearing only a camel-hair girdle for modesty. When he came out of the desert, at about 27 years old, he began preaching throughout Jordan, urging people to repent and receive baptism. John also prophesied the coming of the messiah. "I shall baptize you with water," said John, "but one mightier than I cometh, the latchet of whose shoes I am not worth to unloose: he shall baptize you with the Holy Ghost and with fire" (Luke 3:16). But Jesus insisted that John baptize him in the River Jordan. This event marked the beginning of Jesus' ministry.

DEATH OF THE PROPHET

The outspoken John reprimanded Herod, the ruler of Galilee, for his incestuous behaviour, and for his trouble John ended up in prison. Fearing the wrath of a people who revered John as a prophet, Herod might have left the matter there, but Herodias, Herod's wife and niece, held an unwavering grudge against him. When her daughter, Salome, danced for Herod, he was so pleased that he offered the girl anything she desired: she asked that John the Baptist's head be delivered to her mother on a platter. Afterwards, Jesus himself mourned John's passing alongside his followers.

John baptizes Jesus in the River Jordan.

Salome with the head of John

BORN
Unknown

DIED
First century

CANONIZED
Pre-Congregation

FEAST DAY
1 January
2 February (Purification)
25 March (Annunciation)
15 August (Assumption)
Nativity (8 September)
8 December (Immaculate Conception)

PATRONAGE
(partial list)
humankind
mothers
nuns
travellers
virgins

ALSO KNOWN AS
The Virgin Mary
Mary, Mother of God
Mary, Queen of Heaven
Queen of the Angels
Queen of Peace
Mother of All Sorrows

Saint Mary the Blessed Virgin

Saint Mary holds a uniquely elevated position, honoured with "special veneration" over all other saints. Yet despite her popularity and importance to Christian theology, Mary's biography is largely unknown, reliant entirely on brief mentions in the Gospels and references in scattered apocryphal sources.

Mary ascends into heaven.

Blessed art thou among women, and blessed is the fruit of thy womb.

Saint Elisabeth

Her largest role in the Bible, naturally, surrounds the birth of Jesus. She is also present at other seminal points in her son's life, including Christ's first miracle (John 2:1–5) and the Crucifixion (John 19:25–27). Of her later years and her death nothing is known, other than that Saint John took her in after the death of Jesus; she died either at Ephesus or Jerusalem.

Veneration of Mary

In the first few centuries CE, Mary did not enjoy any particular status among saints: indeed, some Church and, later, some secular authorities, including

In 1917 at Fátima, in a mountainous region in central Portugal, Mary appeared six times to three children, Lucía de Jesus dos Santos and her cousins Jacinta and Francisco Marto.

Miraculous Sightings

Through the centuries, many have claimed to see visions of the Virgin Mary. Of a great number of appearances, the Vatican has declared only a few authentic. Recognized sightings occurred in 1531 near Mexico City (Our Lady of Guadalupe); between 1664 and 1718 in Saint-Étienne-le-Laus, France (Our Lady of Laus); in 1830 in the convent of Rue du Bac, Paris (Our Lady of the Miraculous Medal); in 1846 in La Salette in France; in 1858 in Lourdes, France; in 1917 in Fátima, Portugal; in 1933 and 1934 in Beauraing, Belgium; in 1933 in Banneux, Belgium; and in 1973 in Yuzawadai, near the city of Akita, Japan (Our Lady of Akita).

In art Saint Mary often appears with her son Jesus, either as a young, loving mother of an infant (above), or as a grieving mother, as she is depicted in Michaelangelo's Pietá *(below).*

Constantine of Rome, attempted to deny her cult altogether. Yet other early Fathers, among them Justin Martyr and Irenaeus, applauded Mary as a counterpoint to Eve, balancing her virginity and submission to God's will against Eve's carnality and disobedience.

The cult of Mary spread throughout the Middle Ages, aided by theological developments that named her *Theotokos*, "God-bearer" (Council of Ephesus, 451), proclaimed her Assumption (her corporeal ascent to Heaven, first mentioned in the sixth century and finally declared doctrine in 1950), and established the doctrine of her Immaculate Conception. This last did not formally become Catholic doctrine until 1854. Mary's Immaculate Conception states that she, alone of humankind, was born without original sin, achieved through God's grace at the moment of her conception.

By the Late Middle Ages, the special status of Mary was assured, and in the following centuries the newly converted countries of South America and Central America, in particular, worshipped her fervently. Veneration of Mary rose to even greater popularity in the twentieth century, with numerous sightings verified by the Church and the Second Vatican Council (1962–65) devoting significant energy to elucidating Church doctrine regarding Mary. Study of this pivotal Christian figure has its own name: Mariology. Mary has a long list of patronages, including all of humankind.

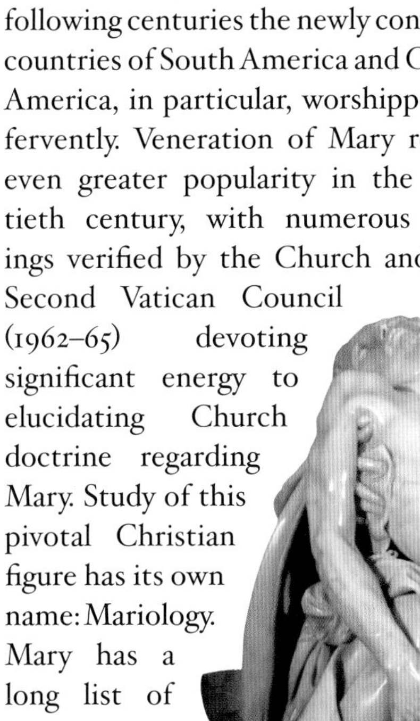

A Closer Look: *Archangels*

Angels appear in many religions, including Christianity, Judaism and Islam, which all recognize angels as spiritual beings who act as intermediaries between God and humans. The word *angel* comes from the Greek *angelos*, meaning "messenger", and it is principally as messengers that angels appear in the Bible. Archangels are angels of high rank, and although they can take on bodily form, they are not human, so do not need canonization to be called "saints".

Saint Michael is often depicted as a winged warrior with a sword and shield, successfully vanquishing the Devil.

The Annunciation. In the Bible, Gabriel is the messenger of God. Many also credit Saint Gabriel as the unnamed angel who spoke to Saint Joseph and proclaimed the birth of Jesus to the shepherds.

WHO ARE THE ARCHANGELS?

The number of archangels varies by religion and denomination, from as few as one to as many as tens of thousands. Roman Catholics name only three: Gabriel, Raphael and Michael. In Christian tradition, Saint Gabriel bestows prophetic visions to Daniel in the Old Testament and announces the births of John the Baptist and, most famously, of Jesus Christ in the New Testament. The scene of Gabriel bearing the news to Mary is frequently depicted in Christian art and is called the Annunciation. Saint Raphael is associated principally with healing and exorcism, both of which stem from his role in the Book of Tobit.

Saint Gabriel is also believed to be the unnamed angel who comforted Jesus in the Garden of Gethsemane.

Saint Michael, the most important of the three named archangels, appears several times in the Bible. He appears in later angelic lore in a militant aspect and more than once engages in battle with Satan. Since at least the second century, his intercessory power has been reckoned so great that he can redeem human souls, even from Hell. Yet since the days of Emperor Constantine, Christians have also venerated Michael as a healer. He is particularly associated with healing waters and is considered the guardian of the Catholic Church.

The Western Church celebrates the Feast of Saints Michael, Gabriel, and Raphael, also known as the Feast of the Archangels, or the Feast of Saint Michael and All Angels – or simply "Michaelmas" – on 29 September.

The Names of Angels

Along with Gabriel, Michael, and Raphael, the Eastern Church venerates four other named archangels: Barachiel, Jegudiel, Sealtiel, and Uriel.

Archangel Uriel

Thomas and the Angels

Saint Thomas Aquinas devoted a hefty amount of ink to angelology, or the theory of the angels. Following Gregory the Great and an anonymous fourth- or fifth-century text attributed at one time to Dionysius the Areopagite, Thomas theorized that the angels existed in nine orders, which were divided into three spheres. In descending order of their nearness to God, these are: seraphim, cherubim and thrones (first order); dominions, virtues and powers (second order); principalities, archangels, and angels (third order). In discussing angels, Thomas touches on such Christian fundamentals as grace, creation and – in the case of fallen angels, whom he considers in detail – temptation. Characteristically, Thomas treats angels logically, entwining revealed truths from God with observed truths from nature.

Archangel Raphael and Tobias. In art Raphael is often shown with Tobias, the son of Tobit.

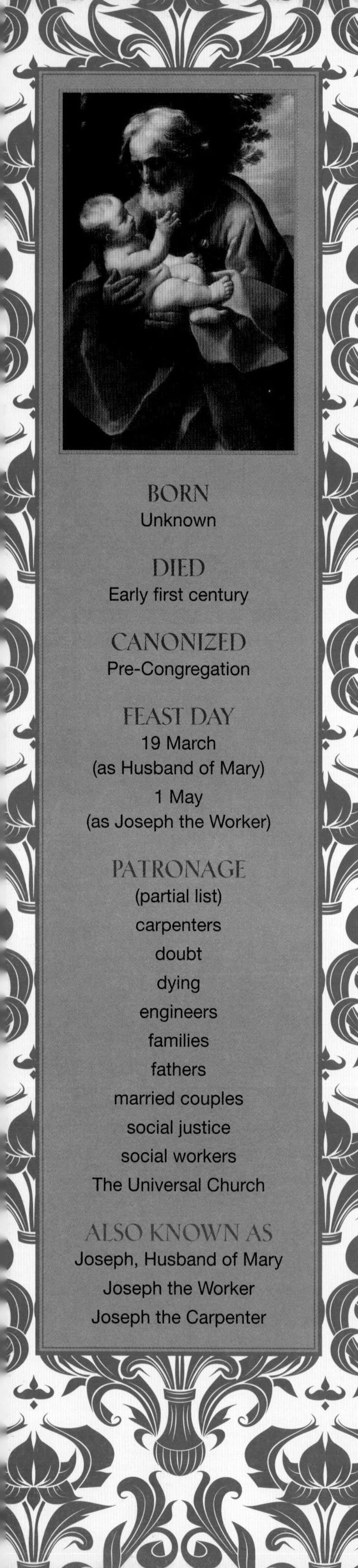

BORN
Unknown

DIED
Early first century

CANONIZED
Pre-Congregation

FEAST DAY
19 March
(as Husband of Mary)
1 May
(as Joseph the Worker)

PATRONAGE
(partial list)
carpenters
doubt
dying
engineers
families
fathers
married couples
social justice
social workers
The Universal Church

ALSO KNOWN AS
Joseph, Husband of Mary
Joseph the Worker
Joseph the Carpenter

Saint Joseph

The husband of Mary and thus earthly father to Jesus, Joseph was a distant descendant of King David and a humble carpenter living in Nazareth. Long tradition suggests that he was rather elderly when he married Mary, and though this is based on an apocryphal source, none of the Gospels mention him after Jesus' youth, indicating that quite possibly he predeceased his son.

When he first learned of his young fiancée's pregnancy his impulse was to hide her to avoid a scandal, but an angel appeared to him in a dream announcing the miraculous birth to come. Therefore, Joseph married Mary (whether before or after she delivered Jesus is not clear) and raised Jesus as his son, even taking his family to Egypt to escape the vengeful King Herod, who searched for the "King of the Jews" (Matthew 2:2) after the holy birth in Bethlehem.

Joseph is often pictured in images and crèches that abound at Christmastime and in other depictions of the Holy Family. He is portrayed as a loving father and husband, watching over his wife and the Infant Jesus with love and awe.

> *Saint Joseph was an ordinary sort of man on whom God relied to do great things.*
>
> 
>
> Saint Josemaría Escrivá

Eastern Christians venerated Joseph as early as the eighth century, but his popularity grew slowly in the West. Eventually, spurred by such devotees as Thomas Aquinas, Teresa of Avila, and Francis of Assisi, his cult grew, gaining strength particularly in the nineteenth and early twentieth centuries.

Saint Mary *Magdalene*

As witness to the crucifixion of Jesus Christ, his burial, and his resurrection, Mary Magdalene emerges as one of the key disciples of Jesus. Yet very little about her can be said with certainty – even in the Gospels her precise identity is unclear. Roman Catholic tradition conflated three Marys: Mary Magdalene at the tomb of Jesus Christ; Mary the penitent sinner (Luke 7:37); and Mary, the sister of Lazarus and Martha (John 11:28–32). Protestant tradition conflates two of these women variously, while Eastern tradition maintains that they are all three separate – a position the Vatican adopted in 1969.

All four Gospels describe Mary Magdalene as a witness to the Resurrection and also describe her telling the other disciples what happened, thereby earning her the title "apostle to the apostles".

She was a popular figure in Gnostic literature and has been widely venerated in many countries, particularly England. An old Eastern tradition took her to Ephesus with the Blessed Virgin Mary and Saint John, where she died; a rival Western tradition names her as one of the evangelists of France, where she and her siblings converted Provence before she retired to a cave and lived as a hermit until her death at Saint-Maximin.

Magdalenes

In the sixth century, Pope Gregory the Great first suggested that Mary Magdalene was a prostitute, a label that followed her through the centuries. Although the Vatican's separation of her from Luke's sinful woman rejects that label, the association between Mary Magdalene and "wayward women" continues to this day.

The Gospels mention Mary Magdalene returning to the tomb of Jesus two days after the Crucifixion to anoint his body. She became the first to see the resurrected Christ.

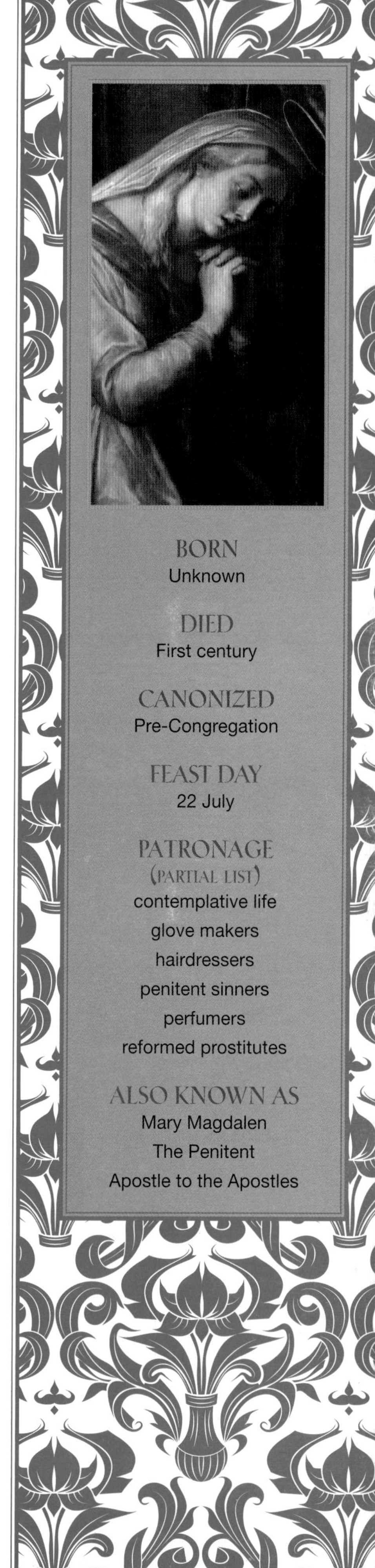

Born
Unknown

Died
First century

Canonized
Pre-Congregation

Feast Day
22 July

Patronage (Partial List)
contemplative life
glove makers
hairdressers
penitent sinners
perfumers
reformed prostitutes

Also Known As
Mary Magdalen
The Penitent
Apostle to the Apostles

BORN
Unknown

DIED
44

CANONIZED
Pre-Congregation

FEAST DAY
25 July

PATRONAGE
(partial list)
Chile
Guatemala
Nicaragua
Spain
Spanish conquistadores
apothecaries
arthritis
blacksmiths
druggists
funeral directors
furriers
knights
labourers
pharmacists
pilgrims
rheumatism

ALSO KNOWN AS
James, son of Zebedee
James the Elder
Jacobus Major
James Boanerges

Saint JAMES *the Greater*

James and his brother Saint John received the name "Boanerges" from Jesus Christ, meaning the "sons of thunder" (Mark 3:17), usually taken to refer to the brothers' impassioned temperaments. To distinguish him from another Apostle James, James Boanerges is usually called "the Greater", because he was the taller of the two.

James was one of the four most important apostles. James, John, and Peter were the only apostles present at three significant points in the life of Jesus: the healing of Jairus's daughter; the Transfiguration; and the Agony in Gethsemane. When King Herod Agrippa I embarked on his persecution of Christians in 44, he had James executed first of all, making James the first apostle, as Christ predicted, to share his suffering.

That James died in Jerusalem is certain; but a medieval tradition spoke of him evangelizing Spain before his death and of an angel transporting the saint's relics to Iria Flavia, Spain. Eventually, they ended up in Compostela, which became a major cult centre and one of the most famous medieval pilgrimage sites. Although it is unlikely that James ever went to Spain, it is possible that some of his relics are indeed at Compostela, while more of his relics may be at Toulouse, France.

According to tradition, John and his disciples were on the banks of the Ebro River near present-day Zaragoza, Spain, when he witnessed an appearance of the Virgin standing atop a marble pillar. She asked John to build a church at the spot, with an altar around the pillar; Mary disappeared but the pillar remained.

Saint Andrew

Andrew is often regarded as one of the foremost apostles. He introduced his brother Simon (Peter) to Jesus Christ, and like his brother lived as a fisherman at Capernaum, on the northern shore of the Sea of Galilee. An immensely popular saint, particularly in Scotland and Russia, very little is really known about his life.

The Bible tells us that Andrew followed John the Baptist before he became an apostle, and that he travelled with Jesus and the other apostles to evangelize the Jews. Once he flees Galilee to avoid incurring the wrath of King Herod Agrippa I (r. 41–44), however, his story becomes murky.

One legend takes him to Greece, where he is crucified on an X-shaped cross; another has him travelling to Kiev, preaching to the Slavic peoples. His association with Scotland stems from yet another legend, in which Saint Regulus carries some of Andrew's relics to Scotland in the fourth century and builds a church in Fife to house them.

One tradition tells how Andrew was crucified on an X-shaped cross, lasting for two days before dying. The X-shaped cross, known since the tenth century as Saint Andrew's Cross, represents Scotland on the flag of the United Kingdom.

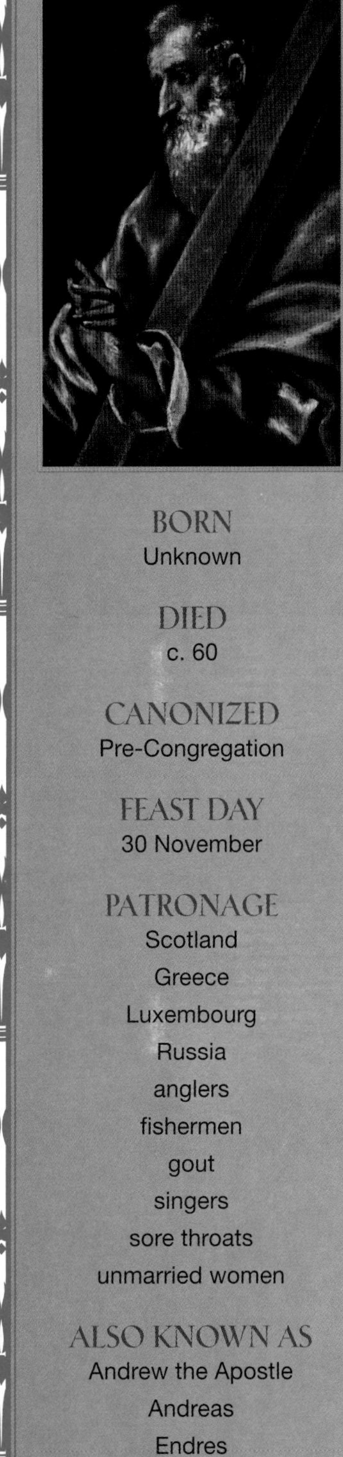

BORN
Unknown

DIED
c. 60

CANONIZED
Pre-Congregation

FEAST DAY
30 November

PATRONAGE
Scotland
Greece
Luxembourg
Russia
anglers
fishermen
gout
singers
sore throats
unmarried women

ALSO KNOWN AS
Andrew the Apostle
Andreas
Endres

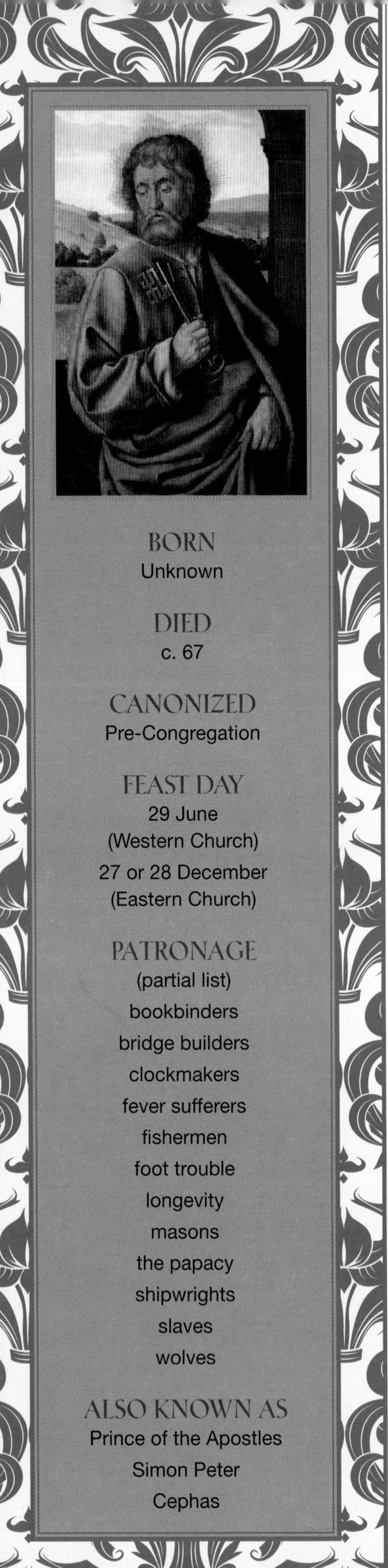

BORN
Unknown

DIED
c. 67

CANONIZED
Pre-Congregation

FEAST DAY
29 June
(Western Church)
27 or 28 December
(Eastern Church)

PATRONAGE
(partial list)
bookbinders
bridge builders
clockmakers
fever sufferers
fishermen
foot trouble
longevity
masons
the papacy
shipwrights
slaves
wolves

ALSO KNOWN AS
Prince of the Apostles
Simon Peter
Cephas

Saint Peter

Born a humble fisherman named Simon, Peter received his new name from Christ himself, who elaborated on its meaning ("rock"): "Thou art Peter, and upon this rock I will build my church; and the gates of Hell shall not prevail against it" (Matthew 16).

Peter became the first among Christ's apostles, speaking for them, leading them, and performing the first miracle after Christ's ascension. In artwork he is often pictured holding the keys to Heaven, which Christ entrusted solely to him. Along with the Apostle Paul, Peter founded the church at Rome, and he became the first pope; it is possible that the tomb below St. Peter's Basilica is indeed his.

The Papal Basilica of Saint Peter in the Vatican City. In Roman Catholic tradition, the huge basilica is the burial site of its namesake.

The First Miracle

The third chapter of the New Testament book, Acts of the Apostles, describes the first miracle performed by an apostle after the ascension of Christ to Heaven. Peter, with John, went to the temple of Jerusalem to pray, encountering a lame man at the door begging alms. Peter, who had no wealth to give him, told him to rise and walk; much to the man's astonishment, he found his lameness cured. Peter insisted the miracle demonstrated the power and holiness of Jesus Christ and afterwards performed many more miracles as he travelled about, proselytizing and converting.

Only one of the several writings attributed to Peter can be verified with any authority, but despite the relative paucity of information about his life, he became – and remains – one of the most widely revered saints in Christendom. By the end of the Middle Ages more than one thousand churches throughout Europe had been dedicated to him, with another two hundred or more dedicated to Peter and Paul together.

THE PRINCE OF THE APOSTLES

The New Testament tells us that Simon and his brother Andrew were fishing one day on the Sea of Galilee when Jesus, preaching throughout the country, discovered them. "Follow me," said Jesus, "and I will make you fishers of men" (Matthew 4:19). Sometime later, after they had both become his apostles and travelled with him, Jesus asked his followers who they thought he was. Simon answered: "Thou art the Christ, the Son of the living God" (Matthew 16:16). As this could only have been revealed through divine intercession, Jesus blessed him and named him Peter, first among his apostles.

Yet even Peter suffered from weakness for, as Jesus himself predicted, the Prince of the Apostles denied he knew Jesus after his arrest in Jerusalem and "wept bitterly" on realizing his betrayal. But after Christ's death and Mary Magdalene's witness to his Resurrection, Christ came alone to Peter, and when he revealed himself to several apostles at Lake Genesareth, he specifically commended the care of his flock – that is, the Church – to Peter.

Peter's movements are not clear after the narrative of the Gospels closes; but he travelled around Israel, possibly founding the church at Antioch, and travelled to Rome. He preached unceasingly, exhorting his fellow Jews to convert; he was also the first to convert gentiles to Christianity. He was imprisoned for his outlawed beliefs by King Herod Agrippa I of Israel but was freed by an angel (Acts 12:3–11), only to die by crucifixion in Rome, a martyr to Emperor Nero's persecution of Christians.

And I will give unto thee the keys of the kingdom of Heaven.

Matthew 16:19

Delivery of the Keys to Saint Peter *by Pietro Perugino is located in the Sistine Chapel, Rome.*

According to all four of the Gospels, during the Last Supper Jesus foretold that Peter would deny him three times before the next day's cockcrow.

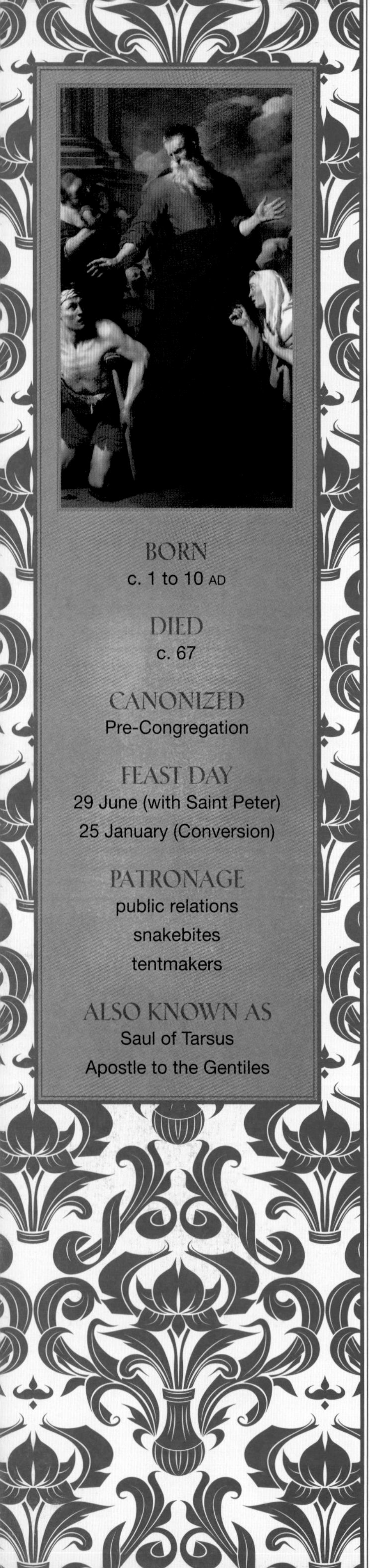

BORN
c. 1 to 10 AD

DIED
c. 67

CANONIZED
Pre-Congregation

FEAST DAY
29 June (with Saint Peter)
25 January (Conversion)

PATRONAGE
public relations
snakebites
tentmakers

ALSO KNOWN AS
Saul of Tarsus
Apostle to the Gentiles

Saint PAUL

After Saint Peter, Paul is likely the most influential of biblical saints. Born a Jew in Tarsus, Paul (called Saul in Hebrew) spent the first part of his adulthood persecuting Christians and participating in the stoning of Saint Stephen (Acts 7:58; 22:20). Sometime during the mid-30s CE, Paul was travelling to Damascus and experienced a powerful vision that elicited perhaps the most famous conversion in Christianity: a brilliant light from Heaven appeared to him and the voice of Christ himself, which Paul alone could hear, spoke to him.

The event left Paul blind until a Christian in Damascus named Ananias cured him, and thereafter Paul fervently dedicated himself to his new religion. In numerous letters and treatises, he laid the groundwork for much of Christian theology, including the relationship of New Testament to Old. Yet he is most remembered for his tireless missionary work, which sent him on three long journeys throughout the Roman Empire. For his work in converting non-Jews he is called the Apostle to the Gentiles.

On several occasions after his conversion Paul ran into trouble. He was arrested and imprisoned but never ceased to preach and publish letters, many of which can be found in the New Testament. Paul finally met his end during the persecution of Christians in Rome under Emperor Nero. As a Roman citizen, he was granted the relative mercy of dying by beheading.

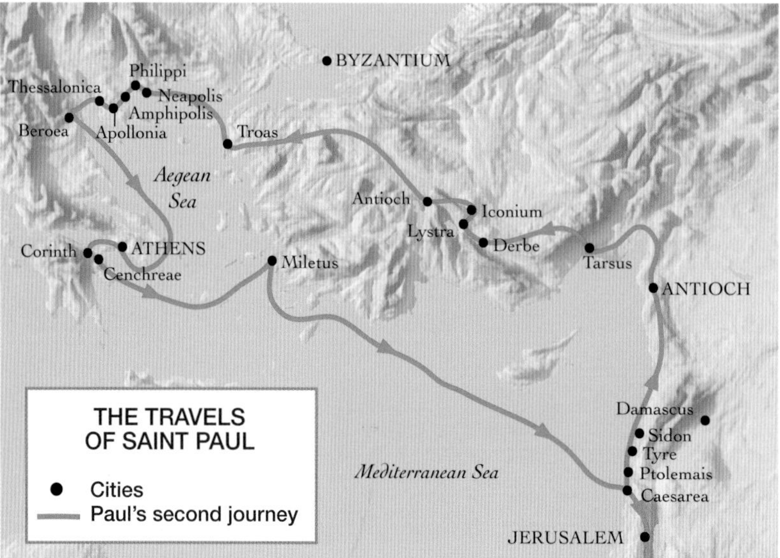

Paul travelled tirelessly on three major missions of conversion. At left is the path of his second journey.

Saint Matthew

Surprisingly little is known about the man who gave his name to the first of the four Gospels. He was most likely a tax collector and customs official before he left to follow Jesus Christ (members in those and related professions have adopted him as their patron). At that point he was called Levi; just as Jesus bestowed the name Peter on Simon and Boanerges on James the Greater and John, so he bestowed the name Matthew on his new convert, a Roman administrator.

> *Where your treasure is, there will your heart be also.*
>
> The Gospel According to Saint Matthew 6:21

Conflicting accounts bedevil the historian of Matthew's life: he was born either in Galilee or Syria, worked in Capernaum – where his profession earned him opprobrium from his fellow Jews – and died in Colchis (east of the Black Sea), Jerusalem, Tarrium, or Tarsuana (the latter two both in modern Iran). Most agree that he was martyred, but he may have been burned, stoned, or beheaded. Supposedly he evangelized "Ethiopia" – meaning not the African country, but a large, vaguely defined area more or less in the Trans-Caucasus.

His relics appeared in the eleventh century; allegedly brought from Ethiopia to Brittany, a Norman lord translated them to Salerno, Italy around 1080.

Matthew, traditionally credited as the author of the first book of the New Testament, was probably a tax collector before he left his profession to became one of the earliest of Jesus' disciples.

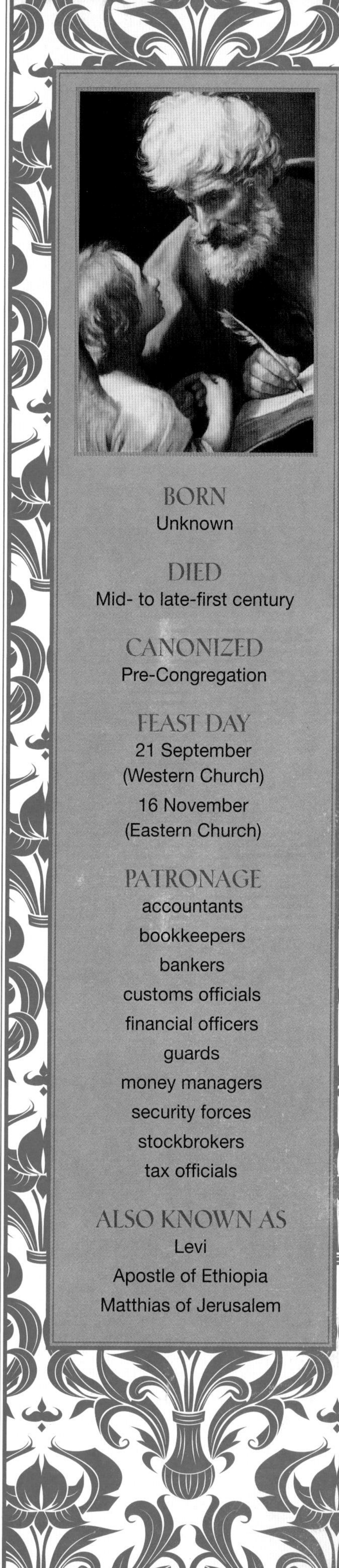

BORN
Unknown

DIED
Mid- to late-first century

CANONIZED
Pre-Congregation

FEAST DAY
21 September (Western Church)
16 November (Eastern Church)

PATRONAGE
accountants
bookkeepers
bankers
customs officials
financial officers
guards
money managers
security forces
stockbrokers
tax officials

ALSO KNOWN AS
Levi
Apostle of Ethiopia
Matthias of Jerusalem

Saint MARK the Evangelist

BORN
Unknown

DIED
c. 70

CANONIZED
Pre-Congregation

FEAST DAY
25 April
(Western Church)
23 September
(Eastern Church)

PATRONAGES
Egypt
Venice, Italy
attorneys and barristers
captives
glaziers
impenitence
insect bites
lions
notaries
scrofulous diseases
secretaries
stained-glass workers

ALSO KNOWN AS
John Mark

Mark authored one of the four Gospels, which, though it is placed second, was probably written first. He may never have known Jesus personally, but his Gospel gains added weight by virtue of the fact that he is said to have been Saint Peter's "interpreter", and his gospel is thus written from the point of view of the Prince of the Apostles.

Eastern churches consider Mark the Evangelist a different person than John Mark, described in the New Testament as the son of Mary, who offered Peter shelter after he escaped the clutches of King Herod Agrippa I. Western tradition maintains that they are one and the same, making Mark a cousin to Saint Barnabas.

Mark travelled with Barnabas and Paul on the first of Paul's evangelizing trips, around 45 CE, but turned back early, apparently due to a quarrel with Paul that was not resolved until approximately 60. A little while later he heeded Paul's request to join him in Rome, and likely saw Paul martyred sometime around 67. It is likely that Mark began his gospel with Peter, also then in Rome, around this time.

A persistent legend holds that Mark founded the Church of Alexandria, where he was martyred, perhaps by strangulation.

Most representations of Saint Mark include a lion, often winged. The lion symbol derives from Mark's description of John the Baptist as a "voice of one crying out in the desert" (Mark 1:3), which artists interpreted as a roaring lion.

Saint THOMAS

Very little can be said with certainty about Thomas, yet this has not prevented the development of a considerable body of legendary material around him. The first three gospels, which mention him simply as one of the Twelve Apostles, are silent about his life and personality; only John provides any details. By far the most famous of these is the story of Thomas's doubting the other apostles' belief that Christ has been resurrected; "doubting Thomas" believes only after Jesus comes to him and tells him to touch his wounds.

A widespread legend has Thomas in India evangelizing after Christ's Ascension. The Christians of Malabar in southern India insist that Thomas proselytized there, before an angry king had him martyred with a spear near Madras. Locals buried him at Mylapore, where Portuguese explorers discovered the tomb in 1522 and translated some of his relics to Ortona, Italy; alternatively, the relics moved to Edessa in the fourth century, and then to Chios before they came to Italy. The Cathedral of Saint Thomas in Mylapore also lays claim to some of the saint's relics.

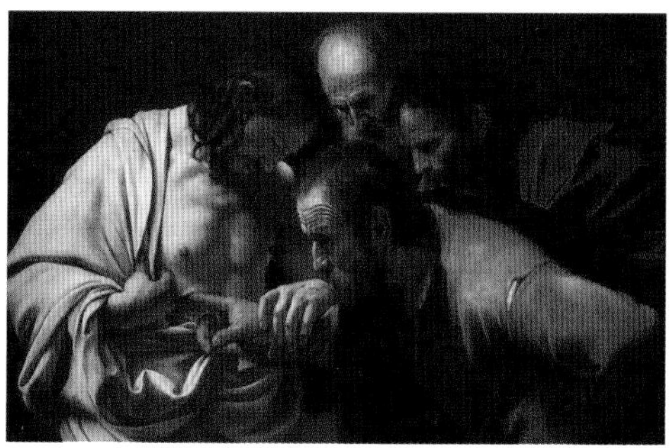

According to the Gospel of John, Thomas doubted that Jesus had been resurrected until he felt inside the crucifixion wounds of Jesus.

> *Thomas, because thou hast seen me, thou hast believed: blessed are they that have not seen, and yet have believed.*
>
> THE GOSPEL ACCORDING TO SAINT JOHN 20:29

BORN
Unknown

DIED
c. 72 (traditional)

CANONIZED
Pre-Congregation

FEAST DAY
3 July or 21 December (Western Church)
1 July (India)

PATRONAGES
India
Pakistan
Sri Lanka
architects
blindness
builders and construction workers
carpenters
doubt
geometricians
masons
stonecutters
theologians

ALSO KNOWN AS
Apostle of India
Didymus (twin)
Doubting Thomas
Judas Thomas
Jumeau

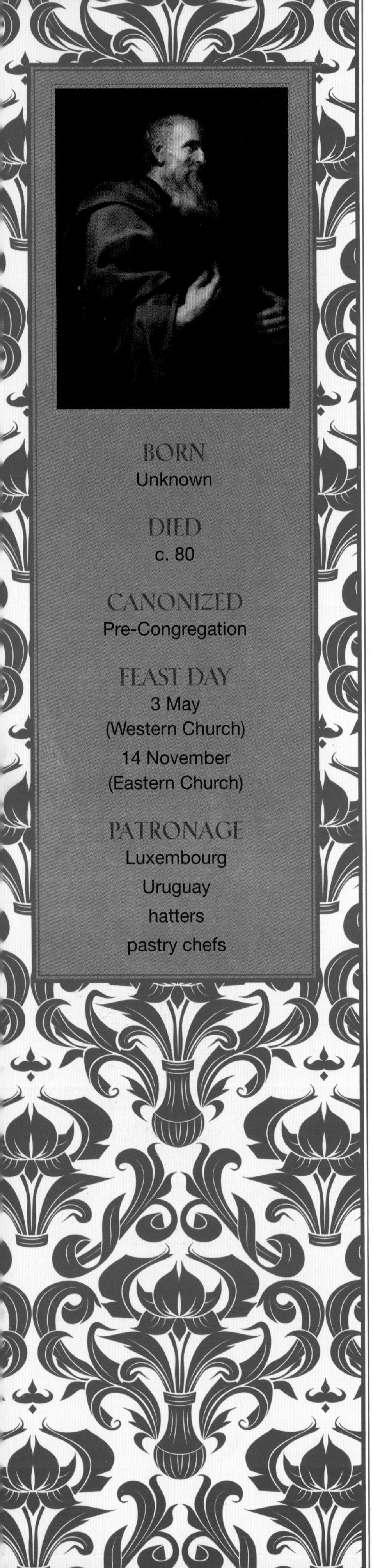

BORN
Unknown

DIED
c. 80

CANONIZED
Pre-Congregation

FEAST DAY
3 May
(Western Church)
14 November
(Eastern Church)

PATRONAGE
Luxembourg
Uruguay
hatters
pastry chefs

Saint Philip

Philip lived in Bethsaida in Galilee and became a disciple of Jesus on the advice of John the Baptist. Later Philip introduced to Jesus his friend Nathaniel, who likely is the same person as the apostle Bartholomew.

The Gospel of Saint John mentions Philip, particularly in the story of the loaves of bread and the fishes with which Jesus miraculously fed a great multitude of his followers (John 6:5–13). For this reason artists often portray John with loaves and fishes, or with a loaf and a cross or book.

Unfortunately, information on Philip even within the New Testament is scanty, and very little outside of it is trustworthy. Early confusion between Philip the Apostle and Philip the Deacon created uncertainty even within Philip's legends. One of the more likely tales, however, explains that Philip proselytized in Greece and Phrygia and suffered martyrdom by inverted crucifixion at Hierapolis.

Saint Bartholomew

Bartholomew's life is as murky as his friend Philip's, if not more so. Born probably in Cana, Bartholomew supposedly proselytized in "India" – a very vaguely understood eastern region, not equivalent to the modern country – and Armenia. Albanopolis claims to be the location of his martyrdom, accomplished by flaying and either beheading or crucifying him. In a rather macabre association, he has thus become the patron saint of tanners, furriers, glovers, and other skin-related industries.

Saints Jude & Simon

Nearly nothing is known about either Jude or Simon. Jude, a fisherman from Galilee, was brother to the Apostle James the Less and the author of the Epistle of Jude, which warns faithful Christians – his audience most likely consisted of converted Jews – away from heresies. Simon is even more shadowy, the only hint to his personality contained in his epithet, "the Zealous".

Lord, how is it that thou will manifest thyself unto us, and not unto the world?

Saint Jude (John 14:22)

One apocryphal source, *The Passion of Simon and Jude,* provides a legendary account of the two saints evangelizing Persia (a vague term including Parthia, Armenia, and surrounding areas). Jude proved himself a miracle worker, casting the demons out of statues to pagan gods while still in Palestine. Meanwhile, Simon proselytized in Egypt, but the two joined forces to travel east. They died in martyrdom, either by the sword or the saw, so that when pictured together one often holds a saw while the other bears a falchion, a kind of short sword. Though the earliest instance of the legend occurs in the sixth century, their shared cult may be older.

The saints, depicted next to the Madonna and child, carry traditional iconographical symbols: Saint Simon a saw, and Saint Jude a lance.

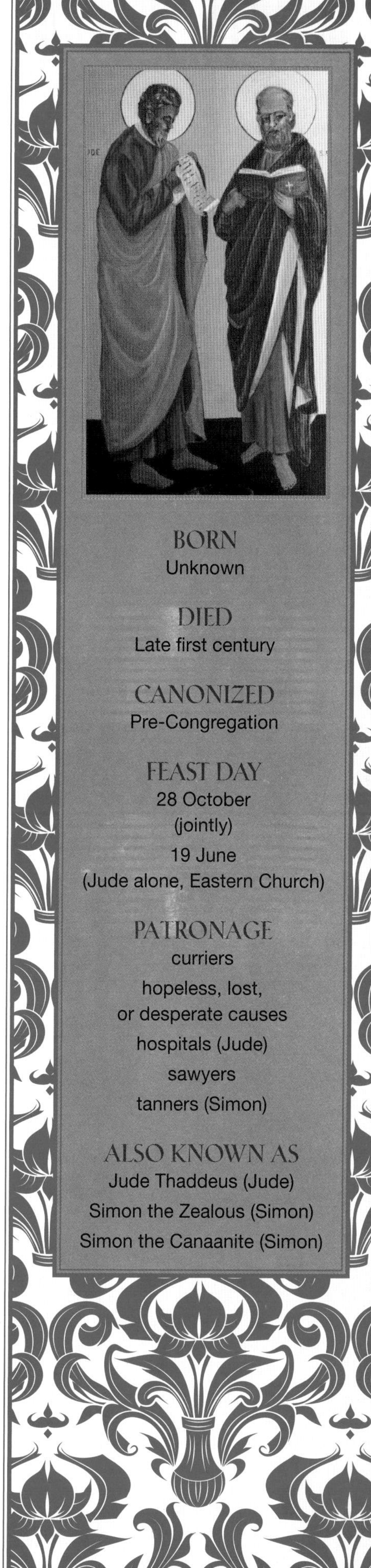

BORN
Unknown

DIED
Late first century

CANONIZED
Pre-Congregation

FEAST DAY
28 October
(jointly)
19 June
(Jude alone, Eastern Church)

PATRONAGE
curriers
hopeless, lost, or desperate causes
hospitals (Jude)
sawyers
tanners (Simon)

ALSO KNOWN AS
Jude Thaddeus (Jude)
Simon the Zealous (Simon)
Simon the Canaanite (Simon)

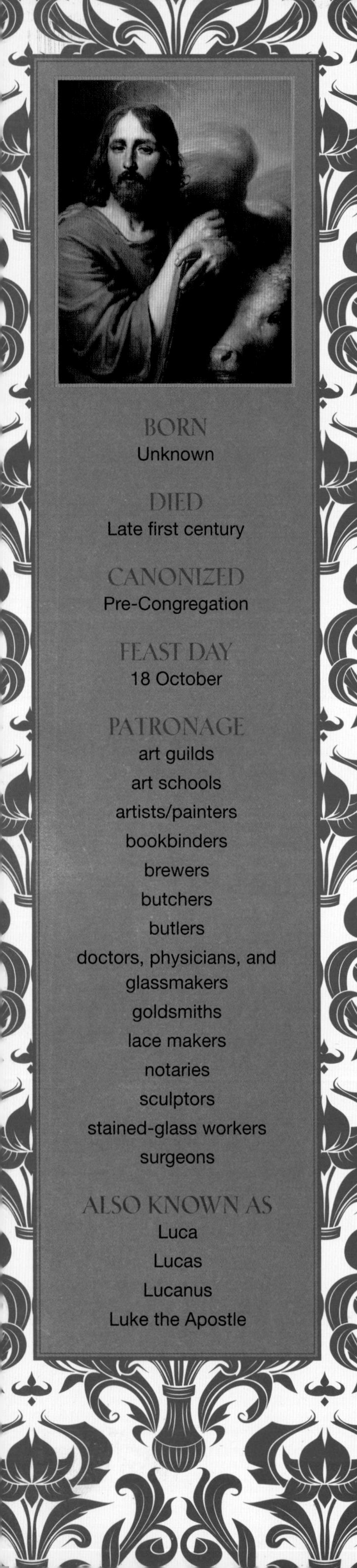

Saint Luke *the Evangelist*

A Greek-speaking doctor from Antioch, Saint Luke was raised in a pagan family and became a Christian convert shortly after Jesus' death (which occurred probably around 30 CE). Although he never knew Jesus, Luke's literary accomplishment stands out in both his contributions to the gospels and the Acts of the Apostles. Luke, who travelled widely with Saint Paul and knew Mark and Peter as well, included in his gospel several iconic parables missing from the other three, notably the Good Samaritan, the Prodigal Son, and the raising of Lazarus. Scholars have also noted with interest Luke's apparent emphasis on women and his overtures to Gentiles.

Luke is often pictured with a bull: a symbol of sacrifice, service, and strength. Another Christian tradition portrays Luke as an icon painter, especially of the Blessed Virgin Mary.

Luke went with Paul on the second of Paul's evangelist journeys but stopped at Philippi for several years to evangelize there. Paul rejoined him on his third trip and the two returned to Jerusalem together. When Paul travelled to Rome after his release from a Caesarean prison, Luke accompanied him again. The details of Luke's life after Paul's martyrdom are vague. An unverifiable tradition from the late second century claims that he died in Bithynia (more likely Boeotia, Greece) at the age of 74 or 84. He was, supposedly, a painter and carried an image of the Virgin Mary with him, but this too cannot be proven.

Saint John the Evangelist

John, author of three Epistles and the fourth gospel (which may have been edited shortly after his death), was brother to James the Greater and with him called Boanerges, meaning the "sons of thunder". The youngest of the Apostles, John nevertheless held a favoured position among them. In his gospel he introduces a theological point of supreme significance, that Jesus was God Incarnate – the eternal given historical specificity.

Like James, Andrew, and Peter, John was a fisherman before Christ recruited him to become a "fisher of men" (Matthew 4:19), and after Christ's Ascension, John proselytized in Ephesus, Samaria, and possibly Parthia. He supposedly survived poisoning and attempts to boil him in oil through the agency of miracles, and is the only apostle to die of natural causes.

He seems to have been close to Peter, with whom he travelled and preached. The two of them prepared the Last Supper and escaped after being imprisoned by King Herod Agrippa I. Along with the other apostles, John returned to Jerusalem by 51 for the first Apostolic Council and spent time on the isle of Patmos, where he received the vision that may have inspired the Book of Revelation.

Saint John the Evangelist was said to have had revelatory visions at Patmos. John, the youngest of the Twelve Apostles, is also often depicted as a youth accompanied by an eagle.

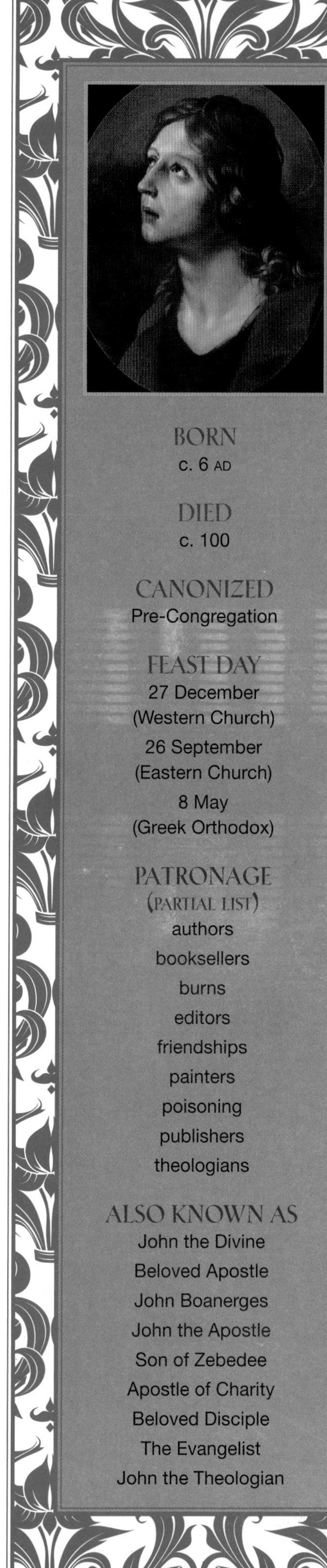

BORN
c. 6 AD

DIED
c. 100

CANONIZED
Pre-Congregation

FEAST DAY
27 December (Western Church)
26 September (Eastern Church)
8 May (Greek Orthodox)

PATRONAGE (PARTIAL LIST)
authors
booksellers
burns
editors
friendships
painters
poisoning
publishers
theologians

ALSO KNOWN AS
John the Divine
Beloved Apostle
John Boanerges
John the Apostle
Son of Zebedee
Apostle of Charity
Beloved Disciple
The Evangelist
John the Theologian

Saints of Vision and Ecstasy

Mysticism produced some of the most famous and controversial saints in the Christian tradition. The mystic's experience is, by definition, private, though certain effects – such as coma-like sleep – can be observed. The occasionally fantastic reports of ecstasy, trances, visions, and miracles can both frighten and arouse suspicion, and led to ridicule for more than one of the following saints. A few, including Bridget of Sweden and Joan of Arc, were even accused of heresy.

Mystics seem to attract miracles, or legends of miracles; many mystics have been seen to levitate. Joseph of Cupertino levitated so frequently that he became known as the "Flying Friar". Others seemed to give off a sweet scent, even in death. Yet mystics are unique in their ability to experience the divine personally, and it is perhaps for this reason that mystics, in particular, exhibit signs of divine favour, such as the holy light that shone from the face of Saint Frances of Rome as she died, or, more commonly, the stigmata, one of the most unusual features of Christian mysticism.

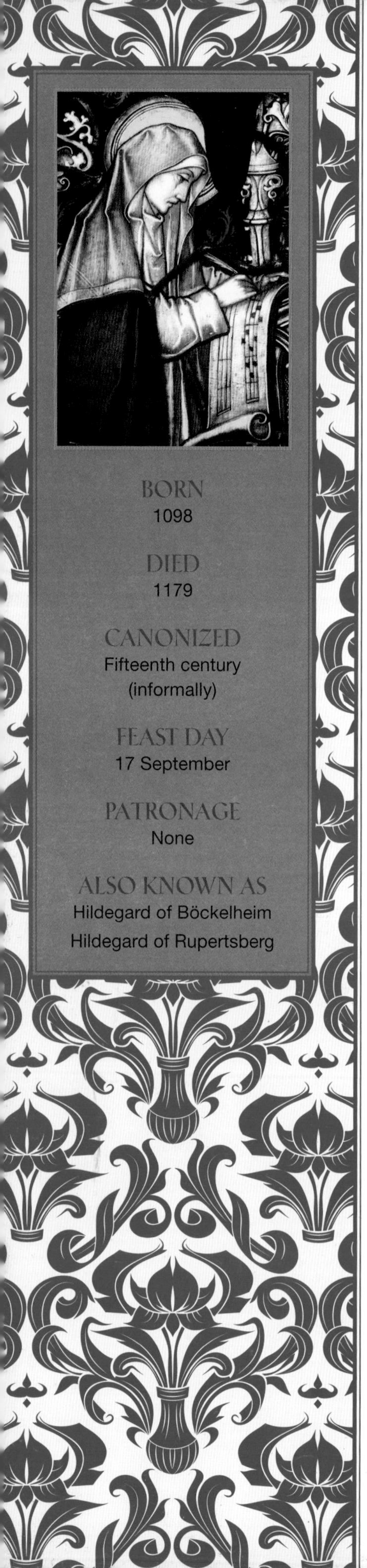

BORN
1098

DIED
1179

CANONIZED
Fifteenth century (informally)

FEAST DAY
17 September

PATRONAGE
None

ALSO KNOWN AS
Hildegard of Böckelheim
Hildegard of Rupertsberg

Saint HILDEGARD of Bingen

Saint Hildegard of Bingen was a Benedictine nun, a theologian who saw visions all her life. From the age of eight she studied with a reclusive nun named Jutta, the mother superior of the convent at Diessenberg, succeeding her as superior when Jutta died in 1136. In 1150 she moved her convent to Rupertsberg, near Bingen, and soon afterwards assumed leadership of Eibingen Abbey.

Hildegard did not promulgate her visions until she was forty years old. Blessed Pope Eugene III declared them legitimate and authentic visions from God. Thus encouraged, Hildegard composed her most famous work, *Scivias (The One Who Knows the Ways of God)*, whose reputation earned her the appellation "Sybil of the Rhine".

Hildegard has been portrayed as an early feminist for her espousal of gender equality and her defence of Eve. She did not shy away from voicing her strong, often uncomplimentary opinions about church reform and morality to the pope, King Henry II of England, or Holy Roman Emperor Frederick Barbarossa.

Efforts to canonize Hildegard failed, for reasons unknown, in the thirteenth and fourteenth centuries, but Church authorities added her name to the Roman Martyrology and her cult, active in Germany virtually since her death, won papal approval.

"Universal Man", an illumination from Liber divinorum operum (Book of Divine Works). *In her three works, written over the course of her lifetime, Hildegard describes all of her visions and interprets their meanings.*

Saint Gertrude the Great

Recognized as one of the most important mystics of the Middle Ages, Gertrude, like Saint Hildegard of Bingen, was never canonized, but her feast is officially celebrated in the Roman Martyrology. Gertrude is often mistakenly described as an abbess, the result of confusion with a second Gertrude who was the actual abbess at the Benedictine nunnery where Gertrude lived.

Gertrude's attachment to the nunnery of Helfta in Thuringia (Germany), began at the age of 5 when she started her education there; by all accounts she lived her entire life in Helfta and died there around the age of 46. Her conversion occurred at age 25, when she abandoned all secular pursuits.

Soften my hard self-opinionatedness, which time has hardened so exceedingly!

Saint Gertrude the Great

A legend of uncertain origin links Gertrude the Great to the souls in purgatory, and prayers to Gertrude are often invoked on their behalf.

Gertrude led an incredibly rich inner life once she embraced mysticism, receiving several vivid visions of Jesus and Mary. In one she was given rings from Jesus' hands, like Catherine of Siena; in another she saw Jesus pushing an arrow of light emanating from the wound in his side into her heart, like Teresa of Avila. Teresa felt a special closeness to Gertrude and chose her as a mentor, while Francis de Sales, among others, recommended Gertrude's writings, in which she discusses her visions and meditates on spiritual exercises and the communal religious life.

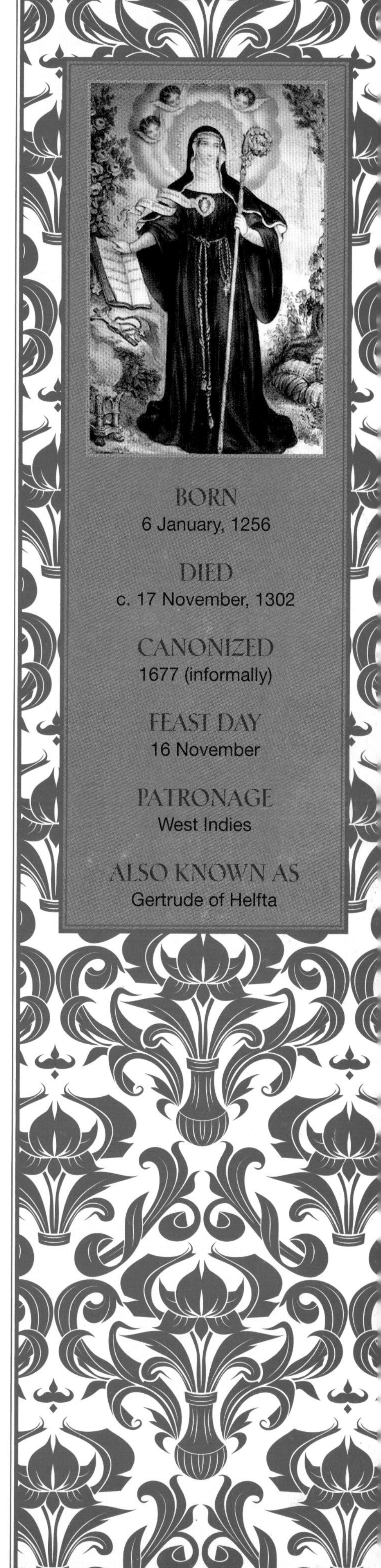

BORN
6 January, 1256

DIED
c. 17 November, 1302

CANONIZED
1677 (informally)

FEAST DAY
16 November

PATRONAGE
West Indies

ALSO KNOWN AS
Gertrude of Helfta

BORN
c. 1296

DIED
14 November, 1359

CANONIZED
1368

FEAST DAY
14 November

PATRONAGE
Thessalonica

Saint GREGORY Palamas

One of the most significant figures in the history of the Eastern Orthodox Church, Gregory Palamas became a monk around the year 1316 and lived in a monastery on Mount Athos, following the Rule of Saint Basil. The monks of Mount Athos practised hesychasm, a form of meditation in which they experienced the so-called "light of Tabor". Hesychasts believed that this light was God himself, identical to the light seen at the Transfiguration. This tradition, first espoused by Symeon the New Theologian (949–1022), came under attack in the fourteenth century, most notably by the Constantinople philosopher Barlaam the Calabrian.

The saint's relics are enshrined at the Cathedral of Saint Gregory Palamas in Thessalonica.

Gregory spearheaded the counter-attack so effectively that the theology of the practice became known as Palamism. Barlaam insisted that God was unknowable, and that the light that the monks saw was created, and therefore not of the eternal God; he dismissed out of hand the physical techniques of hesychasm.

Gregory developed the mystical notion that God is both transcendent and immanent, distinguishing between God's essence and energies – the one utterly unknowable and aloof, the other active and knowable through mystical union. In three church councils at Constantinople in 1341, 1347, and 1351, the issue was settled in Gregory's favour, and in 1347 Gregory became bishop of Thessalonica. He spent the rest of his life there, except for a year he spent in prison due to a Muslim invasion.

Saint Bridget *of Sweden*

Born into a noble family, Bridget married a prince at the age of 13. The happy marriage produced eight children, one of whom would later become Saint Catherine of Sweden. Bridget and her husband, Ulf Gudmarsson, dedicated themselves to a life of continence in the early 1340s; in 1344, Ulf died at his monastery.

Bridget had experienced visions and dreams since about 1335. After Ulf's death she began to fear these as symptoms of demonic attack, until finally – directed by a vision – she told a canon about them; she must have been greatly relieved to learn that her mystical experiences were actually divine in origin. Most of Bridget's visions directed her to speak out against kings, nobles, even the pope, which unsurprisingly made her quite unpopular. At one point an angry crowd in Rome attacked Bridget. Mistrustful of her visions, they accused the saint of witchcraft and threatened to burn her alive.

An illumination from a 1530 folio painted at Syon Monastery, a Bridgettine House in England, shows the risen Christ, displaying his wounds to Bridget and inspiring her to record and interpret her visions on paper.

Bridget's outspokenness did not prevent the Church from recognizing her saintly virtue: Pope Boniface IX canonized her a mere 18 years after her death. She became one of the most popular saints in Sweden and left a lasting legacy in the Bridgettine order, which she founded for women on the strength of a vision. The monastery is located at Vadstena in Sweden, but from 1349 Bridget herself lived in Rome, making short pilgrimages elsewhere.

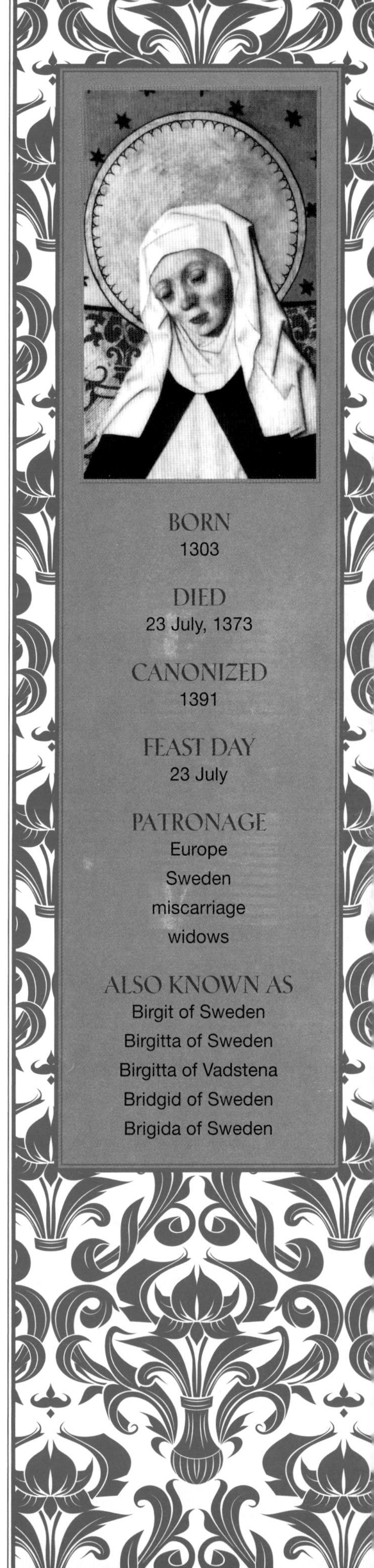

BORN
1303

DIED
23 July, 1373

CANONIZED
1391

FEAST DAY
23 July

PATRONAGE
Europe
Sweden
miscarriage
widows

ALSO KNOWN AS
Birgit of Sweden
Birgitta of Sweden
Birgitta of Vadstena
Bridgid of Sweden
Brigida of Sweden

Saint CATHERINE of Siena

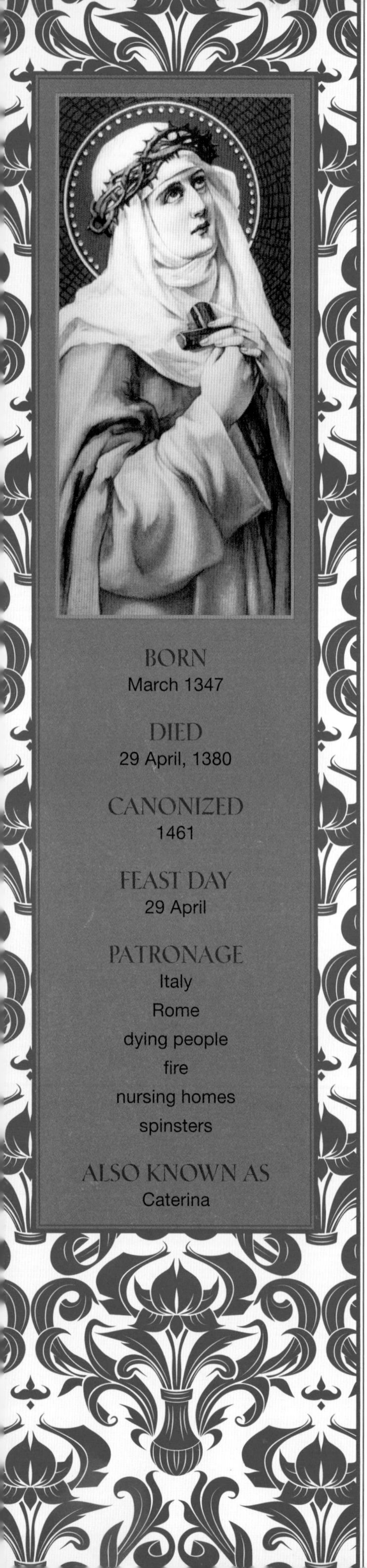

BORN
March 1347

DIED
29 April, 1380

CANONIZED
1461

FEAST DAY
29 April

PATRONAGE
Italy
Rome
dying people
fire
nursing homes
spinsters

ALSO KNOWN AS
Caterina

Catherine, born in Siena to a middle-class family, lived during a tumultuous time in Italy. The Black Death first appeared the year she was born; increasingly powerful Italian city-states vied for wealth and position; Crusaders and Saracens struggled for dominance in Palestine; and the Great Schism, which

As well as receiving the stigmata, by the time of her death Catherine ate almost nothing. She would disgorge her meals, insisting that she found no nourishment in earthly food.

Although Catherine lived with her family, as a tertiary sister she was permitted to wear a Dominican habit. Even at home, though, she isolated herself from her family, devoting herself to prayer and spiritual ecstasy.

saw one pope in Rome and another in Avignon, began in Catherine's lifetime.

The youngest child of a dyer was, perhaps, an unlikely figure to step into the midst of these momentous occurrences, but even as a little girl Catherine felt the hand of God. At six years of age she received a vision of Jesus, and one year later, at only seven years old, she consecrated her virginity. Though far from the desert wilderness where the early Christian anchorites withdrew from the world, Catherine nevertheless mimicked their ascetic lifestyle, joining the Dominican Tertiaries and becoming, as much as possible, a hermit while still living in her father's house.

This period ended in 1366, when Catherine experienced an intense mystical vision of her spiritual marriage to Christ. Attended by the Virgin Mary, the prophet David, and Saints John the Divine, Paul, and Dominic, Christ accepted his spiritual bride in ceremony and granted her a diamond-and-pearl ring, which, though she bore it for the rest of her days, was invisible to everybody except her. Similarly, when she received the stigmata in 1375, her wounds were hidden until after her death.

ABOVE: The Mystic Marriage of Saint Catherine of Siena *by Giovanni di Paolo is one of many artistic interpretations of the saint's visions.*

AUTHOR, DIPLOMAT, AND DOCTOR

At the age of 23 Catherine fell into a mystical trance whose visions inspired her most famous work, *The Dialogue of the Seraphic Virgin Catherine of Siena*. Dictated to scribes between 1377 and 1378, *Dialogue* contains a conversation between herself and God on the spiritual life of humankind and describes her visions of heaven, hell, and purgatory. This trance also marked a new phase in her life, for Catherine obeyed a divinely heard injunction to enter the world.

She began nursing lepers and plague victims and became known to Pope Gregory XI by virtue of the astonishing number of letters she sent to papal legates, princes, and powerful men and women all over Italy, seeking to address failing morality and improve relationships between contentious city-states. The pope himself sent her to various cities as his envoy, and when the next pope, Urban VI, was elected, she became an adviser to him as well. She fought hard for Pope Gregory's call to crusade, for the reconciliation between Avignon and Rome, and for reform throughout the Church, especially in the poorly managed Papal States. She died in 1380, after a three-month bout with a painful disease, leaving behind a group of devoted disciples and a valuable collection of mystical writings, which earned her the title Doctor of the Church in 1970.

Catherine of Siena is one of the two patron saints of Italy, together with Francis of Assisi.

Saint Joan of Arc

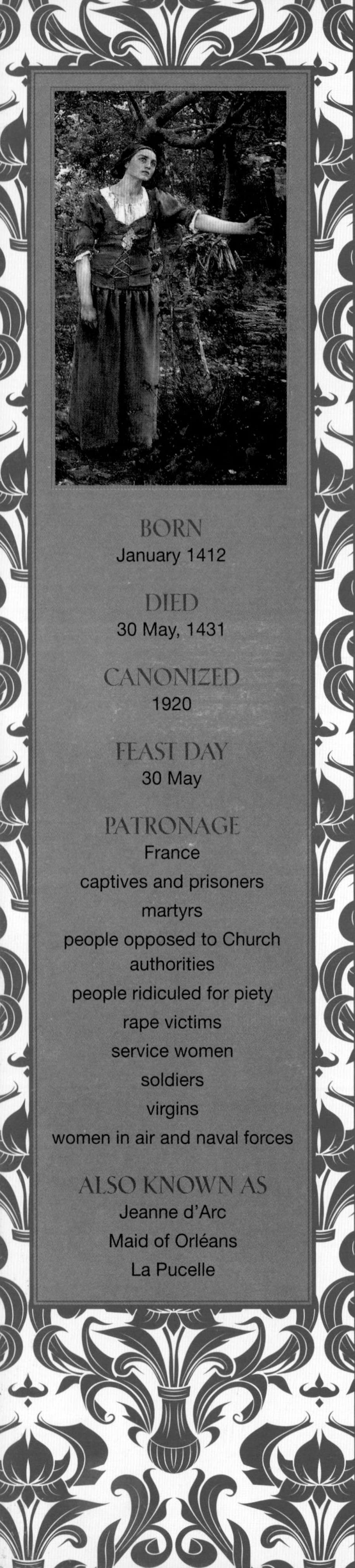

BORN
January 1412

DIED
30 May, 1431

CANONIZED
1920

FEAST DAY
30 May

PATRONAGE
France
captives and prisoners
martyrs
people opposed to Church authorities
people ridiculed for piety
rape victims
service women
soldiers
virgins
women in air and naval forces

ALSO KNOWN AS
Jeanne d'Arc
Maid of Orléans
La Pucelle

At the time of Joan of Arc's birth to a peasant couple in Domrémy, Champagne, France and England had been battling for control of the French throne for 75 years. The world in which Joan grew up looked ominous for the French; major French cities like Rouen, Reims, Orléans, and Paris were now solidly behind English lines.

ABOVE: *Joan identified her most common visions as the Archangel Michael and Saints Catherine of Alexandria and Margaret of Antioch. On a few occasions masses of angels led by the Archangel Gabriel appeared to her.*

GIRL FROM THE OAK WOOD

Rumours began circulating throughout France that a maid from Lorraine would save the country. The source is unclear, but Joan, who was born in the forest tracts of Lorraine and started to hear saints' voices at age 13, certainly fulfilled it. When she prophesied the defeat of the French at the

Bronze statue of Joan of Arc in Paris

The Sword in the Church

Before she left Chinon, Joan discovered a sword in the church of Saint Catherine at Fierbois. She brought it to the church prelates, who rubbed the rust away "without difficulty". Legend claims this sword was that of Charles Martel, the grandfather of Charlemagne and an earlier saviour of France who repelled the Muslims at Poitiers in 732. This remarkable artifact has never been found.

Battle of the Herrings (1429), she was conducted to Chinon, where the dauphin – the heir apparent to the throne of France – was kept in squalor.

The Maid of Orléans

In April of 1429, Joan raised her standard and rode to war in a suit of white armour. She met with little opposition and entered Orléans on 29 April. Her effect on the troops was dramatic, and by 8 May she had successfully captured all of the English forts around Orléans, liberating the city. She moved swiftly to capitalize on her victory, pressing her troops down the Loire Valley. French kings were traditionally crowned at Reims Cathedral, and on 17 June, with Charles VII's coronation, Joan fulfilled her divine mission.

Joan of the Lily

Unfortunately, French leaders – including the newly crowned king – did not support their divinely appointed heroine, and in April 1430 the saints warned that she would be taken captive, which she was, on 24 May. Brought to trial on

charges of heresy, apostasy, idolatry, and invoking evil spirits, Joan was sentenced to burn at the stake.

Joan made a tragic figure as she was led to her pyre on 30 May, 1431. Led before an angry crowd, the convicted heroine – a poorly used girl of 19 – asked for a cross, and one sympathizer fashioned a cross out of sticks for her while another held one before her. She fixed her gaze on this and cried the name of Jesus Christ as she died.

ABOVE: *The Burgundians' capture of Joan began the process by which she would be condemned to death.*

LEFT: *Twenty years after Joan's death at the stake, Pope Callixtus III authorized a posthumous retrial of her case. A formal appeal followed in November 1455. The appellate court declared her innocent in July 1456, describing Joan as a martyr.*

BELOW: *Joan of Arc medallion. Joan is a patron saint of France, along with Saints Louis IX, Denis of Paris, Martin of Tours, and Thérèse of Lisieux.*

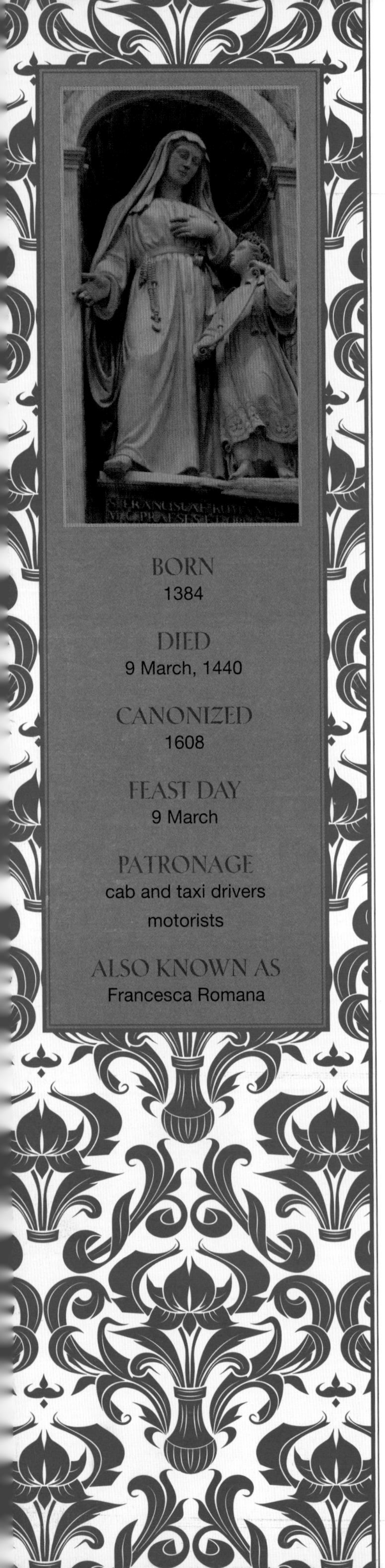

Saint Frances of Rome

Frances' desire to become a nun, expressed when she was only 11 years old, was stymied by her arranged marriage at age 13 to Lorenzo Ponziano. Lorenzo and his brother shared a house, so that Frances became friends with her sister-in-law, Vanozza, also a very pious woman. Together, nursing the sick, they reached out to the impoverished citizens of Rome.

Frances had a number of very powerful mystical visions and ecstasies in her lifetime. She saw, at one time or another, the Virgin Mary, Jesus, Saints Paul, Benedict, and Mary Magdalene, and even God. Her son, Evangelista, who had died at age nine and become an angel, also visited her. Her most famous vision, however, was of her guardian angel, whom she could see at all times. The angel guarded and guided her for 24 years.

The angel has finished his task; he beckons me to follow him.

Saint Frances of Rome, on her deathbed

The Vision of St Frances of Rome *by Orazio Gentileschi depicts Frances, as always with her angel by her side, meeting the Virgin and Child.*

In 1425 Frances founded the Oblates of Mary, later called the Oblates of Tor dé Specchi. This was a group of laywomen attached to the Benedictine order who did not take vows or live in a nunnery. Like Frances herself, the group was dedicated to the poor. Frances worked several miracles and made prophecies (including the day of her own death) but remained a humble, gentle creature to the end.

Saint Juan Diego

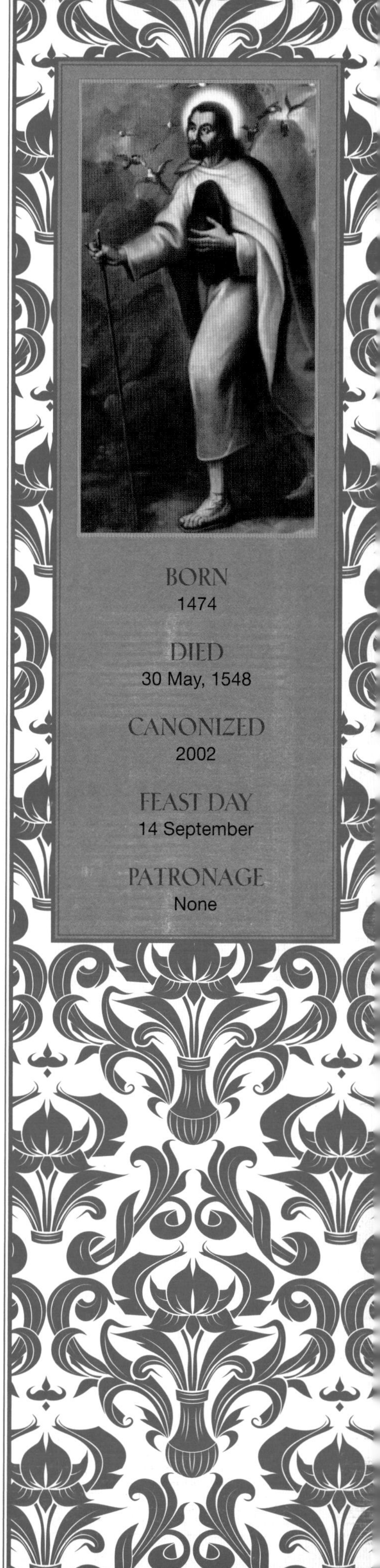

BORN
1474

DIED
30 May, 1548

CANONIZED
2002

FEAST DAY
14 September

PATRONAGE
None

An early convert from the Aztec religion in which he was raised, Juan Diego, born Cuauhtlatoatzin, took his Christian name upon his baptism in 1525. He and his wife were pious Christians, and every Sunday Juan Diego walked several miles from his home to church in Tenochtitlán (Mexico City). On one such walk in early December 1531, he heard a swell of birdsong and a beautiful voice calling to him as he reached the bottom of a hill called Tepeyacac.

At the top of the hill he beheld a lovely woman, and he bowed low before her. Dressed in traditional Aztec clothing and Mexican in appearance, the woman, whom he knew was the Virgin, told him to build a church on top of Tepeyacac. Juan Diego dutifully petitioned the bishop of Tenochtitlán, who was kind but unbelieving. Again Juan Diego saw Mary; again he brought her request to the bishop; again he was rebuffed. Finally, a miracle occurred: on her third appearance, Mary caused roses to grow on top of the hill, which Juan Diego gathered in his *tilma*, a kind of Aztec cloak.

No sooner had he opened his cloak to show the roses than the bishop fell on his knees. For there, imprinted on Juan Diego's *tilma*, was an image of the Virgin Mary herself. The church on top of Tepeyacac was built, and the holy image on the *tilma* can still be viewed there today.

Our Lady of Guadalupe (above). Juan Diego's original tilma *hangs above the altar of the Basílica de Guadalupe, Mexico City (at left).*

Saint Catherine of Genoa

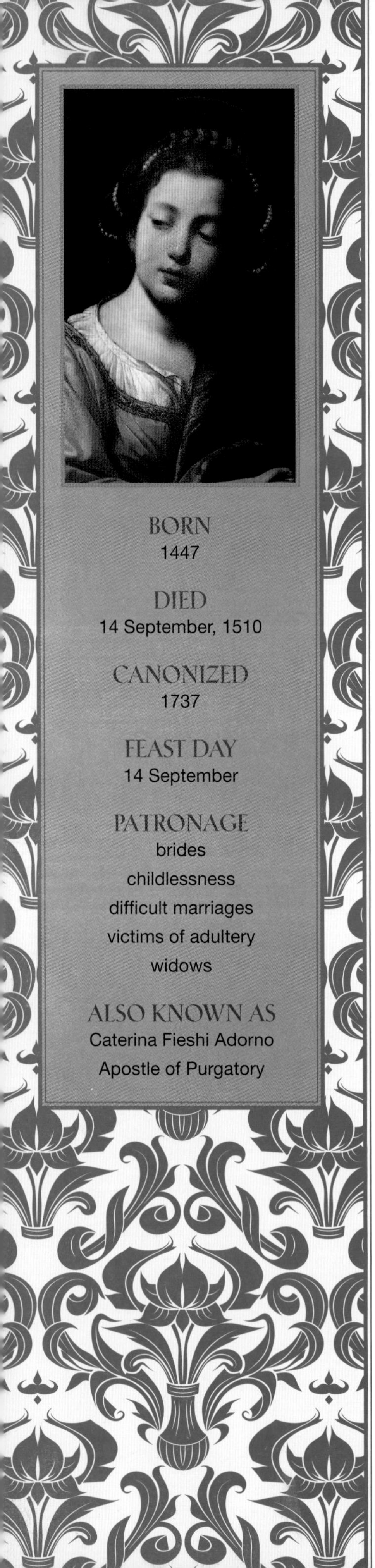

BORN
1447

DIED
14 September, 1510

CANONIZED
1737

FEAST DAY
14 September

PATRONAGE
brides
childlessness
difficult marriages
victims of adultery
widows

ALSO KNOWN AS
Caterina Fieshi Adorno
Apostle of Purgatory

Superficially, Catherine led a mundane life. Born to a well-to-do family, she married the man her parents picked for her, suffered a descent into poverty, volunteered among the impoverished and sick, and died a widow in her old age. Her inner life, however, was nothing short of extraordinary and may well be unique in the annals of Christianity.

As a child she had wanted to join a nunnery, but instead she followed her parents' wishes and married. Her husband, unfortunately, was perfidious and offensive, and Catherine suffered years of deep depression. One day, as she waited for the confessor to arrive, a divine light penetrated her soul. She experienced intense ecstasy and thereafter, for the rest of her life, perceived the purifying holy fires within herself in a kind of astonishingly long-lasting rapture. She had multiple visions of Christ and believed that divine fire consumed her own heart.

Catherine wrote extensively on purgatory, which she believed she suffered on earth – it was the holy fire she felt burning within herself.

Catherine practised extreme mortification and was often sick, but she nevertheless threw herself into the business of nursing others, eventually becoming manager of the hospital of Genoa. Even her miscreant husband reformed and died a repentant Franciscan.

If you are what you should be, you will set the whole world ablaze.

Saint Catherine of Genoa

Saint Felix of Cantalice

A gentle man of humble origin and even humbler character, Felix worked as a shepherd for many years in his home village of Cantalice. He was illiterate but had occasion to listen to a book on the fathers of the desert. The eremitical life appealed to him; failing the desert, he determined to join the Capuchin friary in Cittaducale, overcoming the superior's reluctance with his simple honesty and devotion.

Because of his vision, in art Felix is usually depicted holding in his arms the Infant Jesus.

> *Lead a good life; pray the rosary.*
>
> Saint Felix of Cantalice

He received his habit in 1543 and in 1547 was sent to Rome. There this loving soul, so self-effacing that he referred to himself as the "ass of the Capuchins", won over the city with his mild but constant exhortations to live a more holy life. Children, especially, flocked to him. Although he never learned to read or write he, nevertheless, earned a reputation for inventing verses and songs, always with a Christian purpose.

He rarely spoke of the mystical experiences earned in solitary nighttime prayer, but in his extreme reactions – from weeping to sudden jubilation – observers recognized the presence of the Holy Spirit. Only one of his visions did he relate in full to another brother: as an old man over seventy, Felix beseechingly asked Mary if he might hold the Infant Jesus, and she complied.

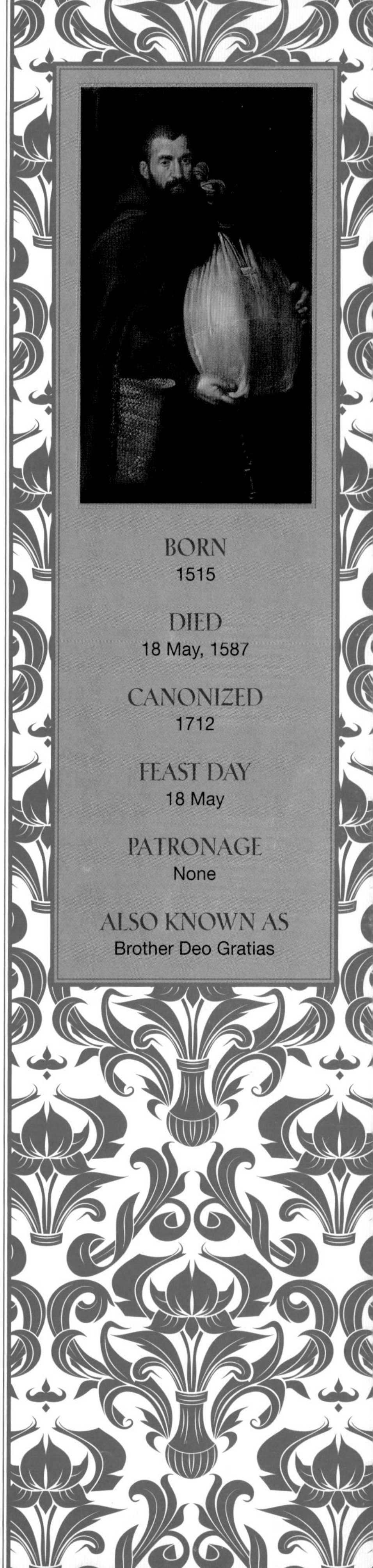

BORN
1515

DIED
18 May, 1587

CANONIZED
1712

FEAST DAY
18 May

PATRONAGE
None

ALSO KNOWN AS
Brother Deo Gratias

A Closer Look: *Miracles*

In the colloquial sense, a miracle is any amazing, unlikely, and beneficial event; but in the more specific sense used by Christians, it refers to an event contradictory to the laws of nature, evident to human observers. Miracles always stem directly from God's will; the miracles "performed" by saints are not a result of human powers but rather result from divine intercession. Saint Augustine, who at one time believed that miracles couldn't occur after the death of Jesus, changed his mind and argued that God's will could suspend the laws of nature whenever he wanted. Today, the Catholic Church considers at least two miracles necessary proof for canonization for saints who are not martyrs; non-martyred saints are thus, by definition, miracle workers.

He restored to Christianity its true face as a religion of hope.

Pope Benedict XVI, about Blessed Pope John Paul II

ABOVE: *Blessed Teresa of Calcutta. Until his own beatification, John Paul II's elevation of Mother Teresa to the Blessed Teresa of Calcutta was the fastest that anyone had ever been beatified. He officially recognized that the healing of an Indian woman's abdominal tumour after the application of a locket containing Mother Teresa's picture was a valid miracle that took place at the intercession of Mother Teresa.*

Statue of John Paul II. Only six years after his death, Pope Benedict XVI beatified John Paul after declaring that a French nun's recovery from Parkinson's disease was a miracle attributable to his predecessor. Benedict waived the typical five-year waiting period to begin the process of canonization.

JAN PAWEŁ II PAPIEŻ 1920–2005

KINDS OF MIRACLES

Miracles come in many forms, but there are a few kinds that appear repeatedly in the lives of saints. Many have manifested the stigmata – the wounds of Jesus inflicted upon the body of the saint. These five wounds are the nail wounds in the hands and feet and the wound in the side, next to the heart. Other saints, such as Julian of Norwich and Catherine of Siena, bore the stigmata of the crown of thorns.

Other miracles include saints who raised the dead or cured the sick. There have been saints with the gift of prophecy or mystical knowledge. Others, such as Padre Pio, were blessed with the gift of bilocation – the ability to be in two places at once. Joseph of Cupertino and Gerard Majella both experienced miraculous levitations. Others have the ability to speak in tongues or understand foreign and ancient biblical languages. John Bosco and Joseph of Cupertino are known for the miracles associated with animals. There are also those saints who survived despite near-complete fasting from food for years, such as Catherine of Siena, and others whose bodies remained incorrupt long after death, including Charbel Makhlouf

Some saints, such as Margaret of Cortona, are said to have had a gift of prophecy. Margaret knew the date of her own death and also had visions in which she spoke with Jesus, who called her poverella, *the "poor one". After renouncing her worldly life Margaret had entered a Franciscan order, living the life of a penitent. She was also instrumental in establishing a hospital for the poor and sick in Cortona.*

Magic and Miracles

The ability to distinguish between miracles – supernormal or supernatural events bestowed by God, sometimes through a human intercessor – and magic – supernormal or supernatural events provoked by human agents – was crucial in early Christian history. Medieval hagiographies often included a battle between the saint and the pagan magician-priest: the saint, whose powers were not his own but actually God's, always bested the pagan, whose magical powers came from demons. (A classic example of this can be found in the apocryphal, second-century text Acts of Peter, which pits Simon Magus against Saint Peter). The association between magical ability and demons began to strengthen in the twelfth century as belief in both intensified. In the Reformation, some Protestants accused Catholics of performing magic; it is partially for this reason that many Protestant sects eschew traditional Catholic rituals.

BORN
23 April, 1522

DIED
2 February, 1590

CANONIZED
1746

FEAST DAY
13 February

PATRONAGE
against illness
sick people

ALSO KNOWN AS
Catherine of Ricci

Saint CATHERINE de' Ricci

Taking the name of Catherine upon becoming a Dominican nun of the Third Order when she was only 14 years old, Catherine de' Ricci was born Alessandra Lucrezia Romola to a wealthy family in Florence, Italy. Even as a child Catherine inclined towards religious contemplation and had visions of a guardian angel instructing her in devotion.

As a nun she practised extreme mortification, fasting often and wearing an iron chain. Frequent illness did nothing to temper her ascetic habits. She had several mystical experiences, most famously a 28-hour-long ecstasy that recurred each week at Thursday noon from 1542 to 1554. Particularly enraptured by Christ's crucifixion, Catherine experienced it herself and exhibited the stigmata, visible to some as the actual bleeding wounds of Christ and to others as reddened, swollen skin.

In another mystical vision, Catherine de' Ricci received a ring from Christ, much as Saint Catherine of Siena had. Legend maintains that she bilocated on one occasion to Rome, and she is rumoured to have had conversations with Saints Maria Magdalena de Pazzi and Philip Neri, whom she never met in the flesh. The latter confirmed that in a vision he once had a long conversation with Catherine.

As did Catherine of Siena, in her visions Catherine de' Ricci saw herself in a marriage to Jesus. She also had weekly ecstasies of the Passion that began when she was twenty and lasted for 12 years. In these, Christ's wounds covered her body, appearing in order from the scourging to the crowning of thorns.

Saint Philip Neri

BORN
22 July, 1515

DIED
26 May, 1595

CANONIZED
1622

FEAST DAY
26 May

PATRONAGE
Rome

ALSO KNOWN AS
Philip Romolo Neri
Second Apostle of Rome
Filippo Neri

Abandoning the career in business that his family had pushed upon him, Philip moved to Rome in 1533 with no money and no connections. He lived there for the next 17 years as an impoverished tutor, studying philosophy and theology, and writing poetry – most of which, unfortunately, he later burned.

Eventually, he began ministering to the sick and needy. His charismatic personality soon attracted followers, and Philip's fame as the "Apostle to Rome" spread. The year 1544 was crucial for Philip: not only did he meet and befriend Ignatius Loyola, but also while praying in the catacomb of San Sebastiano he experienced such an intense union with the Holy Spirit, which he perceived as a "globe of fire", that his heart actually swelled in size, breaking two of his ribs and creating a protrusion on his side. He experienced no pain, but the protrusion was visible for the rest of his life.

Philip Neri is also noted for founding a society of priests and lay-brothers called the "Congregation of the Oratory". There are now more than seventy of these communities worldwide.

Philip finally became a priest in 1551, whereupon numerous ecstatic raptures befell him. He developed the ability to "smell" sin and read the minds of unrepentant people who came to his confessional. Mary saved him from one illness in 1594 – he levitated in rapture – but in 1595 he predicted his own death, even to its hour: "Last of all," said Philip to his final visitors, "we must die."

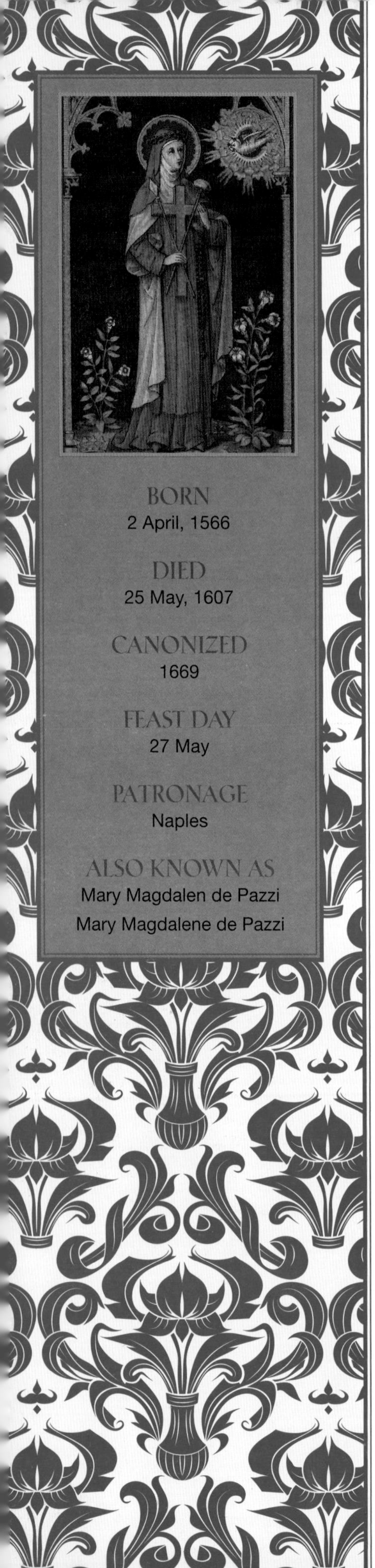

BORN
2 April, 1566

DIED
25 May, 1607

CANONIZED
1669

FEAST DAY
27 May

PATRONAGE
Naples

ALSO KNOWN AS
Mary Magdalen de Pazzi
Mary Magdalene de Pazzi

Saint Maria Magdalena de Pazzi

Born into one of the most famous families of Florence, Maria Magdalena – christened Caterina – renounced the worldly life of luxury she could have led (the more so due to her extraordinary beauty) and instead became a nun.

She entered a Carmelite convent in 1582 and lived, outwardly at least, an unremarkable if sanctified life. A gift for administration moved her rapidly through the ranks until, despite continual bouts of illness, the convent named her its superior in 1604. Around this time she contracted the extremely painful sickness that eventually killed her in 1607.

A depiction of one of the ecstasies of Maria Magdalena de Pazzi in which Saint Augustine of Hippo writes with a quill pen upon her heart.

Her inner life, however, was anything but ordinary. From childhood she demonstrated an unusual and profound love of the Holy Eucharist and felt attracted to her nunnery from the first because it offered daily Communion. More strikingly, she experienced an astonishing number of ecstasies. These could affect her in the way common to mystics, and she would lie as though dead. Unusually however, Maria Magdalena was often capable of working normally while in the throes of rapture. Sometimes, she would speak while enraptured.

Observers recorded these utterances, which included conversations with Jesus Christ and various saints, so that a full seven volumes were eventually published. In recognition of her holiness, and the miracles that followed her death, the Vatican began the beatification process in 1610, only three years after her passing.

Saint Joseph of Cupertino

Joseph of Cupertino rose into the air so often that he became known as the "Flying Friar" for his unrivalled number of witnessed levitations. He was a poor student with a fiery temper and a resentful, impoverished mother. Nicknamed "the Gaper", for his habit of walking about with his mouth open, he gaped, not out of mental incapacity, but because, even as a child, he experienced mystical trances.

Because of his many "flights", this patron saint of those travelling by air, such as pilots and astronauts, is known as the "Flying Friar".

Joseph fell into trances with remarkable ease all his life – virtually every time he saw, heard, or even thought of something holy, which occurred frequently after his priestly ordination in 1628. His levitation during Mass and his repeated ecstasies were of such intensity that even pinpricking or attempts to burn him could not bring him out. This intensity caused much consternation among his superiors, and at one point he was brought before the Neapolitan Inquisition. Despite this official concern, however, Joseph remained popular among the laity.

He lived in various degrees of seclusion – at the demand of his superiors – and in his last ten years went from one monastery to another, finally dying, as he predicted, at Osimo, an ancient town on Italy's eastern coast. In addition to levitation and trances, Joseph displayed other mystical abilities, including a rapport with animals to rival even Saint Francis of Assisi's, and the ability to "smell" sin.

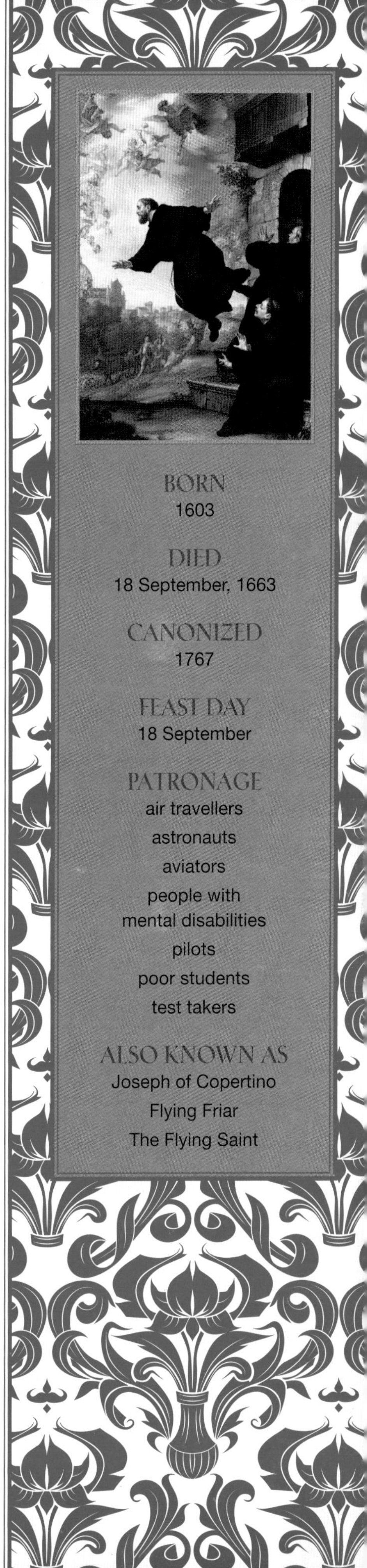

BORN
1603

DIED
18 September, 1663

CANONIZED
1767

FEAST DAY
18 September

PATRONAGE
air travellers
astronauts
aviators
people with mental disabilities
pilots
poor students
test takers

ALSO KNOWN AS
Joseph of Copertino
Flying Friar
The Flying Saint

Saint PETER of Alcántara

BORN
1499

DIED
18 October, 1562

CANONIZED
1669

FEAST DAY
19 October

PATRONAGE
Brazil
watchmen

ALSO KNOWN AS
San Pedro de Alcántara

Peter of Alcántara was born near the Portuguese border of Spain, the son of the governor of Alcántara and a noblewoman. Despite his high birth, he dedicated his life to helping the poor.

Peter himself embraced poverty and chose a very strict eremitical lifestyle. By the time he had risen to provincial of St Gabriel in Estremadura, in 1538, the Protestant Reformation was in full swing and Peter fought hard for the Counter-, or Catholic, Reformation.

At first he met with little success and was so disturbed by the opposition to his reforms that he retired to Arabida, Portugal, in 1540. There he lived in the mountains as a hermit with Saint John of Avila. They began to attract followers, who eventually created a reformed Franciscan order, the Alcatrines. The Alcantrines lived in abject poverty, strictness, and humility.

Peter was prone to outbreaks of mysticism, including rapturous trances, levitation, and walking on water. Pope Gregory XV complimented the treatise he wrote on the subject, calling it a "doctrine prompted by the Holy Spirit". Peter also wrote many letters of interest to students of mysticism, especially his correspondence with Saint Teresa of Avila, to whom he supplied much advice and encouragement.

Statue of Saint Peter of Alcántara in St. Peter's Basilica in Vatican City.

Saint Margaret Mary Alacoque

Few people, even other saints, lived a life as devoted to Jesus Christ as did Margaret Mary Alacoque. She would curb any behaviour upon being told God found it objectionable, even as a child of two. She cherished solitude and prayer and even practised fasting and mortification, consecrating her virginity in childhood.

She joined the Visitation Convent at Paray-le-Monial in 1671, but she did not endear herself to her fellow nuns. When she experienced her most famous visions, between December 1672 and June 1675, she at first met with resistance and ridicule. In these visions, Jesus Christ instructed her in the devotion to the Sacred Heart, calling Margaret Mary his Beloved Disciple of the Sacred Heart. This special devotion to Jesus, which became very popular in France, was adopted by the universal Church in 1856 by Pope Pius IX.

Margaret Mary lived to see her own initially hesitant convent observe the feast of the Sacred Heart for the first time in 1686. When she fell ill she refused all treatment, and she died at only 43 years of age. She had, in fulfilment of her own desires, lived a life of suffering. To Margaret Mary, suffering was a means of showing love for Jesus Christ – she used to worry that she could not crucify herself for him, as he had for her.

The Sacred Heart is an enduring religious devotion, which uses Jesus' physical heart as the representation of his divine love for humanity.

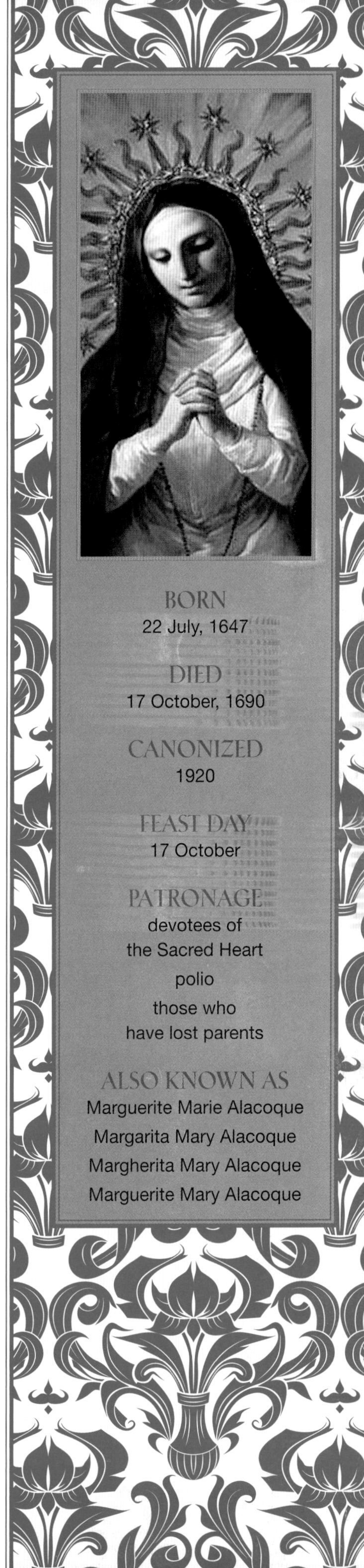

BORN
22 July, 1647

DIED
17 October, 1690

CANONIZED
1920

FEAST DAY
17 October

PATRONAGE
devotees of the Sacred Heart
polio
those who have lost parents

ALSO KNOWN AS
Marguerite Marie Alacoque
Margarita Mary Alacoque
Margherita Mary Alacoque
Marguerite Mary Alacoque

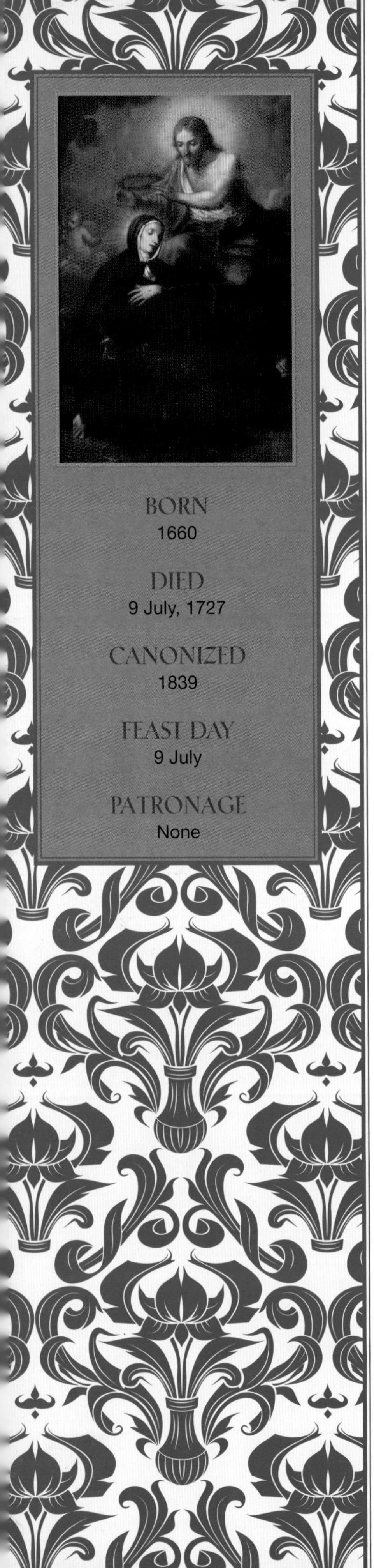

Saint VERONICA *Giuliani*

Veronica Giuliani suffered more than most mystics. In addition to visions – one of which, in revealing her heart made of steel, convinced her to soften her character – she also developed stigmata, suffering pain from the crown of thorns from 1694, when the wounds first appeared, until her death in 1727.

She received the crown of thorns (and later, stigmata on her hands, feet, and side) after she accepted in a vision the chalice of suffering from Christ. She immediately felt pain in her heart; when examined after her death, it appeared it had been stamped with a cross.

Despite this physical pain, as well as the misery inflicted by ecclesiastical authorities who subjected her mysticism to humiliating tests, Veronica served her nunnery well. She fought with her father to be allowed to enter when just 17 years old, but after she fell ill he relented. Veronica joined the Poor Clares, a reformed order of Capuchins – and immediately recovered from her sickness.

She served as novice-mistress for 34 years, rising to abbess in 1716. Remarkably, she kept a diary of her mystical experiences for 33 years (published posthumously in ten volumes) but never allowed her novices to read it.

Veronica's Namesake

Upon becoming a nun, the young Ursula Giuliani took the name Veronica in honour of Saint Veronica. According to legend, Veronica – identified as Berenike in the East – was a Jerusalem matron who accompanied Jesus Christ as he bore his cross to the crucifixion, giving him her veil to wipe his perspiring forehead. The "Veil of Veronica" thereafter bore Christ's imprinted image, and from the eighth century St. Peter's in Rome reportedly kept the relic. The image of Veronica wiping Christ's face eventually became one of the 14 Stations of the Cross in the popular Franciscan devotion commemorating Christ's Passion.

Saint GERARD Majella

Gerard took holy vows only three years before the end of his short life but became famous for his charity, dutifulness, and miracles. Among the kinds of miracles attributed to him are the ability to levitate, read hearts, and command the weather. He was born to a tailor, apprenticed to another, and finally opened his own tailoring business in 1745. Even in this worldly life he displayed remarkable sanctity, bequeathing one portion of his earnings to his mother and a second to the poor, for whom he showed a special affinity.

Rejected by the Franciscan Capuchins, Gerard Majella found a place with the newly formed Congregation of the Most Holy Redeemer.

I see in my neighbour the Person of Jesus Christ.

Saint Gerard Majella

He tried to join the Franciscans but was turned away; however, Saint Alphonsus Liguori, founder of the Redemptorists, accepted him into his new order in 1749. Scandal threatened the reputation of this holy mystic when a pregnant woman accused the young priest of fathering her child. Fortunately, she retracted her calumny, and Gerard bore the shame of the accusation with such gentle grace that Alphonsus declared him a saint.

As other mystics, Gerard had the gift of prophecy, predicting the hour of his death and naming the cause: tuberculosis. He was only 29 years old, but the many miracles he performed earned him the sobriquet "the Wonder-Worker".

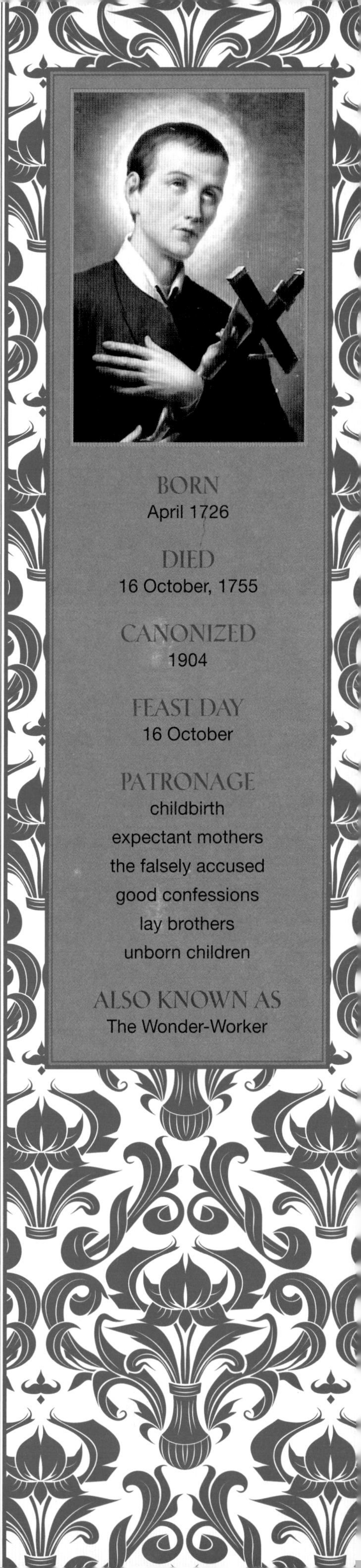

BORN
April 1726

DIED
16 October, 1755

CANONIZED
1904

FEAST DAY
16 October

PATRONAGE
childbirth
expectant mothers
the falsely accused
good confessions
lay brothers
unborn children

ALSO KNOWN AS
The Wonder-Worker

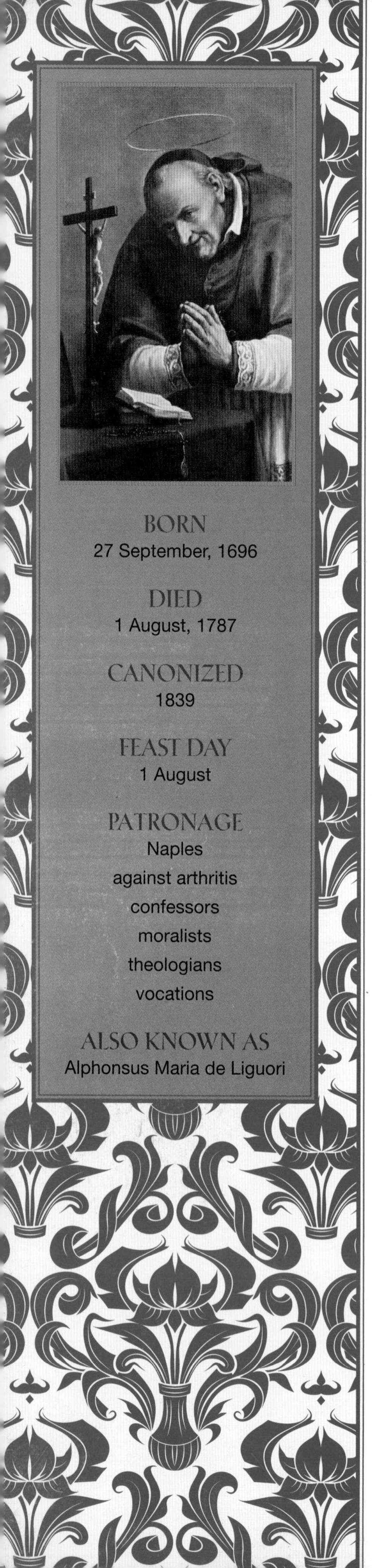

BORN
27 September, 1696

DIED
1 August, 1787

CANONIZED
1839

FEAST DAY
1 August

PATRONAGE
Naples
against arthritis
confessors
moralists
theologians
vocations

ALSO KNOWN AS
Alphonsus Maria de Liguori

Saint ALPHONSUS Liguori

Intelligent and scholarly, Alphonsus became a lawyer at the tender age of 19, having earned his degree three years previously. He enjoyed incredible success for a period of eight years, despite his youth, and though he was pious by nature he showed no inclination towards a religious career until a humiliating scene in court, where he made a gross error, threw him into a state of inconsolable grief. He was 26 years old.

Later that year, on 28 August, Saint Alphonsus was visiting a hospital when he experienced a revelation accompanied by a bright light and twice heard the words, "Leave the world and give thyself to me." Obediently, and over his father's intense opposition, Alphonsus joined the Fathers of the Oratory in October 1723; he was ordained in 1726.

Venerable Maria Celeste Crostarosa, founder of the Redemptoristines, the companion female order to Alphonsus Liguori's Redemptorists.

In 1732, another mystic, Sister Maria Celeste Crostarosa, told him that a divine revelation had made it known to her that Alphonsus should found an order to teach and preach in the slums of cities. While she set up a companion congregation of nuns, Alphonsus founded the Congregation of the Most Holy Redeemer.

The order was wracked by internal dissension, the death of Sister Marie Celeste, and a schism in 1780 that sadly did not heal until after the saint's death. Alphonsus travelled with unceasing missionary zeal throughout Naples, becoming a famous preacher and mystic, and at the age of 49 began to write on theology and devotion. He published his most famous work, *Moral Theology*, in two volumes, in 1753 and 1755. These writings eventually convinced Pope Pius IX to declare him a Doctor of the Church in 1871.

Saint Jean-Marie-Baptiste Vianney

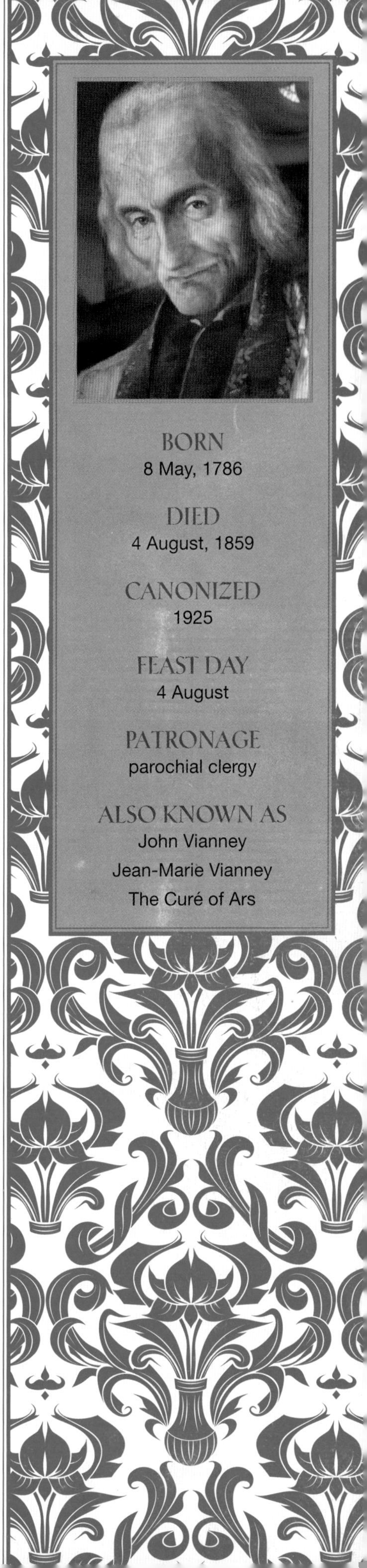

BORN
8 May, 1786

DIED
4 August, 1859

CANONIZED
1925

FEAST DAY
4 August

PATRONAGE
parochial clergy

ALSO KNOWN AS
John Vianney
Jean-Marie Vianney
The Curé of Ars

Jean-Marie-Baptiste grew up on his father's farm near Lyons, and he worked as a shepherd throughout his childhood. His studies at a school for ecclesiastical students were interrupted when the army drafted him during Napoleon's Peninsular War. He deserted and might have faced charges, but his brother took his place in the army.

His inadequate education haunted his attempts to join the priesthood, yet despite his meagre learning, Vianney ultimately passed his exams, taking his orders in 1815. Two years later he became curé, or parish priest, in the tiny village of Ars. He soon became known for his preaching and for his skill in the confessional, where he was reputed to have the ability to read the hearts and minds of those who wouldn't reveal all. He could also prognosticate and multiply food and money, especially for the Providence, a catechetical school he founded for orphaned girls. He battled regularly with Satan, who attacked him physically and on one occasion set fire to his bed.

The Sanctuaire de St Jean-Marie Vianney, the shrine to the saint in Ars. Between 1830 and 1845 an average of 300 people visited the tiny village every day to meet with the curé.

He had achieved such renown that, by the end of his life, Ars hosted twenty thousand visitors every year; Vianney spent upward of 16 hours a day in the confessional hearing them. Yet he never lost his incredible humility: he refused a knighthood, and when he was promoted to canon he sold his robes to feed the poor. For forty years he lived on nothing but a potato or two and two hours of sleep a day. His survival is testament to the mystical endurance of this holy man.

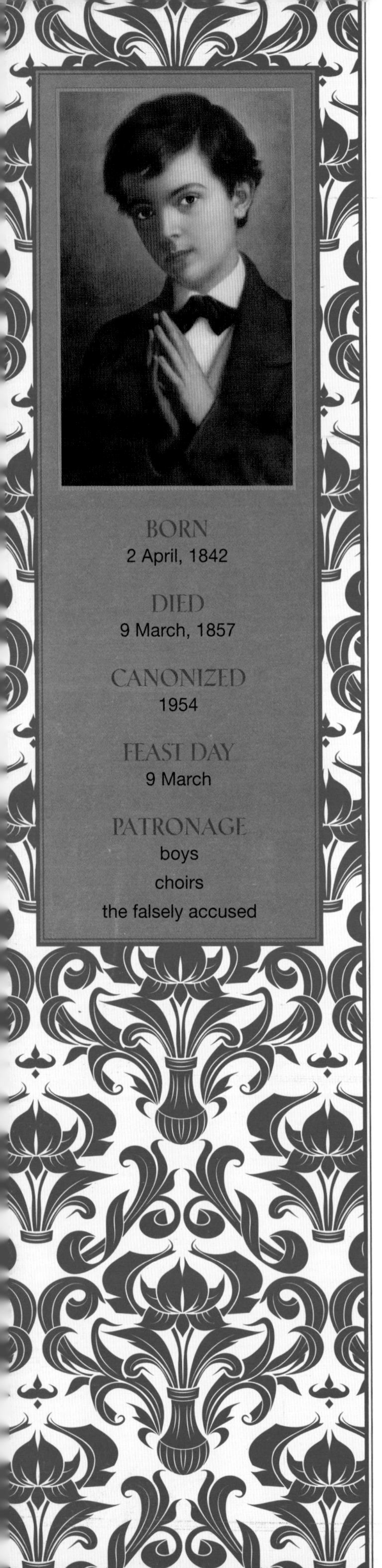

BORN
2 April, 1842

DIED
9 March, 1857

CANONIZED
1954

FEAST DAY
9 March

PATRONAGE
boys
choirs
the falsely accused

Saint DOMINIC *Savio*

A student of Saint John Bosco, Dominic displayed an intense religiosity at a very young age, praying in solitude when just four years old and becoming a choirboy at five. He experienced periods of ecstatic prayer, which he referred to as his "distractions". John Bosco records one such occasion when the boy prayed for six hours without moving or noticing the passage of time.

Although Dominic's manifest sanctity did not always win him friends at John Bosco's school, his example nevertheless produced beneficial results on several occasions, as when he formed a group called the Company of the Immaculate Conception, which performed religious devotions and made itself useful in practical matters.

His teacher – and fellow saint – John Bosco wrote the first biography of Dominic Savio.

John Bosco related a mystical vision of Dominic's to Pope Pius IX in which a bishop carried a torch across a misty English plain; the remarkable child and the pope both recognized the vision as an injunction to return the Catholic faith to England.

I can't do big things, but I want all I do, even the smallest thing, to be for the greater glory of God.

SAINT DOMINIC SAVIO

On the occasion of his first Communion, Dominic resolved to die before sinning, and in this, sadly, he was wholly successful. He died smiling one month before his fifteenth birthday with a vision of Heaven before his eyes, declaring, "What wonderful things I see."

Saint Catherine *Labouré*

After losing her mother when just nine years old, Catherine Labouré – nicknamed Zoe by her family – looked after her siblings and her widowed father. She joined the Sisters of Charity in 1830 and spent the rest of her life as an unremarkable nun of rather distant, reserved character.

Not until the year of her death, 1876, did Catherine reveal to her Mother Superior her incredible mystical experiences. As a young woman she had several intense visions, including one of an elderly, saintly priest whom she discovered, after joining the nunnery, to be none other than Saint Vincent de Paul, the Sisters of Charity's founder.

Her most famous visions occurred in a series in 1830 and were all of the Virgin Mary. Few people knew about these, but in 1836 an ecclesiastic review found them to be genuine. In one, Mary showed Catherine the design for the so-called Miraculous Medal, which was endorsed by the Church and became extraordinarily popular.

ABOVE: *Saint Catherine Labouré's relics lie in a glass coffin in the Chapel of Our Lady of the Miraculous Medal in Paris.*

LEFT: *The Miraculous Medal, also known as the Medal of the Immaculate Conception, is worn by many who believe that the Virgin will intercede for them at the hour of death, granting them special graces.*

Catherine predicted her own death as well as several other events, including the anticlerical protest in Paris in 1870 and possibly the execution by radicals of Archbishop Darboy in 1871. Her body – still incorrupt – can be found at the Chapelle Rue du Bac in Paris.

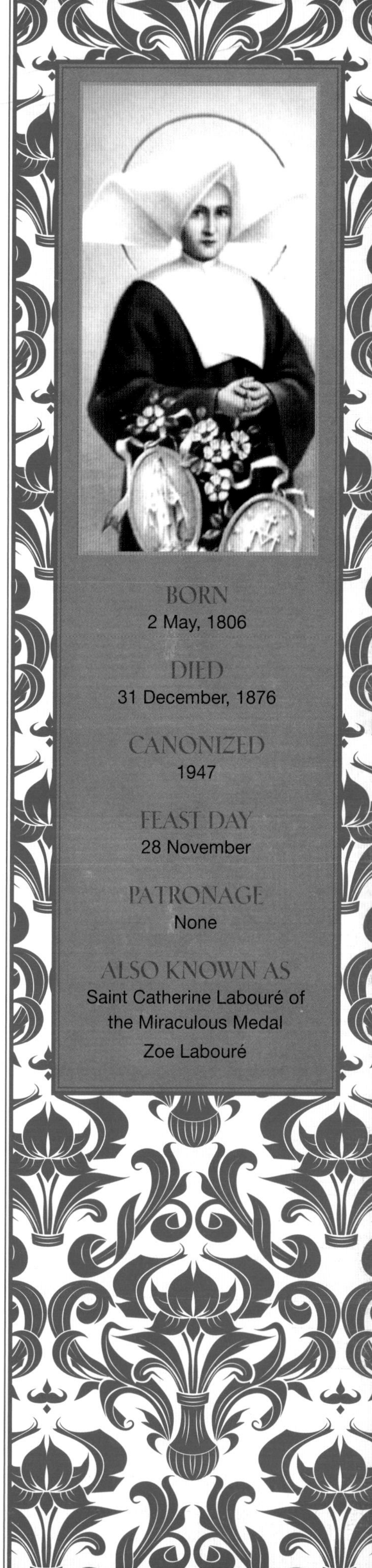

A Closer Look: *Stigmata*

Stigmata, marks resembling the wounds of the crucified body of Christ during the Passion, said to be supernaturally impressed on the bodies of certain persons, are an unusual element of Christian mysticism. Most saints who bore the stigmata also experienced ecstasy – generally, but also in specific relation to the first appearance of their wounds.

It ought not be that suffering should adapt itself to us, but we ought to adapt ourselves to suffering.

Saint Gemma Galgani

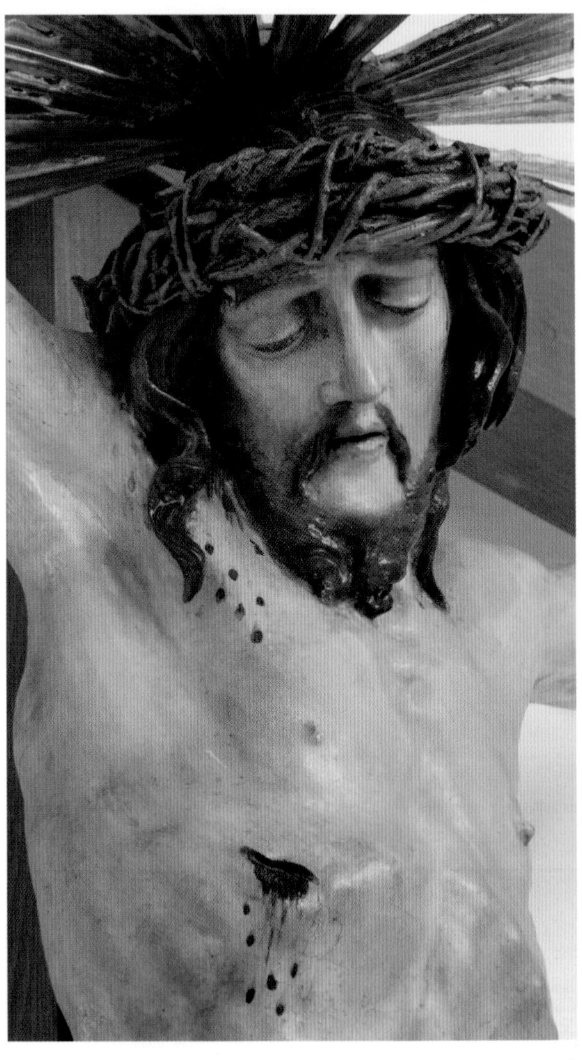

Visible stigmata may include wounds on the hands, feet, side (from the spear which pierced Jesus), and head (from the crown of thorns). They may or may not bleed and may disappear and reappear. Less dramatically – for observers, if not for the victim – saints may also suffer invisible stigmata, where the saint perceives them but the signs do not appear physically.

Some stigmatics, including Catherine of Siena and Catherine de' Ricci, had both in succession, the visible wounds becoming invisible after prayer. Other notable stigmatics are Saints Francis of Assisi, Gemma Galgani, Veronica Giuliani, John of God, Rita of Cascia, Faustina

Saint Pio of Pietrelcina

One of the most remarkable cases of stigmatism occurred in the last century on the person of Francesco Forgione (1887–1968), known to the world as Padre Pio. Padre Pio was ordained in the Capuchin Order on 10 August, 1910. Eight years later, on 20 September, 1918, his stigmata appeared. Forgione bore the wounds on his hands, feet, and side for the rest of his life, the longest known duration in history. In his lifetime, the Catholic Church considered his purported miracles a fake and the wounds self-inflicted forgeries; he was silenced in 1923, although he could still say Mass and hear confessions. Despite these restrictions, his fame spread and brought many visitors. One of these, in 1947, was a Polish priest named Karol Wojtyla. Wojtyla became Pope John Paul II in 1978 and reversed the Church's position, beatifying Padre Pio in 1999 and canonizing him in 2002.

Kowalska, and Marie of the Incarnation, along with Blessed Lucia Brocadelli of Narni, Blessed Anne Catherine Emmerich, Sister Marcelline Pauper, Sister Therese Neumann, Father Zlatko Sudac, Marthe Robin, and Marie Rose Ferron.

Saint Francis of Assisi was the first to record his stigmata, which first manifested after a vision of a crucified angel appeared to him while he prayed.

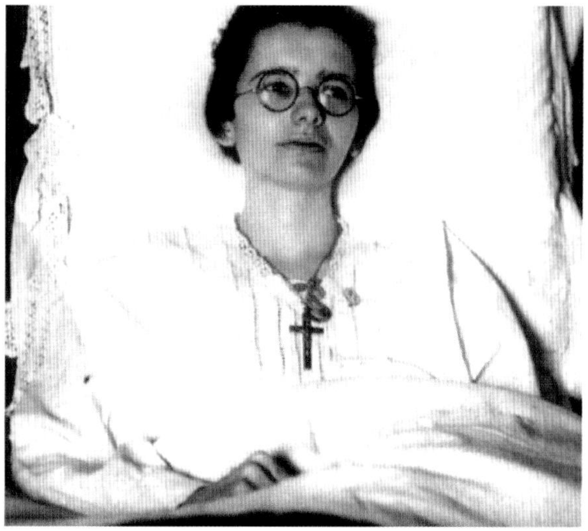

For more than fifty years, as well as suffering stigmata, Marthe Robin did not ingest anything except the Eucharist that was brought to her once or twice a week. Marthe was like many other stigmatics, such as Anne Catherine Emmerich, Marie Rose Ferron, and Therese Neumann, who remained bedridden for long portions of their lives.

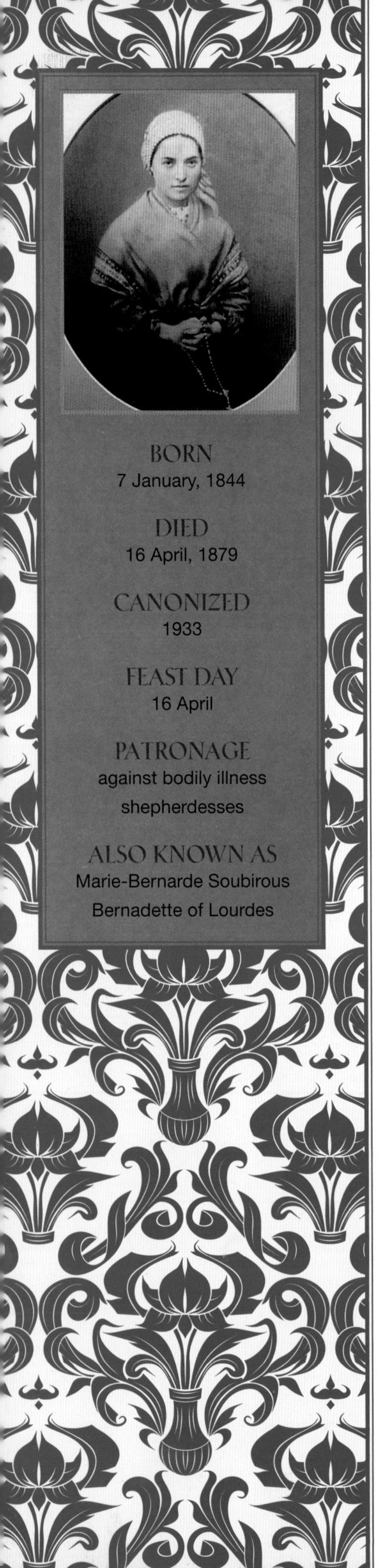

BORN
7 January, 1844

DIED
16 April, 1879

CANONIZED
1933

FEAST DAY
16 April

PATRONAGE
against bodily illness
shepherdesses

ALSO KNOWN AS
Marie-Bernarde Soubirous
Bernadette of Lourdes

Saint Bernadette Soubirous

In the course of six months, at the age of 14, Bernadette experienced an astonishing 18 visions in the course of six months. Each occurred near Lourdes at Massabielle. In each of them a "small woman" appeared and gave Bernadette instructions; not until the final vision did the woman reveal herself as "Mary of the Immaculate Conception". Only recently declared by the pope, the doctrine of the Immaculate Conception was unknown at the time to Bernadette, who lived in abject poverty and could only speak a rural French dialect.

Following the Virgin's instructions, Bernadette persuaded the local authorities to build a church at the place where she had her visions. In another vision, Mary told Bernadette to drink from a spring and pointed to a spot on the ground. Bernadette was obliged to dig before she found water, but the spring continues to flow today. To date the water has affected 67 miraculous cures, all of them vetted by medical practitioners.

In 1862, after rigorous investigation, the Church declared Bernadette's visions – during which she would sometimes fall into ecstatic trances for up to an hour – authentic. Bernadette retired from the world to become a nun, dying of tuberculosis at the age of 35; she refused to drink the healing waters of Lourdes. Even more than her visions, her sobriety, humility, and simplicity convinced the Church to canonize her in 1933.

Statue of the Blessed Virgin of Lourdes, also known as Our Lady of Lourdes, in the Grotte de Massabielle. Today, Lourdes is one of the world's most popular Catholic pilgrimage spots.

Saint John Bosco

Born into terrible poverty, John Bosco dedicated his life to improving the spiritual and material lives of poor youth. He became a priest in 1841 and soon began attracting destitute boys to his oratories. He taught them Catholicism and gave workshops offering classes in tailoring, shoemaking, and other technical skills. By 1856, his pupils and dependants numbered 650; in 1874, Pope Pius IX approved the formation of Bosco's new order dedicated to caring for impoverished children, the Society of Saint Francis de Sales, or Salesians.

Bosco's life and much of his work was guided by lucid dreams in which he met with saints, angels, the Virgin Mary, and possibly Christ himself. In 1858, Pope Pius IX requested that Bosco keep a record of these dreams; more than 150 eventually made it into print. In addition to this mystical guidance Bosco performed several miracles, including multiplying food for his young charges, levitation, and prophesying. Having done so much for the youth of Turin, his love was reciprocated when much of the city – some forty thousand people – turned out to attend his funeral.

Grigio

Working among the poor, John Bosco frequently travelled in unsafe parts of the city. On one occasion, when thugs threatened his life, a great grey dog came out of nowhere and defended him and then vanished as soon as Bosco was out of danger. From that time on, for more than a decade, whenever Don Bosco came home late, "Grigio" would appear to walk him home. Described variously as an Alsatian, German shepherd, mastiff, or mutt, Grigio – "grey" in Italian – earned a place of honour in Bosco's legend. Some believe he was an earthly canine inspired by God to defend the saint, while others believe God sent the dog from heaven, and still others maintain the dog was Bosco's guardian angel taking canine form.

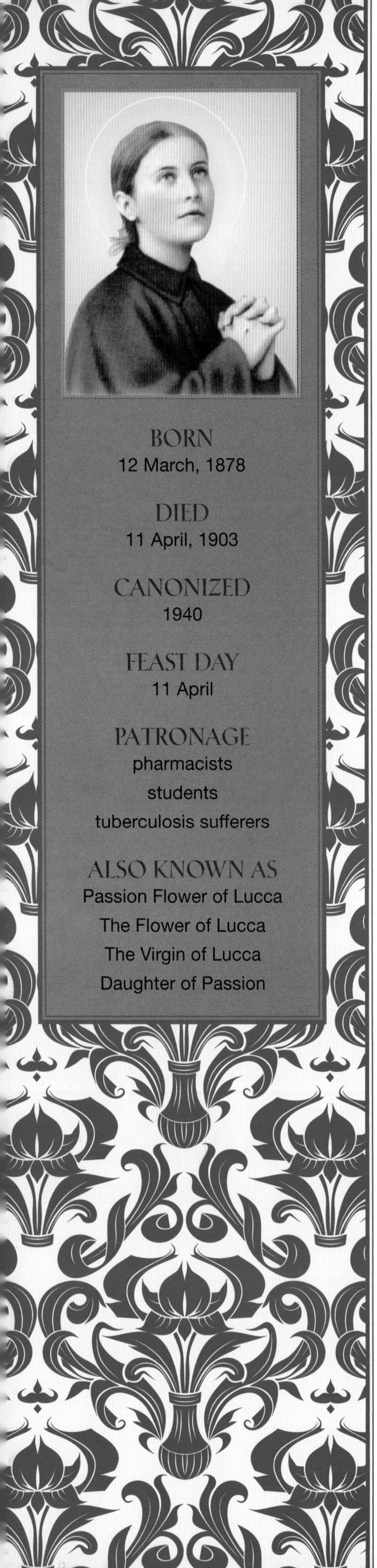

BORN
12 March, 1878

DIED
11 April, 1903

CANONIZED
1940

FEAST DAY
11 April

PATRONAGE
pharmacists
students
tuberculosis sufferers

ALSO KNOWN AS
Passion Flower of Lucca
The Flower of Lucca
The Virgin of Lucca
Daughter of Passion

Saint GEMMA Galgani

Gemma Galgani, who lost her mother when just 7 years old and her father at 18, suffered from poor physical health but had a vibrant inner life. She wished to join the Passionist order, and though she was denied because of her infirmity, Gemma continued to devote herself to Christ's Passion, developing stigmata in 1899 after she had a vision of the Virgin Mary and Jesus Christ in which fires issued from his wounds.

Every week thereafter, the stigmata wounds would appear on Thursdays, only to close again by Sunday. They did not vanish until 1901 when, in obedience to Father Germano, the Passionist priest who attended her, Gemma prayed for them to stop.

In addition to Christ and Mary, Gemma often saw her guardian angel and sometimes Father Germano's angel as well. She maintained a remarkably prosaic relationship with her angel, who delivered messages for her, scolded her when she strayed from the spiritual path, and watched over her while she slept. On occasion Gemma also battled with the Devil and once seemed possessed by a demon, who made her spit on a crucifix and break a rosary.

Today, Saint Gemma Galgani has an intense Passionist following, with many finding inspiration in her short but holy life.

Gemma died, aged 25, of tuberculosis of the spine. Impressed by her acceptance of suffering, both materially and physically, and by her obedience, Pope Pius XI beatified her only thirty years later.

Saint FAUSTINA *Kowalska*

Born Helenka Kowalska to a poor Polish family in 1905, Faustina took the name Sister Maria Faustina of the Most Blessed Sacrament upon entering a Warsaw nunnery in 1925. She felt drawn to the religious life in childhood and had the first of many visions of Jesus Christ in 1924.

Apart from her superiors and confessors, Faustina kept silent about her mystical experiences as a nun, including her visions of Jesus and Mary and her stigmata. In 1934, one of her confessors prompted her to keep a diary; published as *Divine Mercy in My Soul*, it eventually formed the basis of Faustina's widespread cult and led to her subsequent canonization.

According to *Divine Mercy*, Faustina had her most famous vision in 1931. In it, Jesus instructed her to commission a painting to spread his message of mercy. The resulting painting shows Christ, his right hand raised with two beams of light streaming from his heart, one red, one white, above a banner reading, JESUS, I TRUST IN YOU. The painting has since been reproduced many times by various artists.

Faustina died young, only 33 years old, but thanks to the publication of her diary, her enormously rich mystical life has had a resounding influence throughout the Catholic faith.

Images such as this, based on the vision of Saint Faustina Kowalska, are immensely popular.

REGVLA CARME
RDINIS RITARVM
REGVLA CA
LBERTV DEI
BROCARDVS
CAMINO DE PERFECCION

Saints of the Cloth

The following saints were not only men and women of great holiness but also of great vision and skill. They include bishops, abbots, priests, monks, and nuns who founded religious orders, led reforms, or sought ways to improve the lives of not only religious but also of laity and of the poor and ill. The monastic orders they founded – including the Benedictines, Dominicans, and Jesuits – had large and lasting effects on the development of Christianity. The Benedictines, for example, planted the kernel of cenobitic, or communal, monasticism that would dominate the West. The Dominicans systematically combated heresy in the ignoble period of the Inquisition; and the Jesuits sent extraordinary numbers of missionaries to convert South America and Central America, with profound results.

Some of these saints, Simeon Stylites and Romuald, for instance, had no intention of founding new orders. Others, like Dominic and Teresa of Avila, were consumed by the drive to reform existing orders or start afresh. Still others – like Saint Nicholas – were neither reformers nor founders, but rather remarkable men and women who sought to help the needy and glorify God; their sanctity was made manifest by miracles.

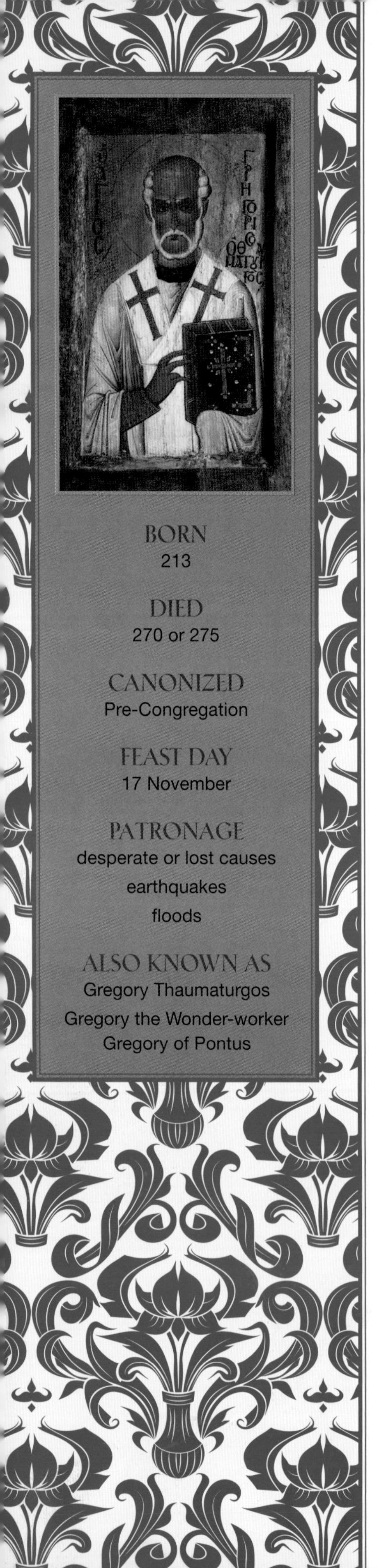

BORN
213

DIED
270 or 275

CANONIZED
Pre-Congregation

FEAST DAY
17 November

PATRONAGE
desperate or lost causes
earthquakes
floods

ALSO KNOWN AS
Gregory Thaumaturgos
Gregory the Wonder-worker
Gregory of Pontus

Saint Gregory of Neocaesarea

A student of the vaunted Christian scholar Origen, Gregory became the first bishop of Neocaesarea, his native city, at the age of 40: at the time, his entire Christian flock numbered only 17. In an amusing coincidence that shows a glimpse of his charisma and oratory skills, by the time he died in the 270s only 17 pagans remained in the city.

Born into a pagan family, who called him Theodore, Gregory did not become a Christian until around 233, when he met Origen, already a famous scholar, while studying philosophy and law at Caesarea. Unfortunately, few authentic writings of Gregory's survive, but his influence on Christianity in Cappadocia sounded long echoes. Through Saint Macrina the Elder, his theology and history came to Saint Gregory of Nyssa and Saint Basil.

Gregory contended with persecution, plague, and Gothic raids, but his success in these areas paled next to his miracles, which so dominated that he became known as the Wonder-worker or Thaumaturgos (the "miracle worker"). In his legends he moves a mountain, shifts the course of a river (to avert an imminent flood), and cures the sick. These miracles are of doubtful historicity, but it is undeniably true that this early bishop played an enormous role in the history of Anatolian Christianity.

According to legend, Saint Gregory of Neocaesarea, as his nickname the "Wonder-worker" suggests, could perform miracles. He was said to heal by a laying-on of his hands. His gift was so powerful that he not only cured the illness but converted the sufferer on the spot.

Saint Anthony

Often called the founder of monasticism, Anthony abandoned his worldly riches in order to live an eremitic life.

When Anthony's parents died, the young Egyptian (he lived in Coma, near Memphis) sold his many possessions and retired to a nearby desert tomb. There he famously battled voracious demons that sometimes attacked him as wild beasts and on one occasion nearly killed him. He also waged inner battles against temptation, emerging victorious after fifteen years.

Now Anthony intensified his seclusion, confining himself to a deserted fort on a mountain at Pispir. He saw no one for twenty years; the man who brought him food threw bread over the wall. Yet his fame spread and disciples gathered on the mountain, imitating his asceticism and asking him to guide their development. Finally, in 305, Anthony emerged and a few years later founded Christianity's first monastery, Der Mar Antonios. Except for a trip to Alexandria in 311 to support persecuted Christians and another in 355 to combat Arianism, Anthony lived in strict seclusion at his monastery for the remainder of what was, if the sources are accurate, an extremely long life.

Saint Paul the Hermit

According to legend, Anthony thought himself the first hermit until directed by a vision to Paul the Hermit. To avoid the Decian persecution Paul had fled to the desert as a youth. Anthony found Paul in his cave, and they greeted each other in brotherhood. That evening, the raven sent by the Lord to feed Paul brought an entire loaf of bread, instead of the usual half, and Paul recognized Anthony as God's true servant. Paul sent Anthony to fetch him a cloak given by Emperor Constantine to Saint Athanasius, but when Anthony returned, Paul was dead. Anthony dressed Paul in Constantine's cloak but lacked the strength to dig a grave. While wondering how to bury him, two lions walked into the cave and dug a grave (whose location was afterward concealed by God) with their claws, and Anthony buried the body.

BORN
251

DIED
356

CANONIZED
Pre-Congregation

FEAST DAY
17 January

PATRONAGE
amputees
basket weavers
brush makers
butchers
domestic animals
epilepsy
ergot sufferers
gravediggers
hermits
monks
pestilence
skin diseases

ALSO KNOWN AS
Antony
Anthony of Egypt
Anthony of the Desert

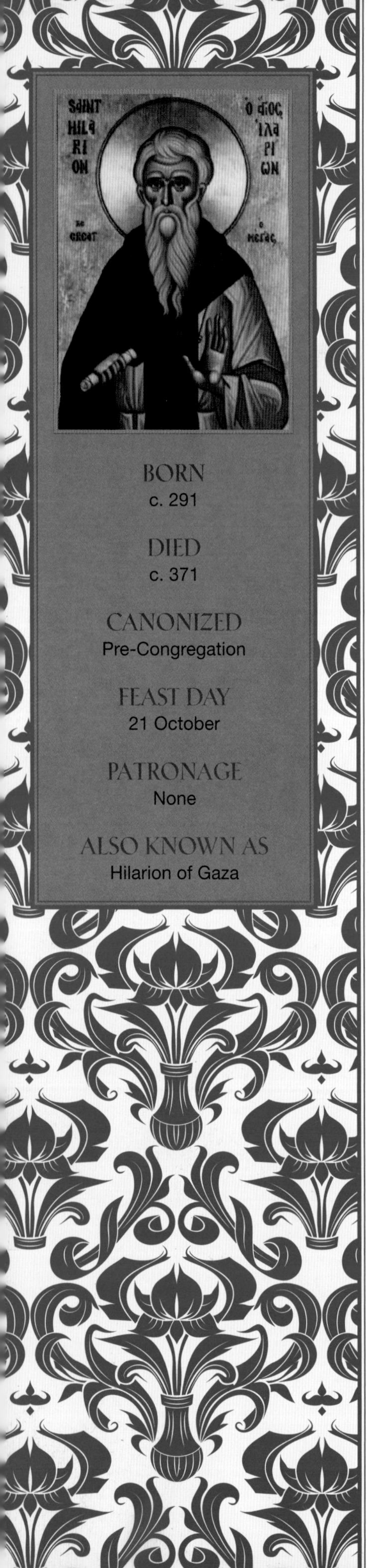

BORN
c. 291

DIED
c. 371

CANONIZED
Pre-Congregation

FEAST DAY
21 October

PATRONAGE
None

ALSO KNOWN AS
Hilarion of Gaza

Saint Hilarion

Around 305, when Hilarion was fifteen, he converted to Christianity and joined the monkish community in the Egyptian desert that was following the example of Saint Anthony. Upon returning to his hometown of Thabatha in Palestine at age sixteen (he had spent his school years in Alexandria), he discovered that his parents had died.

Further inspired by the example of Saint Anthony, he sold off his inheritance and embarked on the eremitic life that would bring him unwelcome fame and earn him a reputation as the founder of anchorite life in Palestine.

Hilarion first built a house of reeds in the desert of Majuma, near Gaza, which he later replaced with a tomb-like cell. He earned a meagre livelihood selling woven baskets. In the desert, he managed to conquer demonic temptations through his rigid adherence to Anthony's asceticism. For example, he fasted his entire adult life, surviving on a single meal per day consisting variously of figs, bread, or vegetables. His rigour left him wasted and malnourished, yet he lived until age eighty.

He found pleasure in the vast and terrible wilderness with the sea on one side and the marshland on the other.

Saint Jerome
The Life of Saint Hilarion the Hermit

Hilarion's ascetic way of life and the many miracles attributed to him attracted crowds of eager disciples. Looking to find solitude, he moved several times – first to Egypt, then Sicily, then Dalmatia, and finally to Cyprus, where he died. His disciple Hesychius translated his relics to Majuma, near Gaza.

Saint Nicholas

Very little can be stated with historical certainty about this bishop of Myra, despite his long-standing, widespread, and enduring popularity. Nicholas was most likely born in Parara, a Lycian city, travelled to Egypt and Palestine, and suffered imprisonment in the Diocletian persecution. Behind these bare facts lie a host of legends and miracles, including bilocation, the resurrection of three murdered boys (or young clergymen), and the distribution of gold for their dowries to young women who would have otherwise become prostitutes.

Despite the scanty information about him, the cult of Nicholas was popular by the sixth century in the East and by the tenth in the West. His Western cult grew enormously in the eleventh century when Saracens invaded the eastern city of Myra (modern Kale, Turkey), and Italian merchants translated his relics to Bari.

ABOVE: The Dowry for the Three Virgins *shows the saint anonymously dropping coins into the home of a poor nobleman.*

LEFT: *His reputation for generosity has forever linked him with gift-giving and made him the model for the American Santa Claus, the Anglo-Canadian and British Father Christmas, and the Dutch Sinterklaas. In many countries, Saint Nicholas Day is a festival for children.*

In the West, Saint Nicholas is most famous today for his identification with Santa Claus. The web of Christmas traditions entangling the two is complex but of fairly recent origin, probably dating to the Early Modern Period and stemming primarily from Germanic, Nordic, and Dutch folk traditions.

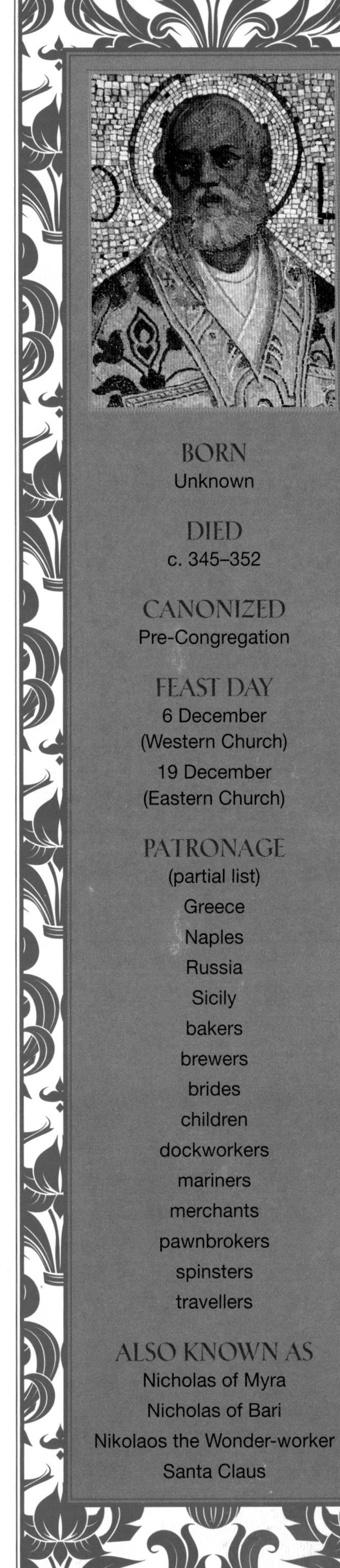

BORN
Unknown

DIED
c. 345–352

CANONIZED
Pre-Congregation

FEAST DAY
6 December
(Western Church)
19 December
(Eastern Church)

PATRONAGE
(partial list)
Greece
Naples
Russia
Sicily
bakers
brewers
brides
children
dockworkers
mariners
merchants
pawnbrokers
spinsters
travellers

ALSO KNOWN AS
Nicholas of Myra
Nicholas of Bari
Nikolaos the Wonder-worker
Santa Claus

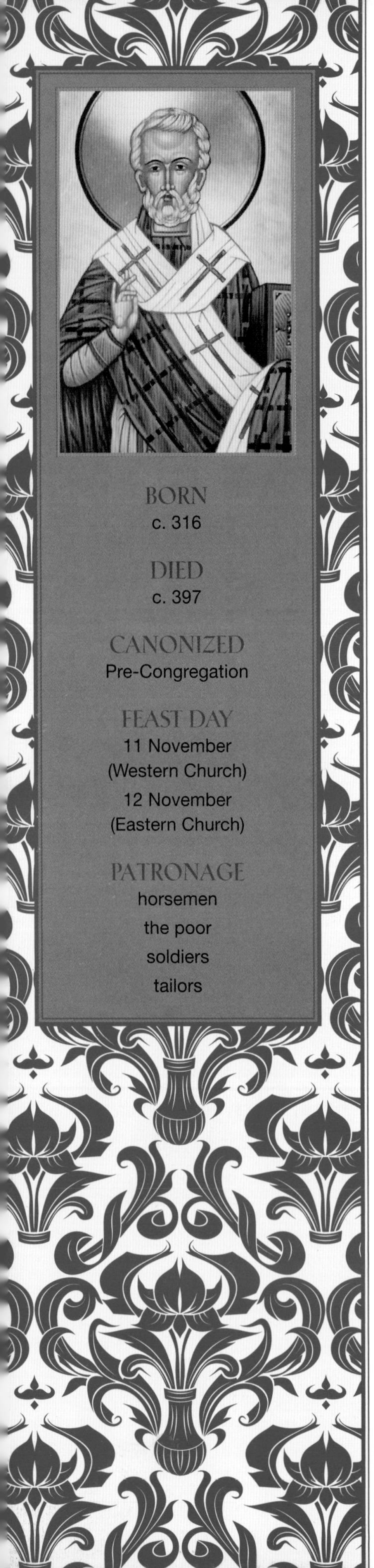

BORN
c. 316

DIED
c. 397

CANONIZED
Pre-Congregation

FEAST DAY
11 November
(Western Church)
12 November
(Eastern Church)

PATRONAGE
horsemen
the poor
soldiers
tailors

Saint Martin of Tours

Martin became one of the most popular saints of the Middle Ages, especially in the West, where he was hailed as the founder of Western monasticism. He is called after the city of Tours, France, where he served as bishop for 25 years, but he was born in Sabaria, Pannonia (modern Hungary). He was not born Christian, but at his request he became a catechumen in childhood. The Roman army drafted him when he was only fifteen, but after his baptism he became convinced that Christianity was incompatible with warfare. Imprisonment did not deter him, and he was discharged in 357.

Artists most often depict Martin of Tours as a soldier on horseback splitting a cloak with his sword. This is based on the legend that tells how while Martin was still a Roman soldier, a nearly naked beggar approached him as he arrived at the gates of the city of Amiens. On impulse he sliced his military cloak in half and shared it with the beggar. In a dream that night, Jesus came to Martin wrapped in the half-cloak.

Having travelled through Gaul as a soldier, Martin became attached to Saint Hilary of Poitiers. When the Arians banished Hilary, Martin, too, fled and lived alone on Gallinaria; when Hilary returned to Poitiers, in 360, Martin returned as well. Hilary granted him some land near Poitiers, where Martin – now accustomed to a solitary life – established the first monastery in Gaul. He attracted followers of his own and had such a reputation in Tours that the city tricked him into the bishopric in 372. At Marmoutier he established the second monastery of several and spent the rest of his life travelling through Gaul, converting the pagans of the countryside. He died at Candes, which subsequently became a major pilgrimage site.

Saint SIMEON *Stylites*

Simeon became the first of the stylites, ascetics who practised extreme austerity on top of pillars, after the rigour of his penance so alarmed the abbot of his monastery at Eusebona (modern Tell'Ada) that he was asked to leave.

Simeon's extreme penance included mortification of the flesh, extraordinary fasting (on one occasion leaving him unconscious until followers revived him with the Eucharist and lettuce leaves), and, perhaps most remarkably, very long periods of standing upright. During Lent, with his practice of austerity at its most extreme, he would remain standing for two weeks.

He retired to his first pillar, nine feet high, in 423, when his reputation for extreme penance attracted crowds. The pillar only encouraged more visitors, however, so he increased its height several more times until it stuck up fifty or sixty feet. Even then he was not alone: recorded miracles and spectacular conversions of pagan gawkers increased Simeon's fame to the point where even emperors and other notables visited him for advice. A ladder allowed the occasional visitor to attend his words or bring him food and water. Other stylites followed his example, including Saints Daniel, Alypius, and Luke the Younger. Though never practised in the West, the tradition of the stylites endured in the East into the Early Modern Period.

The Church of Saint Simeon Stylites, located northwest of modern-day Aleppo, Syria, was erected on the site of the pillar of Saint Simeon Stylites. Built in the fifth century, it is the oldest surviving Byzantine church in the world.

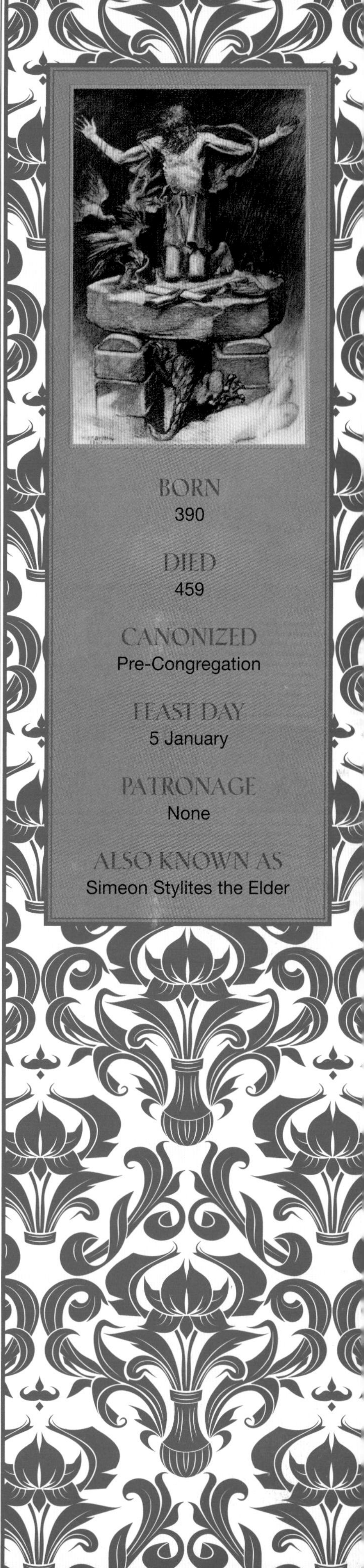

BORN
390

DIED
459

CANONIZED
Pre-Congregation

FEAST DAY
5 January

PATRONAGE
None

ALSO KNOWN AS
Simeon Stylites the Elder

Saint Benedict *of Nursia*

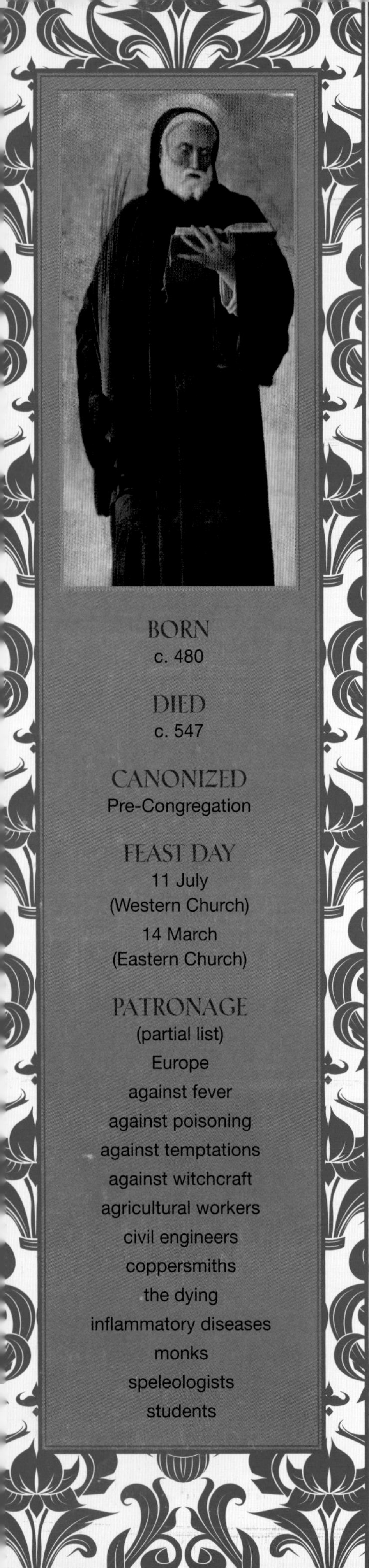

BORN
c. 480

DIED
c. 547

CANONIZED
Pre-Congregation

FEAST DAY
11 July
(Western Church)
14 March
(Eastern Church)

PATRONAGE
(partial list)
Europe
against fever
against poisoning
against temptations
against witchcraft
agricultural workers
civil engineers
coppersmiths
the dying
inflammatory diseases
monks
speleologists
students

Benedict generated an enormous legacy, far outstripping what he could have imagined himself, yet he was, in his own way, a visionary. Details of his life are few, but we do know that he was born in Nursia, Italy. As a youth he travelled to Rome for his education, but at 14, disgusted with the city and its iniquities, he retired to a cave at Subiaco, where he lived the life of a hermit.

Let them prefer nothing whatever to Christ. And may He bring us all together to everlasting life!

Saint Benedict of Nursia

It is said that Benedict died while standing at prayer in the monastery at Monte Cassino. Most of what little is known about Benedict of Nursia comes from a character sketch of the saint written by Pope Saint Gregory I.

Disciples began to gather around him, and with the genius for organization that would characterize his life, he divided them into 12 deaneries under his general direction. Thus, the Subiaco community became a sort of proto-monastic order.

Around 525, Benedict moved from Subiaco to Monte Cassino, where he founded the first true monastery in the West. There he wrote his Rule, and with such success that Benedict became known as the Father of Western Monasticism; the Benedictine order became the example for all other Western monastic orders.

The Benedictine Rule

The Rule of Saint Benedict, like Saint Benedict himself, married wisdom with austerity, flexibility with orthodoxy, order with humility. Its 73 chapters lay out guiding precepts for many aspects of monastic life. Yet, for all its detail, the Rule is not overly rigorous or prescriptive, and gradually through the Middle Ages it became the backbone of monasteries everywhere despite changing social needs and political pressures.

The monasteries came to fulfil these pressing social needs, in part, because the Benedictine Rule not only lent itself across a broad range of necessary activities, from farming to meals and administration to hospitality, but also because it set the gaze of monasticism on the general populace. In Late Antiquity, Christianity was still centred on Rome's old urban centres: it was, for the most part, a religion of the elites. Benedict himself envisioned his monks as laymen, however, not priests (as most monks still are in the Eastern Orthodox Church).

Saint Scholastica

Benedict's twin sister, Scholastica, lived at Plombariola, five miles away from Monte Cassino. Like her brother, she founded a religious community and also like him governed it herself, albeit under Benedict's direction. She is considered a pioneer of nuns but was hardly the first woman to live in something like a nunnery. Women may, in fact, have been the first to commit to an ascetic religious life: when Saint Anthony decided to retire to the desert he first ensconced his sister in a parthenon, an exclusively female community of virgins. Very little is known of Scholastica's life, less even than Benedict's, but she died only a few months before her brother, and their relics were entombed together.

A twelfth-century illuminated manuscript from the Benedictine Abbey of Saint-Gilles near Nîmes, France, shows Benedict delivering his Rule to other monks of his order.

The Rule spread gradually through Europe, aided particularly by Saint Boniface in the eighth century. Many other monastic orders were formed after Benedict's, with rules of their own, but even today Benedict's Rule remains the standard.

A Closer Look: *Monasticism*

Monasticism developed in the early history of Christianity, with both its forms, solitary (recluses) and communal (cenobites), already in evidence by the fourth century. Monks and nuns played important but changing roles over time, especially in the Middle Ages, and monasticism developed differently in the East than it did in the West. After the eleventh century, especially, Western monasticism became communal, while in the East the solitary holy person was ever the more usual. In the East, where they followed Saint Benedict's intention that every monastery be independent, there were no monastic orders. Additionally, Eastern monasteries never became centres of scholastic or pedagogical activity, as their Western cousins did; but in both halves of Christendom, monasteries functioned as hospitals, hospitality centres, charitable offices, and – most importantly – places of worship.

Saints Benedict and Scholastica. Among the list of saints who were Benedictines are Augustine and Lawrence at Canterbury, Justus at Rochester, Mellitus at London, and Paulinus at York, as well as Boniface, Hildegard of Bingen, Bede the Venerable, and Gregory the Great.

Religious Orders

In general, religious orders fall into one of the following four categories:

- Monastic: Self-sufficient monks and/or nuns live and work at their monastery and engage in communal prayer.
- Mendicant: Friars (clerics or lay people) live and pray in common, but also engage in a more active apostolate, depending on alms for their livelihoods.
- Canons regular: Canons (clerics) and canonesses regular sing the liturgy in choir and may run parishlike apostolates.
- Clerks regular: Priests take religious vows and usually have an active apostolate.

"In the World, but Not of It"

Each order has its own aim and its members must adhere to the particular way of life of the order, whether "contemplative" or "active". Those in contemplative orders, such as the Benedictines, Carmelites, Trappists, Carthusians, Cistercians, and Poor Clares, usually spend more time in community prayer. These orders tend to be self-supporting, with income generated from endeavours such as beekeeping, candlemaking, winemaking, and brewing. Active orders like the Franciscans and Dominicans interact with the word, and their adherents are often teachers, nurses, or missionaries.

The larger orders were given popular names, derived usually from the colour of their habits and cloaks or other distinguishing marks of their dress. The Carmelites, shown above with their founder Saint Berthold at far right, came to be known as the White Friars for the colour of their cloaks. Franciscans are known as Grey Friars (top left) and Dominicans as Black Friars (bottom left).

Major Religious Orders of the West

Order	Type	Founder	Date
Benedictines	monastic	Saint Benedict	c. 525
Camaldolese	monastic	Saint Romuald	c. 1000–27
Premonstratensians	canons regular	Saint Norbert	1120
Carthusian	monastic	Saint Bruno of Cologne	1084
Cistercians	monastic	Saint Robert	1098
Carmelites	mendicant	Saint Berthold	1155
Trinitarians	mendicant	Saint John of Matha	1198
Augustinians	mendicant	various	1200s*
Franciscans	mendicant	Saint Francis of Assisi	1210
Poor Clares	mendicant	Saints Francis of Assisi and Clare of Assisi	1212
Dominicans	mendicant	Saint Dominic	1216
Mercedarians	mendicant	Saint Peter Nolasco	1218
Bridgettines	mendicant	Saint Bridget of Sweden	c. 1350
Minims	mendicant	Saint Francis of Paola	1470
Ursulines	mendicant	Saint Angela Merici	1535
Jesuits	clerics regular	Saint Ignatius Loyola	1539

*Date rules were written or founder organized first

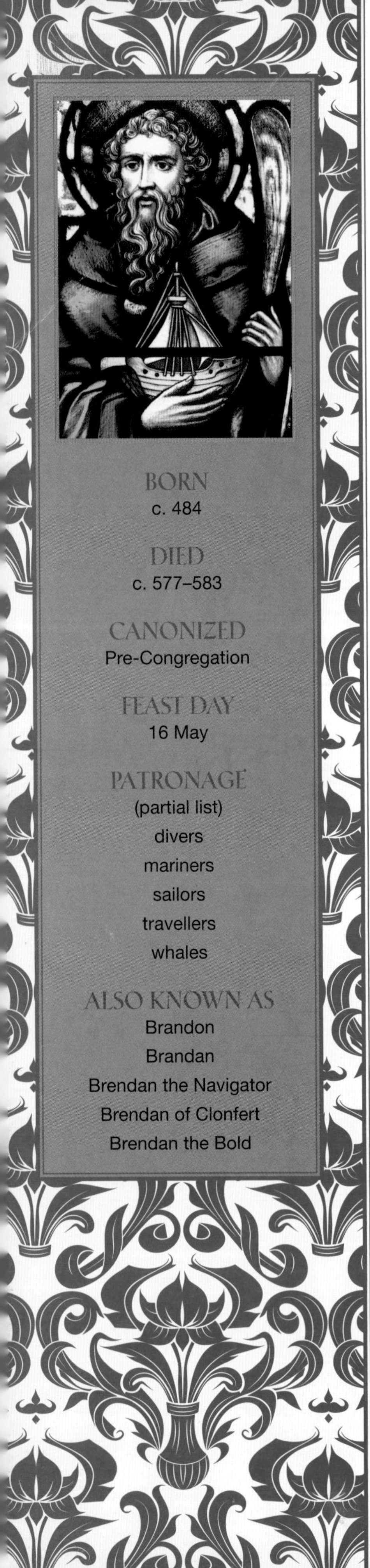

BORN
c. 484

DIED
c. 577–583

CANONIZED
Pre-Congregation

FEAST DAY
16 May

PATRONAGE
(partial list)
divers
mariners
sailors
travellers
whales

ALSO KNOWN AS
Brandon
Brandan
Brendan the Navigator
Brendan of Clonfert
Brendan the Bold

Saint BRENDAN *the Voyager*

This peripatetic, energetic abbot of Clonfert travelled widely throughout Ireland, studying under Saints Ita and Erc and visiting (according to legend) Saints Columba and Malo. In the Middle Ages Ireland became justly famous for its monasteries, which Brendan did much to encourage by founding important monasteries at Clonfert, Annaghdown (where he died), and Ardfert, among others.

The Voyage of Saint Brendan *by Edward Reginald Frampton depicts the saint's encounter with Judas Iscariot, who, for a good act performed in life, is released from Hell for one hour each Christmas Eve.*

Brendan's great claim to fame, however, lies not with his remarkable legacy of monasteries but rather with a ninth-century text, *The Voyage of Saint Brendan.* This imaginative, gripping tale of a voyage to a pseudomythical, semi-magical "Isle of the Saints", which takes Brendan and his monks on a seven-year trek across the Atlantic Ocean in the small Irish boats called "curraghs", belongs to a long tradition of sacred or semi-sacred Irish storytelling dating to pre-Christian times. The leitmotif of a voyage to an Otherworld is itself pre-Christian and appears in other early Irish and Welsh texts.

The Voyage represents an outstanding and enduringly popular example of this tradition, and if it cannot be taken as historically accurate, it nevertheless signifies the peculiar wealth of Irish Christianity in the Middle Ages. Little beyond the rough dates of his birth and death and a vague outline of his education and monastic accomplishments can be stated for the historical Brendan. The last alone, however, verifies his sanctity.

Saint DAVID

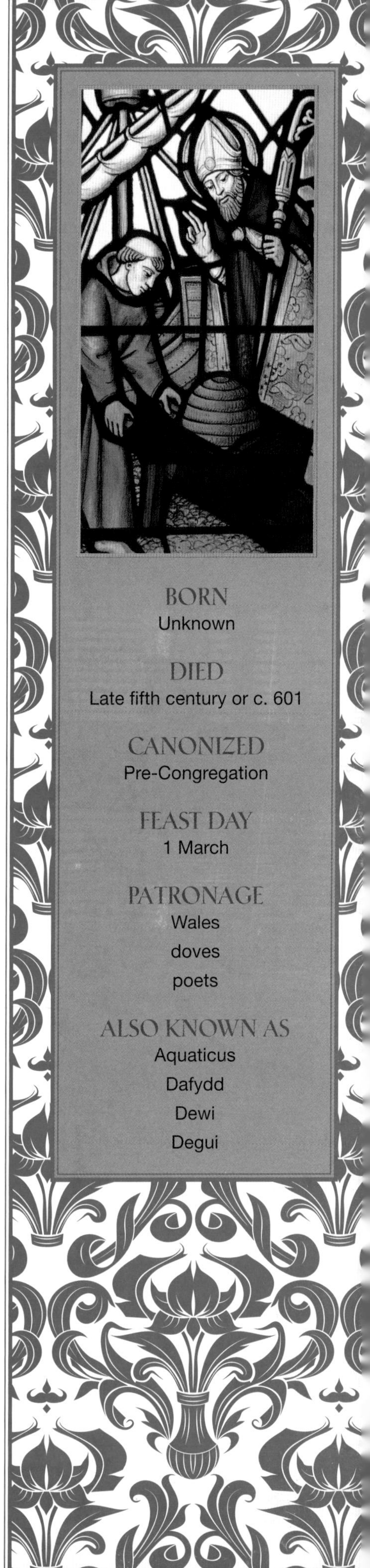

BORN
Unknown

DIED
Late fifth century or c. 601

CANONIZED
Pre-Congregation

FEAST DAY
1 March

PATRONAGE
Wales
doves
poets

ALSO KNOWN AS
Aquaticus
Dafydd
Dewi
Degui

Although a very popular British saint and one of Wales's patrons, David's life is shadowy and most of the information about him legendary. His cult probably began in Dyfed and spread through South Wales, Dumnonia, and Cornwall.

Anglo-Saxon tribes had established themselves in southeastern Britain in David's day and were pushing the remaining Celts west. To the extent that King Arthur is a historical figure, he likely belongs to this period – Geoffrey of Monmouth calls David "Arthur's uncle". One popular legend has David instructing Welsh warriors to distinguish themselves from their Saxon enemies by wearing leeks in their hats. Leeks remain one of Saint David's primary symbols.

David's first hagiographer, writing some four hundred years after the saint's death, claims he founded ten monasteries, among them Menevia (the Roman name for Saint David's) and Glastonbury. According to his hagiographer, David attended the Synod of Brevi (likely true) and there so impressed his colleagues that he was declared archbishop (likely untrue).

David was buried at the site of the present Saint David's Cathedral in Pembrokeshire, Wales, which was begun in 1181. During the Middle Ages, this shrine became a centre of pilgrimage.

Other legends explain that his nickname Aquaticus ("Waterman") resulted either from his insistence on temperance among his monks or from the great number of baptisms he performed, and that angels prophesied his birth and David, himself, prophesied his death.

Saint THEODORE of Sykeon

Improbably, Theodore was born to a travelling acrobat and a prostitute who lived in an inn with her mother and sister. When Theodore was six years old his mother had a vision of Saint George, who scolded her into educating him.

> *The trembling of the cross forecasts a crowd of misfortunes and perils for us.*
>
> Saint Theodore of Sykeon

Theodore himself had visions of Saint George and venerated the great saint all of his life. At around age 12 Theodore was stricken with plague. When Saint George cured him he retired as a hermit, first to a chapel at Arkea and then to a remote cave, which he sealed. There he lived in solitude for two years, visited only by a deacon who brought him food. But his family persuaded the deacon to betray his location, and they rescued him from his regimen of extreme austerities.

He was now 18, and his feat compelled the bishop of Anastasiopolis to ordain him as a priest. Theodore went on a pilgrimage to Jerusalem and settled at Mossyna upon his return. Eventually, after the bishop of Anastasiopolis died, Theodore, by popular demand, replaced him. He remained bishop for ten years but longed for a life of contemplation. He worried about his monks, and when the pressures of administration began to overwhelm him, he retired to Akreina, near Heliopolis. A trip to the emperor's court at Constantinople produced several results, including the emperor's decision to bestow the power of sanctuary on all monasteries. Theodore is renowned as a miracle worker, particularly for healing, exorcising demons, and reconciling troubled marriages.

Saint HILDA of Whitby

The young Hilda, along with other Northumbrians and family members, converted to Christianity through the missionary Saint Paulinus. She started to follow her sister Hereswith to Gaul, where Hereswith had become a nun, but Saint Aidan, the "Apostle of Northumbria", presumably recognizing her worth, asked her to return.

Hilda became a religious leader, first of a small community on the Wear River, then of a double monastery – after the Gaulish fashion, in which two unmixed communities of men and women operated under a single rule and a single superior and shared a church – at Hartlepool, and finally at Whitby.

Whitby quickly became an important centre under Hilda's capable guidance, earning a reputation for producing learned, pious men and women. Hilda herself received kings, nobles, and common folk alike; all valued her guidance and advice.

The newly Christian Anglo-Saxons found themselves caught between Ireland and Rome, whose leaders disagreed with each other about the all-important date of Easter, then the holiest day in the Christian sacred year. The issue threatened to tear the Celtic Church away altogether, but at the crucial Synod of Whitby, held under Hilda's aegis in 664, the Roman calendar prevailed. Hilda herself preferred the Irish date, but in the interests of avoiding schism agreed with the rest of the Irish party to abide by the decision.

The ruins of the second Whitby Abbey overlook the North Sea on the East Cliff above Whitby in North Yorkshire. During Hilda's tenure as abbess, Whitby Abbey was a centre of learning.

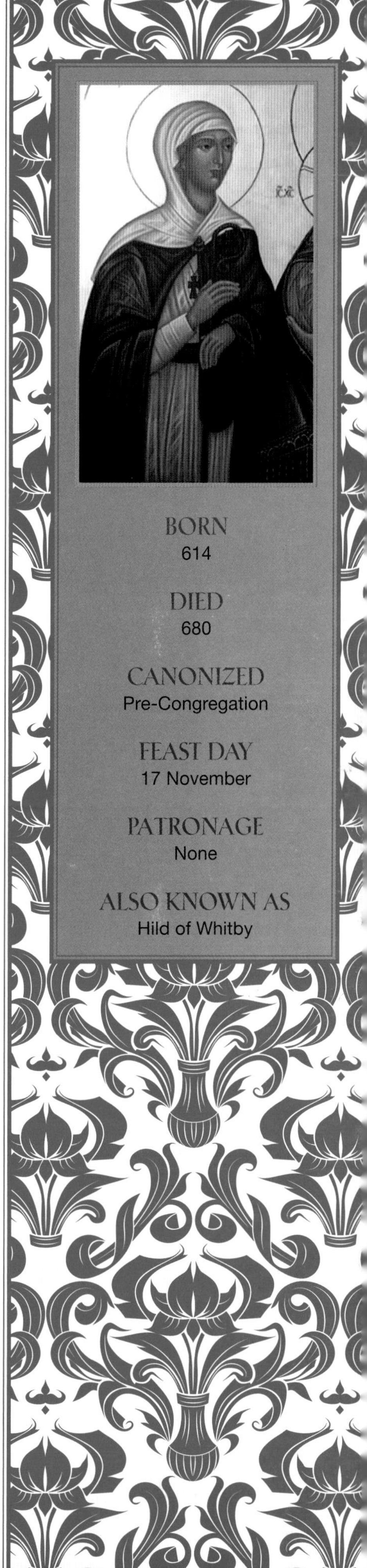

BORN
614

DIED
680

CANONIZED
Pre-Congregation

FEAST DAY
17 November

PATRONAGE
None

ALSO KNOWN AS
Hild of Whitby

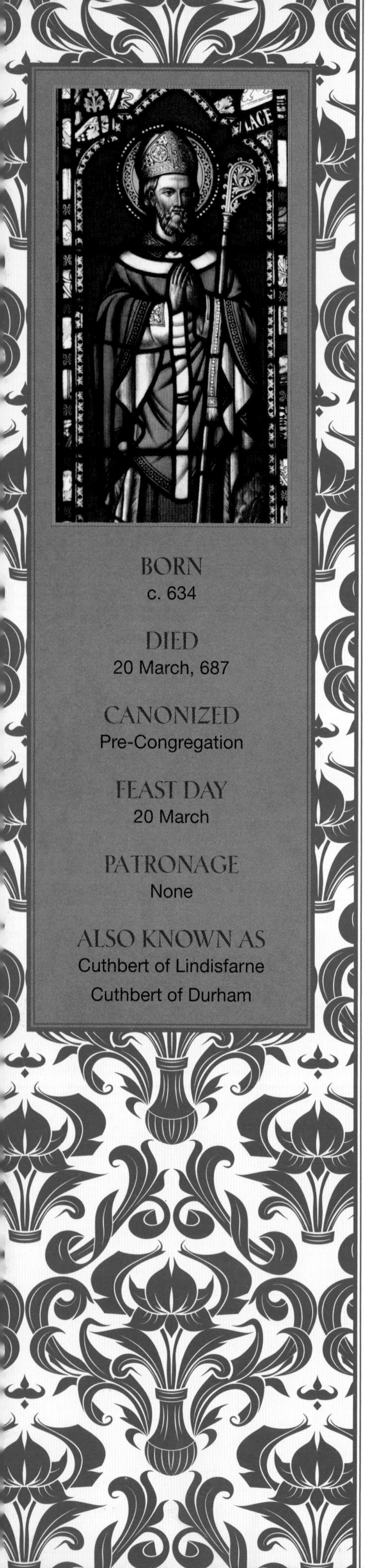

BORN
c. 634

DIED
20 March, 687

CANONIZED
Pre-Congregation

FEAST DAY
20 March

PATRONAGE
None

ALSO KNOWN AS
Cuthbert of Lindisfarne
Cuthbert of Durham

Saint Cuthbert

Cuthbert was instrumental in the conversion of Anglo-Saxons, especially in the area around Lindisfarne where he served as prior and, later, bishop. He also played an important role in convincing the monks of Lindisfarne, an old and famous monastery, to adhere to the decision of the Synod of Whitby regarding the date of Easter. Having been educated in the Celtic tradition, to which Lindisfarne belonged, he was uniquely suited to persuade his fellows to change their minds, as he had.

An Anglo-Saxon, Cuthbert was born near the Tweed River and seems to have worked as a shepherd and a soldier before becoming a monk at Melrose in 651. He became prior in 661 and moved to Lindisfarne as prior in 664. After a few years in that position Cuthbert withdrew from the world, becoming a hermit on Inner Farne Island.

His holiness and good reputation encouraged the king and archbishop to name Cuthbert bishop, though he acceded to their request with great reluctance. The bishopric to which he had been elected, Hexham, went instead to Saint Eata; Cuthbert then took over Lindisfarne.

Although he ministered gently and well at Lindisfarne, he survived but two more years. He again retired to Inner Farne, where he died shortly thereafter.

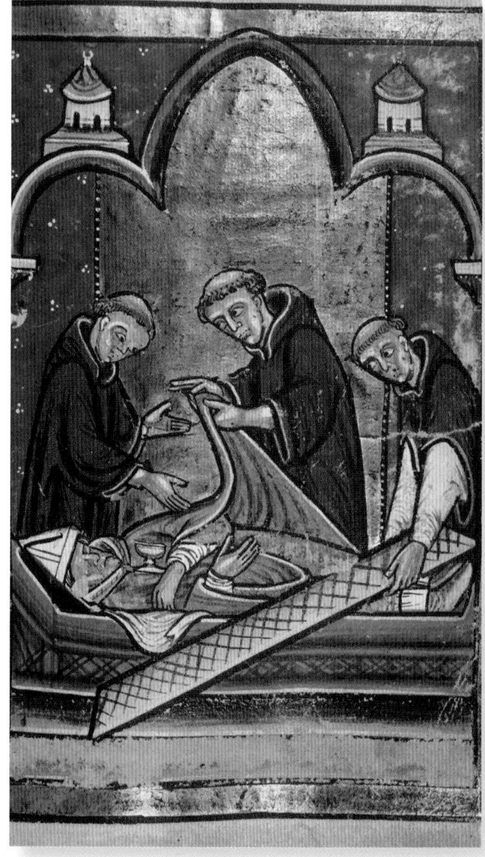

A twelfth-century illuminated manuscript of Bede the Venerable's Life of St Cuthbert *shows a group of monks discovering that the body of Cuthbert had remained incorrupt.*

Cuthbert's great fame came posthumously: four times, in approximately 697, 875, 1104, and 1537, his casket was opened, and his body was found incorrupt and sweet-smelling. Finally, upon exhumation in 1827, all that remained of the saint were his bones.

Saint Wilfrid

Wilfrid championed the jurisdiction of Rome in the early Anglo-Saxon Church, then heavily influenced by the dominant Celtic Church through the powerful monasteries of Iona and Lindisfarne. He studied at Lindisfarne before travelling to Gaul and Rome, where he received instruction from Archdeacon Boniface.

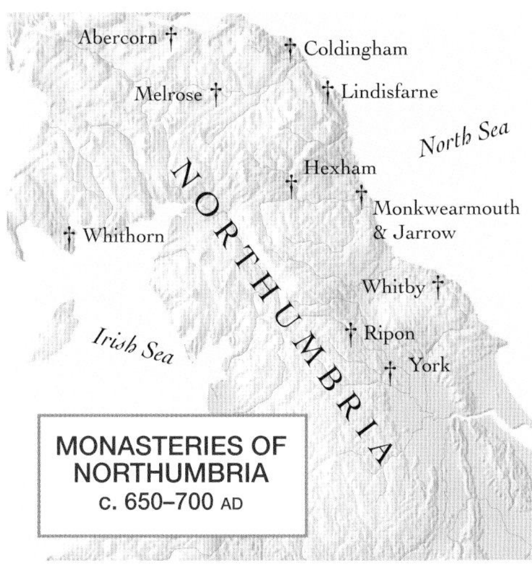

Hexham Abbey. Wilfrid established this monastery in the seventh century, adding to the rich wealth of learning in Anglo-Saxon Northumbria (see *map at left*).

Wilfrid became deacon at Ripon on returning to England, imposing the Rule of Saint Benedict and the Roman date of Easter (he became the leading proponent for the Roman date at the Synod of Whitby in 664). In 669, he ascended to bishop of York, overseeing the whole of Northumbria. There he established numerous Benedictine monasteries, notably the excellent Hexham. Politics troubled his life, however, beginning in 672 when he angered the king by encouraging the queen to become a nun.

The Archbishop of Canterbury, Thomas, overstepped his power and divided Wilfrid's diocese, prompting a second trip to Rome. Though vindicated by the pope, the irascible king imprisoned Wilfrid and then exiled him. From 680 to 686 Wilfrid evangelized Sussex, then still pagan, before returning to Northumbria with Theodore's blessing. Disputes about his monasteries and jurisdiction continued, however, and he travelled to Rome a third time, in 703. In 705, he returned to Northumbria and stayed until his death, his holdings ultimately reduced but his legacy of strict adherence to Roman rule intact.

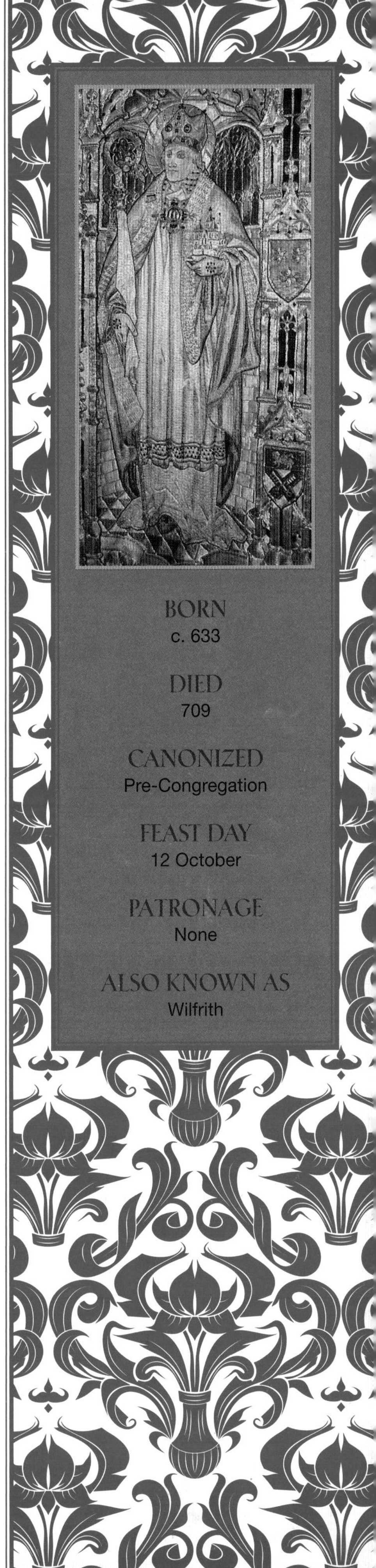

BORN
c. 633

DIED
709

CANONIZED
Pre-Congregation

FEAST DAY
12 October

PATRONAGE
None

ALSO KNOWN AS
Wilfrith

Saint DUNSTAN

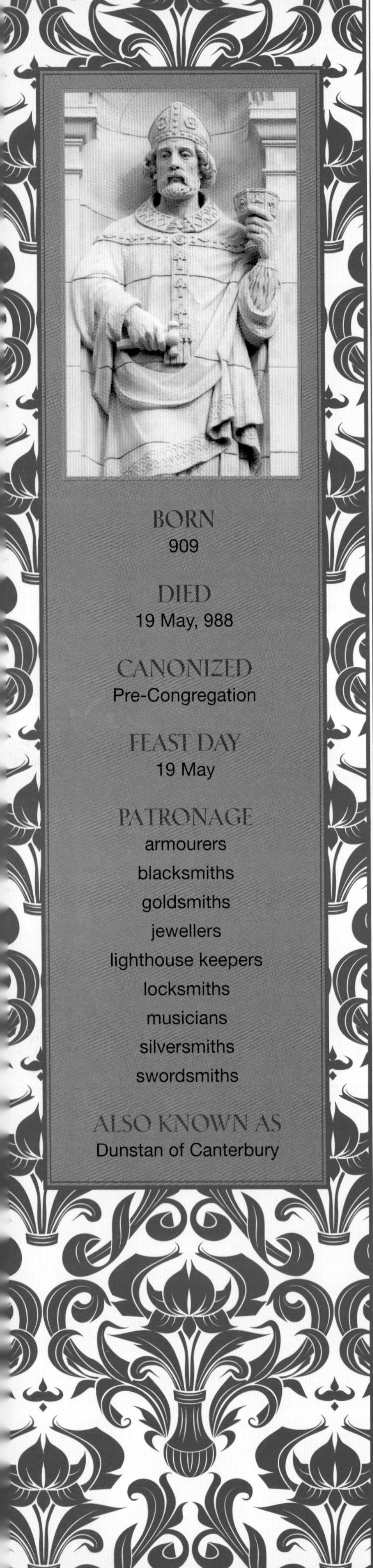

BORN
909

DIED
19 May, 988

CANONIZED
Pre-Congregation

FEAST DAY
19 May

PATRONAGE
armourers
blacksmiths
goldsmiths
jewellers
lighthouse keepers
locksmiths
musicians
silversmiths
swordsmiths

ALSO KNOWN AS
Dunstan of Canterbury

Dunstan exercised enormous influence over the Church in England even before his consecration as archbishop of Canterbury in 960. His family boasted multiple positions in the ecclesiastic hierarchy and at court, although Dunstan's fortunes rose and fell as he fell in and out of favour.

He made his first appearance at court as a young man, but conspirators, perhaps jealous of his influence, levelled spurious charges and drove him away in 935. He became a monk, showing skill at illumination and metalwork. In 939, the new king recalled Dunstan to court, then rapidly expelled him; later, after a near-fatal accident, he repented and installed Dunstan as abbot of Glastonbury. From then until 978, when the king, whom Dunstan had supported, was assassinated, Dunstan enjoyed great influence and power apart from a brief exile from 955 to 957.

Under Saint Dunstan's guidance Benedictine monasteries flourished, and the monastic life, much stunted in England, entered a golden age. The monasteries at Glastonbury, Bath, and Westminster, among others, owed their greatly improved situation to him. His *Regularis Concordia,* published around 970, contained the highlights of his innovations for England's monasteries: great reliance on the monarch, to the detriment of potentially hostile and fickle local rulers; emphasis on the scriptorium (where the monks produced their manuscripts); and an insistence on conformity in practice and liturgy.

It is highly likely that Dunstan at least commissioned this drawing of Christ, even if he did not execute it as well, as was long believed. An inscription identifies the small kneeling monk in the right corner as Dunstan himself.

Saint Romuald

Born into a noble family in Ravenna, Italy, Romuald felt no compulsion to join the monastic life until his father, Sergius, killed a relation in a duel. As a man of rather demanding character, Romuald struggled to find a monastery strict enough to accommodate his intense penitential desires.

He first tried Sant'Apollinare in Classe, but finding the rule there too lenient he travelled to Venice, attaching himself to Marinus, a hermit known for imposing rigorous severities. Romuald and Marinus went to the Benedictine abbey of Saint-Michel-de-Cuxa in 978. Romuald stayed at Cuxa for ten years, gathering disciples.

Meanwhile, Sergius had also become a monk, but he was filled with doubt about his new profession. Romuald travelled to Ravenna to reassure his father (Romuald strongly believed that in monkish solitude lay salvation) and then spent his remaining decades travelling throughout Italy, founding hermitages and monasteries as he did so. The most famous of these was Camadoli, granted to Romuald by the land's owner on the strength of a dream about monks ascending to heaven on the spot.

Camadoli is considered the birthplace of Romuald's Camaldolese Order, which wedded the communal, cenobitical monastery with the solitary, eremitical hermitage. Although the order has never become popular it has nevertheless persisted, and Romuald has been credited with reintroducing eremitical life into Western monasticism.

Romuald, the white-bearded man at right, in the habit of the Camaldolese, a loose white garment with wide sleeves. The inspiration for the habit is said to have been a dream in which Romuald saw the monks of his order climbing a ladder to heaven, clad in flowing white.

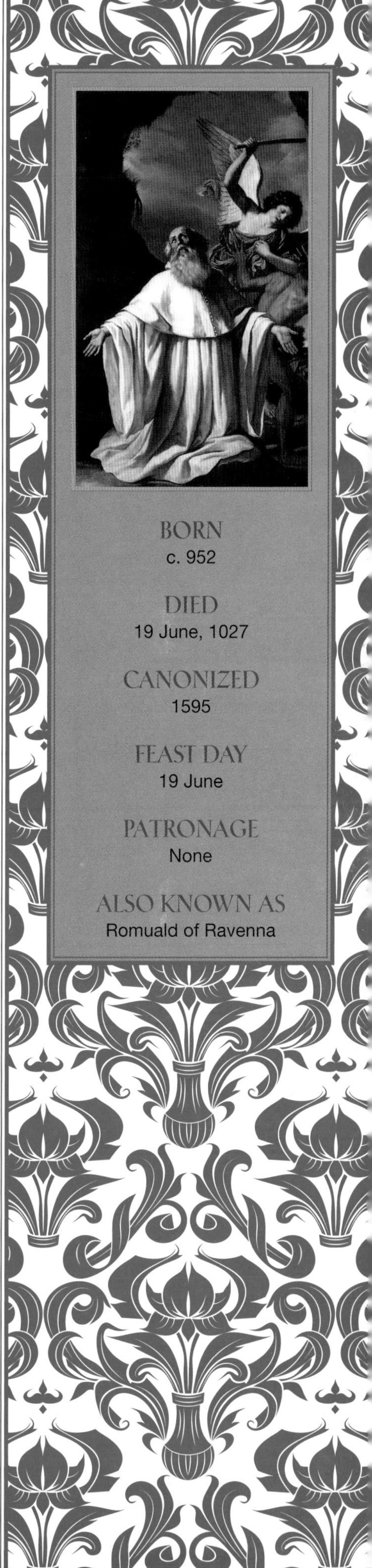

BORN
c. 952

DIED
19 June, 1027

CANONIZED
1595

FEAST DAY
19 June

PATRONAGE
None

ALSO KNOWN AS
Romuald of Ravenna

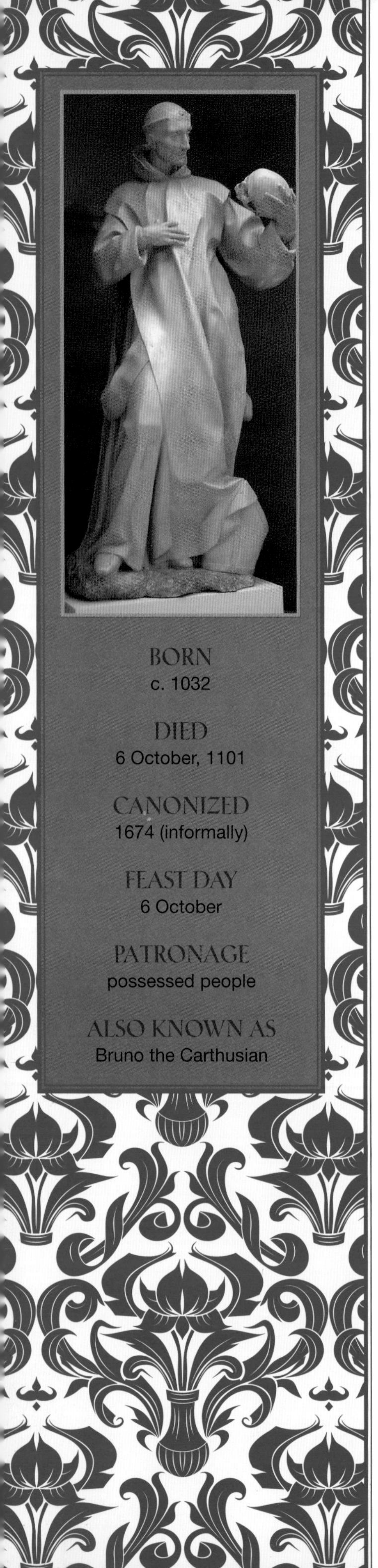

Saint BRUNO of Cologne

Bruno lectured for 18 years at the renowned school of Reims, from 1057 to 1075. One of his pupils later became Pope Urban II, who strove to continue the reforms championed by Pope Gregory VII. Urban insisted that Bruno, who by then had retired to the Chartreuse Mountains near Grenoble, advise him, and though the specific role Bruno may have played in the reformation is unknown, the pope's reliance on him strongly attests to his influence. Bruno stayed with Pope Urban for five years before again retiring, in 1095, this time to La Torre in Calabria.

Bruno is better known, however, for the order he founded in the Chartreuse and Calabria. The Carthusians, like the Camaldolese, embrace an eremitical life, instead of the Rule of Saint Benedict; they live in extreme poverty. The austere practices of the Carthusians, including living in near silence, fasting once a week, and engaging in hard manual labour, did nothing to prevent the order from achieving widespread and enduring popularity. Bruno's canonization never occurred formally in the church; but when Pope Leo X authorized his cult for the Carthusians, in 1514, and Pope Gregory XV authorized it for the Church in general, in 1674, he achieved sainthood.

Saint Bruno is best known for founding the Carthusians, an austere order that demands a contemplative and simple way of life. Although, since 1740, Carthusian monks have produced the cordial liqueur Chartreuse, they themselves never partake of alcohol.

Saint BERNARD of Clairvaux

Bernard became a monk in 1112 or 1113 after a vision of his deceased mother appeared to him. He received an excellent education and possessed a charismatic, energetic character that would have an enormous effect on his Cistercian order, founded in 1098 at Cîteaux, as well as on many important matters of the early twelfth century.

Give Him glory once

for offences pardoned;

give it again for

virtues conferred.

Saint Bernard of Clairvaux

Saint Robert founded Cîteaux with an eye to reforming the Benedictine Order, but the monastery struggled until Bernard entered, bringing some thirty companions with him. Within three years Bernard became the abbot of a new Cistercian house, Clairvaux. Bernard founded 163 monasteries in his lifetime; Clairvaux alone held seven hundred monks. The Cistercian explosion of the twelfth century is largely the result of Bernard's influence, in particular his close relationship with Pope Eugenius III, who had once been Bernard's disciple.

Bernard did not shy away from the contentions of his time. From 1130 to 1138 he strove tirelessly to win support for Pope Innocent II, whose election was contested by the antipope Anacletus; twice he engaged in public disputes with leading scholars. Most famously, however, Bernard was a vociferous advocate of the Second Crusade (1147–9), whose disastrous results greatly disheartened the saint. A crusader's son himself, Bernard perceived the need for a knightly body in the Holy Land to care for the sick, defend pilgrims, and bear arms, and he worked hard in 1128 to gain recognition for the Knights Templar. His many letters and writings earned his designation in 1830 as a Doctor of the Church.

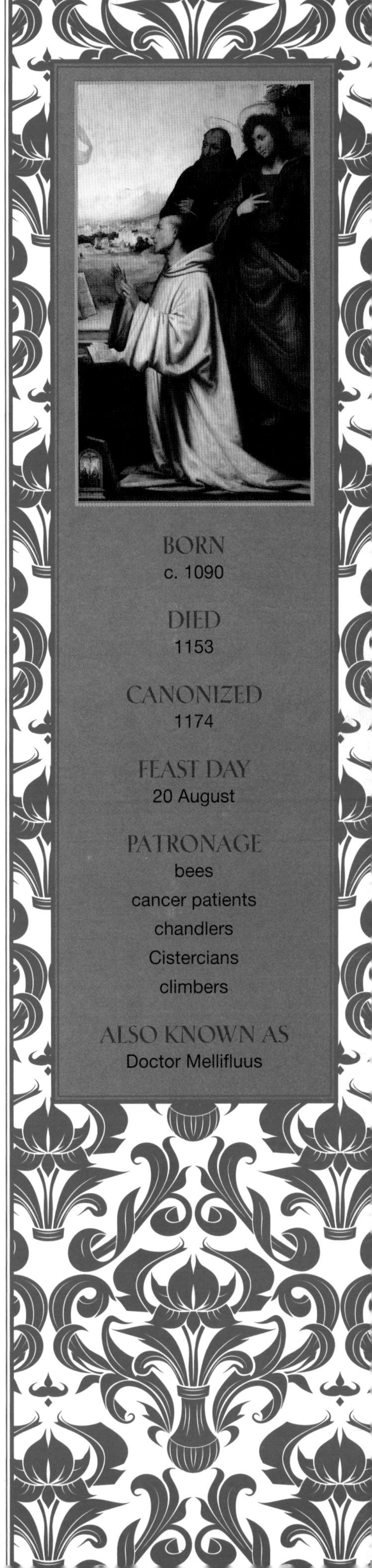

BORN
c. 1170

DIED
6 August, 1221

CANONIZED
1234

FEAST DAY
8 August

PATRONAGE
astronomers
the falsely accused

ALSO KNOWN AS
Dominic of Osma
Dominic de Guzmán
Domingo Félix de Guzmán

Saint Dominic

Saint Dominic founded the Order of the Preachers in Toulouse, France, in 1215. Better known as the Dominicans, after their founder, the Order of the Preachers quickly won prominence throughout Europe, gaining papal approval just a year after its founding. Dedicated to combating heresy, Dominicans were soon associated with the inquisitions begun in 1231 by Pope Gregory IX.

The Life of Dominic

Born in Castile (then called Caleruega), Dominic became a canon at Osma Cathedral sometime before 1199. Dominic committed himself to poverty and rigorous study from the first. He impressed Osma's bishop, Diego, so that Diego took Dominic with him on a long voyage to Denmark, where the churchmen were to help arrange the marriage of the prince. The journey proved formative for Dominic, who witnessed firsthand the lax state of religion in outlying regions and, more importantly, the Cathars.

The Cathars were a dualistic sect, purportedly following ancient traditions, whose popularity had spread to various places in Europe since 1143. By Dominic's day they were especially prominent in two regions of Europe: Lombardy, in northern Italy, and Languedoc in southern France, where they were called Albigensians.

Appalled, Diego and Dominic, who had been deputized to preach against the heresy, joined the Cistercians in Lombardy but found them lenient and

Saint Dominic (at left) and Francis of Assisi, who both established major mendicant orders.

ineffective, due in part to a lack of education. Dominic's pleas to found a new order of preachers, well educated and

To praise,

to bless,

to preach.

Motto of the Order of Preachers

dedicated to the abolition of heresy, went unheeded in Rome at first, but Dominic continued to preach.

When he finally succeeded in his effort to found a new order, Dominic devoted himself wholeheartedly to its promulgation. He had a talent for administration and journeyed to Rome, Bologna, Spain, and throughout France from his home base in Toulouse. As Dominic himself did, the order insisted on higher education (and established relationships with universities), poverty, and preaching. Dominic died in 1221 in Bologna while on one of his trips.

Among the symbols artists usually show with Saint Dominic are a stalk of lilies, to represent chastity, and a book and staff, which refer to the story, recounted in The Golden Legend, *in which Peter and Paul give him these items with the message that he should take them and preach to the world.*

The Inquisition

In 1231, Pope Gregory IX issued the first order for an inquisition into heretical beliefs. Although nominally called "the Inquisition", inquisitors did not belong to a single monolithic institution but rather followed one of many individual commissions. Dominicans played a large role in the Inquisition, especially in the first commissions, which sent them to Germany, France, and Italy. The Cathars were their special concern at first, but soon inquisitors began to tackle other troublesome belief systems, including the "heresies" of Jews and Muslims. The thirteenth century saw the first large-scale persecutions of these groups, particularly Jews, many of whom lived in Europe's cities.

Although there is only slender evidence that Dominic took an active role in the Inquisition, long tradition casts him as its founder and first inquisitor-general. This circa 1495 painting by Pedro Berruguete depicts Saint Dominic presiding over an auto-da-fé, the ritual of public penance of condemned heretics.

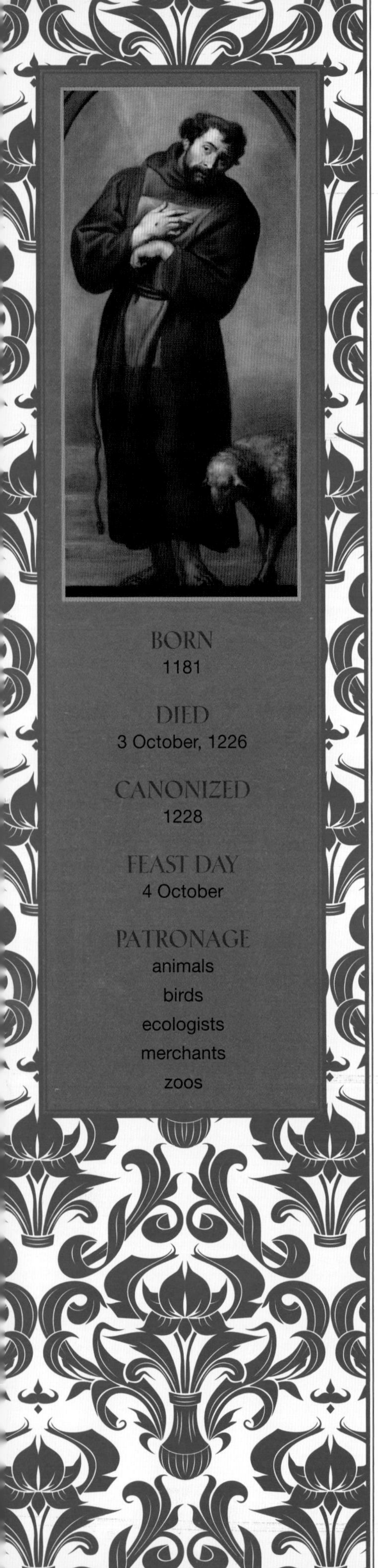

BORN
1181

DIED
3 October, 1226

CANONIZED
1228

FEAST DAY
4 October

PATRONAGE
animals
birds
ecologists
merchants
zoos

Saint FRANCIS *of Assisi*

As a youth Francis betrayed remarkably little of his future sanctity. His thoughts turned to religious contemplation after he was wounded in battle in 1201 and spent a year in captivity. While praying at San Damiano, a small, neglected church in Assisi, Francis received divine auditory instruction. From a crucifix mounted in the church issued the command: "Go and repair my house, which you see is falling down."

Saint Francis is credited with staging the world's first crèche, a living re-creation of Christ's nativity in 1223 at Greccio, Italy.

CHURCH REPAIRS

Francis took the injunction literally and sold his father's possessions to rebuild the church. Battling with his father, Francis renounced his inheritance, took a vow of poverty, even stripped

Lord, grant that I might not so much seek to be loved as to love.

SAINT FRANCIS OF ASSISI

off his clothing. Yet his extraordinarily charismatic, yet humble, personality soon attracted followers, and in 1210 Francis wrote the first Rule for his little order, emphasizing obedience, poverty, and orthodoxy.

Around 1211, after a trip to Rome, the friars made crude homes in Porziuncola, near Assisi. They travelled incessantly, preaching and living as labourers, farmers, and occasionally beggars. They distinguished themselves through their steadfast devotion to poverty; because they were utterly dedicated locals, who could cement opinions among the poor and uneducated, the Church, in turn, effectively used the Franciscans to counter heresy.

FRANCIS LATER LIFE

Francis attempted to travel to Syria and then Morocco, to convert Muslims, but circumstances frustrated him. Eventually, in 1218 or 1219, Sultan al-Kamil received him gracefully but refused to convert.

Returning to Italy in 1220, Saint Francis found his order in chaos. The Franciscans, now numbering more than five thousand, needed leadership and organization, and Francis, humbly recognizing that he did not possess these abilities, stepped down as vicar-general.

Francis had a remarkable mystical experience in 1224, when he saw a fiery, six-winged seraph and the crucified Christ. Waking, he discovered stigmata – the first verified account. In 1225, Francis composed the song "Canticle of Brother Sun", still popular today. Although only 45, Francis was infirm, nearly blind, and ill. He died in Assisi in 1226.

SAINT FRANCIS AND THE ANIMALS

Francis' rapport with animals and love for nature are well known: he hoped the Holy Roman Emperor would enact an animal-welfare law. One legend claims Francis tamed a ravening wolf by insisting that townspeople feed the beast, whose terrorizing had been dictated by hunger. The townsfolk even buried the animal in their church. In artwork Francis is often attended by birds, which, several sources say, came to hear him preach.

The Three Franciscan Orders

In addition to the "First Order" of mendicant monks, Francis formed a tertiary order, for which he wrote a Rule in 1221. This so-called Third Order did not take vows but was dedicated to the Franciscan ideal. Saint Clare of Assisi, a noblewoman devoted to Francis and who renounced worldly life in order to form an order of nuns, formed the Second Order. As the First Order spread throughout Europe so did the Second Order, better known, after its founder, as the Poor Clares.

ABOVE: *Saint Clare of Assisi. Clare was one of the first followers of Francis. She founded the Order of Poor Ladies, based on the Franciscan model. Ten years after her death, the order became known as the Order of Saint Clare.*

LEFT: *Saint Francis of Assisi is the patron saint of animals, and artists often depict him surrounded by birds or with a wolf at his feet.*

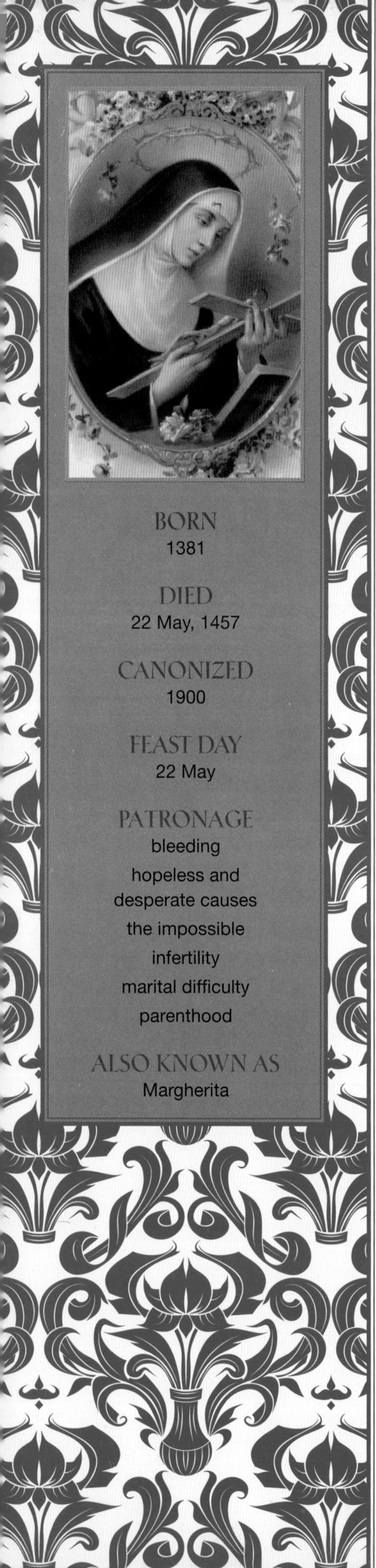

BORN
1381

DIED
22 May, 1457

CANONIZED
1900

FEAST DAY
22 May

PATRONAGE
bleeding
hopeless and desperate causes
the impossible
infertility
marital difficulty
parenthood

ALSO KNOWN AS
Margherita

Saint Rita of Cascia

Saint Rita's cult spread through Italy soon after her death, receiving local approval in 1457 – although Rita was not beatified until 1626 and canonized in 1900. Her cult has retained its popularity, due in part to her association with victims of marital trouble. Rita married young, in obedience to her parents' wishes; unfortunately, her husband badly mistreated her and proved unfaithful, dying in a knife fight 18 years later.

Rita's two teenage sons wished to avenge their father's death, but Rita persuaded them to forgive the murderer. Tragedy soon followed, however, with both boys dying from an illness shortly thereafter. Nonetheless, Rita welcomed their reconciliation with God.

Please let me suffer like you, Divine Saviour.

Saint Rita of Cascia

In art, Rita is usually depicted with the wound from the crown of thorns clear on her forehead.

Rita had wanted to be a nun since childhood, but her arranged marriage prevented it. Now widowed and childless, she applied for admission to an Augustinian convent in Cascia. Reluctant to admit a non-virgin, the convent refused her three times before finally accepting her. She became a model nun – obedient, pious, and penitent. In 1441, praying after listening to a sermon on Christ's crown of thorns, she received an unusual stigmata: she felt a thorn pierce her forehead, which left her with a visible wound for the rest of her days.

Saint ANGELA Merici

Angela lost many family members at a young age, including both parents and an older sister. After a vision in which she saw her sister with the Virgin Mary, Angela became a Franciscan tertiary. She returned to her home village of Desenzano in the 1490s with several companions, starting a programme to educate the girls there, especially in the Catholic religion.

She opened two schools, one in Desenzano and one in Brescia; her efforts inspired many other young women to follow her. Angela journeyed to Crete (where, legend has it, she was struck blind but cured on her return trip), the Holy Land, and Rome, where she met Pope Clement VII (r. 1523–34). Her heart remained with her work, however, and she dreamed of founding an order of tertiary women to continue teaching.

Her dream was realized in 1535, when she and 28 followers in Brescia dedicated themselves to God. Called the Ursulines after their patron, Saint Ursula, the women initially lived simple but informal lives, committed to the education of girls, and teaching and praying together. In later years the order became a formal congregation and adopted a cloistered way of life, though never losing sight of its pedagogical mission and playing a large role, in the seventeenth and eighteenth centuries, in the conversion and education of Native Americans.

> *Charity wins souls and draws them to virtue.*
>
> Saint Angela Merici

Saint Angela Merici, founder of the first teaching congregation of women in the Church.

BORN
24 December, 1491

DIED
31 July, 1556

CANONIZED
1622

FEAST DAY
31 July

PATRONAGE
Jesuit Order
soldiers
spiritual retreats and exercises

ALSO KNOWN AS
Ignatius of Loyola

Saint IGNATIUS *Loyola*

Ignatius' early life did not begin to hint at the enormous impact he would later have on Catholicism. The youngest child of Basque nobility, at 16 Ignatius joined the household of the king of Castile's treasurer, where he lived the indulgent life of a courtier. In 1517, he became a soldier and fought for four years before a catastrophic injury to his right leg ended his service.

While recuperating in his family castle at Loyola from this injury, and the truly gruesome attempts to repair it, Ignatius asked for a distraction: the courtly romances with which he was familiar. All that his sister-in-law had on hand, however, were Spanish translations of *The Golden Legend,* a medieval collection of hagiography, and Ludolph of Saxony's *Life of Christ.*

Ignatius Loyola turned his militancy as a soldier into his passionate service of Christ.

> *Go forth and set the world on fire.*
>
> Saint Ignatius Loyola

It was a turning point for Ignatius, who read and reread the books and found in them a peace and meaning he missed elsewhere. He converted; and after recovering fully (though the surgery left him with a permanent limp), he travelled to Montserrat, a famous abbey in Catalonia. He followed this with nearly a year spent in a cave in Manresa, where he lived a contemplative life, suffering illnesses, remorse, and austerities. While at Manresa he began his most famous work, *Spiritual Exercises* eventually published, with papal approval, in 1548.

PILGRIM AND PRIEST

In 1523, Ignatius resolved to make a pilgrimage to the Holy Land, controlled since 1516 by the expanding Ottoman Empire, where he hoped to preach the rest of his life. The Franciscans – who maintained tenuous control of the Holy Places (sites significant in the Gospels) and could neither risk antagonizing their hosts with fiery preaching nor afford an expensive ransom should such a prisoner be captured – immediately thwarted this ambition. Disappointed but obedient, Ignatius returned to Spain in 1524.

He decided to become a priest, first studying at the University of Alcalá, then the University of Salamanca, and finally at the Sorbonne, achieving ordination in 1534 and a master's degree in 1535. Acquiring an education had proven difficult: Ignatius had been imprisoned both at Alcalá and Salamanca, first for daring to teach before earning his degree, later by an overzealous Dominican inquisitor. In Paris he acquired a small group of followers who also became priests and included among their number Saint Francis Xavier.

ABOVE: The Vision at La Storta. *While in Italy, Ignatius had a vision of Jesus placing him at the service of Christ and his cross, inspiring him to form the Society of Jesus.*

LEFT: *In summer 1534, the first seven companions pronounce their vows at Saint-Pierre de Montmartre, one of the oldest churches in Paris. Ignatius Loyola had gathered six of his university companions to become the first Jesuits.*

THE SOCIETY OF JESUS

In 1539, this small group, led by Ignatius, determined to become a new religious order; the following year their Society of Jesus won papal approval. The Jesuits, as they became known, took vows of poverty and chastity as well as an unusually rigorous vow of complete obedience. Emphasizing education, they also vowed to travel anywhere and to perform any duties required by the pope. Almost immediately the Jesuits became one of the most visible and active missionary arms of the Church.

Ignatius died after a brief bout with fever, but by then, thanks to his immovable will and powers of organization, his order numbered more than one thousand. Today, the Jesuits make up the largest Catholic order and are known for their efforts in education, research, and social justice.

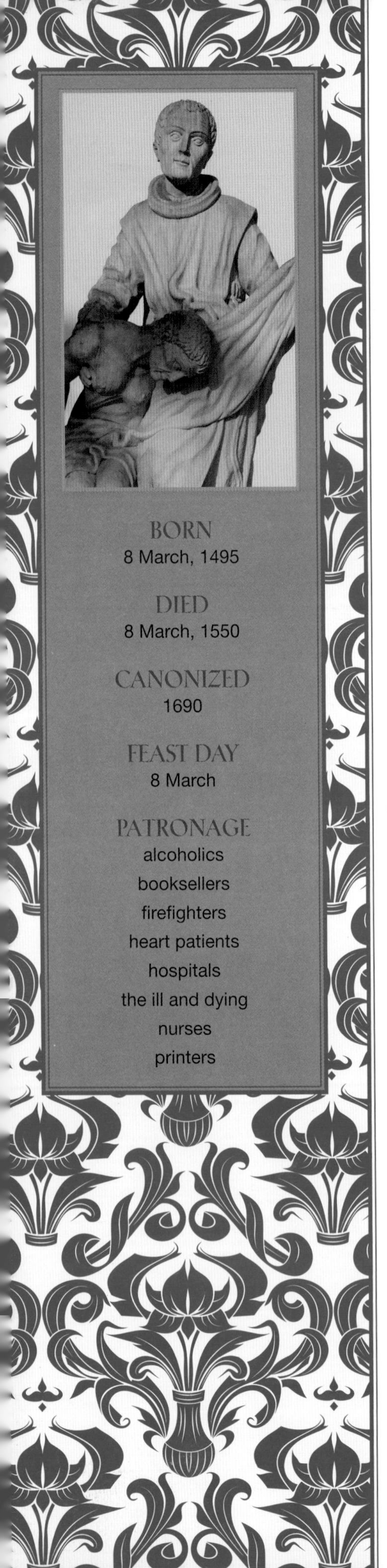

BORN
8 March, 1495

DIED
8 March, 1550

CANONIZED
1690

FEAST DAY
8 March

PATRONAGE
alcoholics
booksellers
firefighters
heart patients
hospitals
the ill and dying
nurses
printers

Saint JOHN of God

For a saint, John had an unusual childhood: as a child he ran away from home, worked as a shepherd on an estate, and later joined the Spanish army, where he lived a life of decidedly low moral standards.

John changed his ways after leaving the army. He planned to travel to Northern Africa to aid Christians imprisoned by the Muslim Moors, but he was dissuaded from this path and instead moved to Gibraltar, where he sold religious books for meagre profit. A vision at the age of forty of Mary and the Infant Jesus (she called him John of God, the name by which he is now known) strengthened his desire to make amends for the sins of his youth, and John moved to Grenada.

There he encountered Saint John of Avila, whose preaching both inspired and shamed him. He went through a period of intense distress, making such a spectacle of himself by running through the streets and wailing that the authorities eventually placed him in an asylum. In 1539, John finally found his true calling, caring for Grenada's sick in his own home with such devotion that he soon inspired followers. After his death these followers organized themselves as the Brothers Hospitallers, or the Brothers of Saint John of God, whom they named as their founder.

So intense was John's religious conversion that those who saw him feared for his sanity. His time in an asylum inspired him to dedicate his life to helping the poor and sick.

Saint JOHN *of the Cross*

Reckoned with Saint Teresa of Avila as a founder of the Discalced Carmelites, Saint John of the Cross suffered greatly for his order, even at the hands of some of his fellow friars.

Born Juan (John) de Yepes, John was apprenticed to a silk weaver in his youth. He was drawn to the religious life, however, and he joined the Carmelites in 1563.

> *In the evening of life, we will be judged on love alone.*
>
> SAINT JOHN OF THE CROSS

While studying in Medina he met Teresa, who persuaded him to join her reform movement. He took over the deeply impoverished house of Duruelo. After that he served as rector at Alcala and then, in 1572, confessor to the nuns of Avila. He served in that post until 1577, but in 1575 some unreformed Carmelites imprisoned him in a tiny, dark cell for nine months, subjecting him to beatings, humiliation, and near starvation.

John faced persecution even after the scuffle between Carmelites and reformers had settled, this time from his own vicar-general. His enemies in the order wished him expelled altogether, but instead his offices were stripped and he was exiled, first to La Peñuela and finally to Ubeda, where he died.

John had a special reverence for the Virgin Mary, whom he saw several times and to whom he attributed his survival on no fewer than four life-threatening occasions: twice from drowning as a child, once from prison, and once when a wall of his monastery fell.

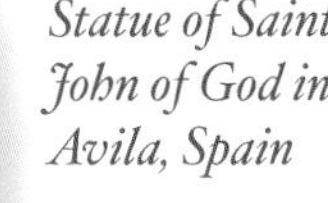

Statue of Saint John of God in Avila, Spain

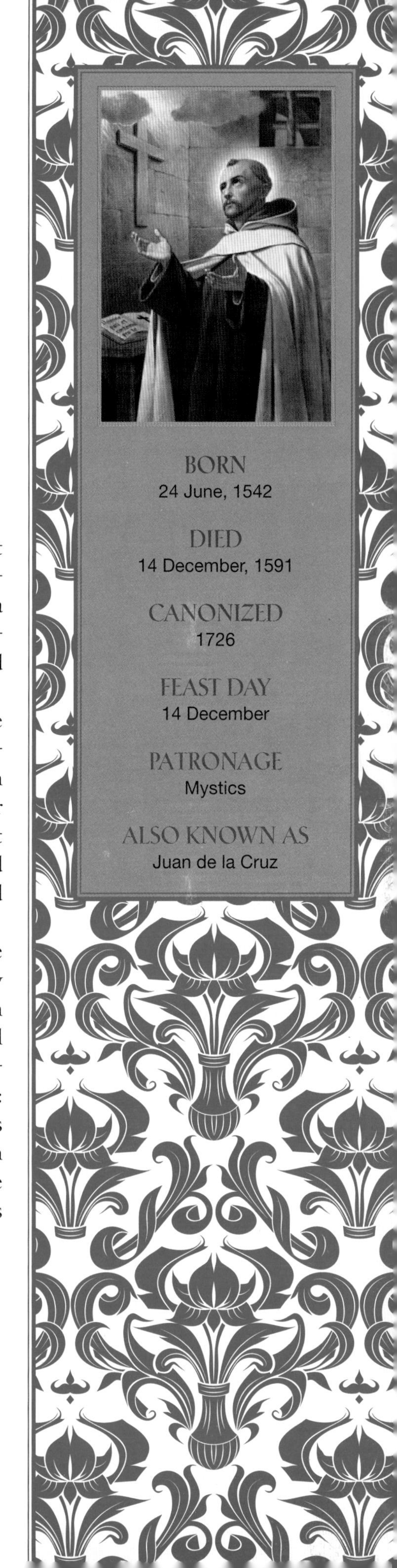

BORN
24 June, 1542

DIED
14 December, 1591

CANONIZED
1726

FEAST DAY
14 December

PATRONAGE
Mystics

ALSO KNOWN AS
Juan de la Cruz

Saint Teresa of Avila

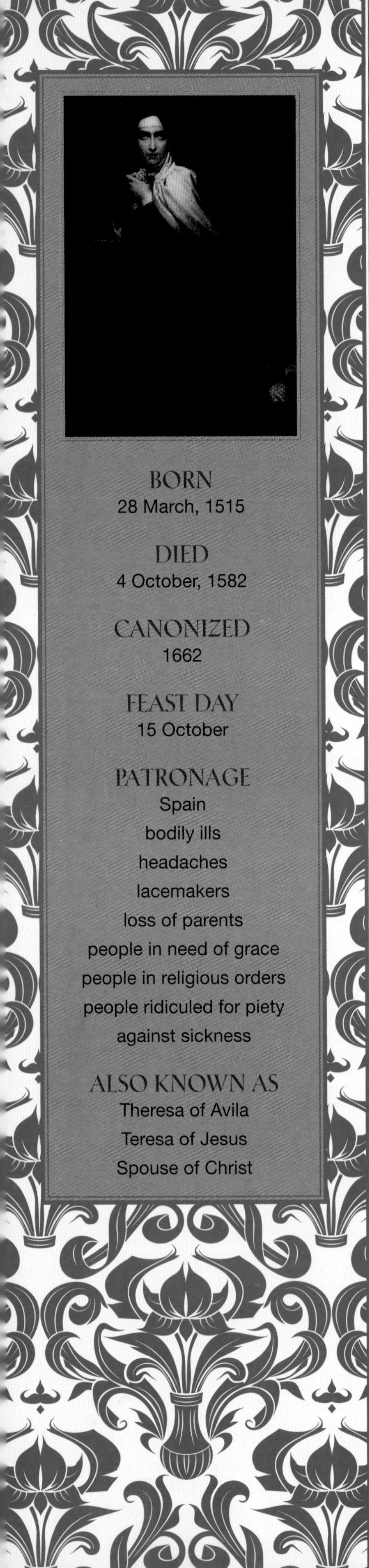

BORN
28 March, 1515

DIED
4 October, 1582

CANONIZED
1662

FEAST DAY
15 October

PATRONAGE
Spain
bodily ills
headaches
lacemakers
loss of parents
people in need of grace
people in religious orders
people ridiculed for piety
against sickness

ALSO KNOWN AS
Theresa of Avila
Teresa of Jesus
Spouse of Christ

Teresa became a nun at age twenty, entering the Carmelite convent at Avila over her father's objections (though he dropped them afterward). A scion of Castilian nobility, the young Teresa demonstrated an inclination to the religious life, once even running away from home with her brother to Moorish Africa where the pair intended to die as martyrs.

After entering the convent, Teresa fell victim to a serious illness that lasted three years. On one occasion she hovered so close to death that rites were performed, a grave was prepared, and Teresa made full confession. This was her low point, however, from which she began a slow recovery, the disease remaining with her in some form until she was forty years old.

Today it is believed Teresa suffered from malignant malaria; she attributed her illness to God's punishment for her sins, her recovery to Saint Joseph's intercession. The long illness and convalescence opened her mind to introspective prayer, and eventually she became a practised mystic. Unfortunately, however, and despite her warm and gracious personality, the promulgation of her remarkable experiences generated contempt and ridicule, even among her fellow nuns.

THE DISCALCED CARMELITES

Teresa founded her first reformed Carmelite nunnery in 1562, after struggling with both secular and ecclesiastical authorities. She was dissatisfied with

Although often ridiculed for her intense mysticism, her analytical writings on visionary experience were deeply thoughtful, leading her to be named a Doctor of the Church for her profound insights on contemplative prayer.

the relaxed rule at her Carmelite house, standard throughout the order, and wished to return to a far stricter way of life. Joining in her effort to reform the order was Saint John of the Cross, himself a Carmelite focused on the need to reform the friars.

After 1575, when the General Chapter abolished the reform, resistance to the Discalced Carmelite reformers (so-called for their habit of going barefoot or wearing sandals instead of shoes), was intense. Persecution followed, during which Saint John and others were imprisoned, but the reformers persisted until, in 1580, the Discalced Carmelites were reinstated; in 1593, they became a separate order.

Suffering is a great favour. Remember that everything soon comes to an end . . . and take courage. Think of how our gain is eternal.

Saint Teresa of Avila

ABOVE: *Saint Teresa of Avila depicted with her followers in the Discalced Carmelite order, also known as the Barefoot Carmelites. Teresa formed this offshoot of the Carmelites in an attempt to return to a stricter eremitic way of life.*

BELOW LEFT: *Statue of Teresa in one of the two shrines dedicated to the saint in Avila, Spain.*

FOUNDER AND DOCTOR

Teresa died in 1582. By then she had founded seventeen reformed religious communities, led her infant order through its painful persecution, and laid the groundwork for lasting reform. She had also written several books on her life, her mysticism, and – in her most famous work, *The Interior Castle*, the result of a mystical vision – her doctrine for personal spiritual development. Pope Paul VI declared her a Doctor of the Church in 1970, the first female saint so honoured.

Saint ROSE of Lima

BORN
20 April, 1586

DIED
24 August, 1617

CANONIZED
1671

FEAST DAY
30 August
(Peru);
23 August
(general)

PATRONAGE
(partial list)
Native Indian peoples of the Americas
Latin America
India
Peru
Philippines
West Indies
florists
gardeners
needle workers
people ridiculed for piety

ALSO KNOWN AS
Rosa de Lima

Christened Isabel, Saint Rose was born in Lima, Peru, to Gaspar Flores, a cavalryman from San German, Puerto Rico, and his wife, Maria de Oliva, a native of Lima. She was the first person from the Americas to be canonized, 54 years after her death. She died young, at only 31 years old, after living a life of extreme penance and sanctity.

Apart from the cross, there is no other ladder by which we may get to heaven.

SAINT ROSE OF LIMA

Rose was a very beautiful girl of Spanish and Incan descent. Her parents wished her to marry, and her beauty attracted much interest from suitors, but Rose was determined to remain a virgin and deliberately spoiled her looks. She entered the Third Order of Saint Dominic at the age of twenty,

Rose used to rub her face with pepper to produce disfiguring blotches. Although she was admired for her great beauty, Rose feared that her looks were a threat to her chastity.

retiring in semi-seclusion to a hut in the family garden. To help support her impoverished family, she grew flowers and sewed beautiful embroidery and lace for the market.

When not engaged in such necessary pursuits, Rose lived the life of an ascetic. She fasted often, wore a crown of metal spikes, and lay on a bed of broken glass and pottery, rocks, and thorns. She flogged herself daily and wore gloves filled with nettles. She became something of a mystic, experiencing religious ecstasy and receiving visions of Jesus Christ. Despite living in seclusion she became known for fighting the corruption of colonial Peru and caring personally for the poor and sick. When she died, after a long illness, the people of Lima poured into the cathedral to pay her respect.

Rose with The Blessed Virgin and the Holy Child. Her parents' refusal to allow Rose to leave home to enter a convent did not deter her from living a life of piety. She joined a tertiary Dominican order, which allowed her to dwell with her family while she devoted herself to prayer.

Saint John Macías

Even though late sixteenth- and early-seventeenth-century Lima was marked by political turmoil, it was also a place of deep religious conversion. During the short life of Rose of Lima, there were others who stood out for their holiness and dedication, including her contemporaries – and friends – Saint Martin de Porres and Saint John Macías.

Just a year older than Rose, John Macías was born Juan de Arcas Sanchez in Spain. He was 25 years old when he first ventured to the New World under the employ of a wealthy merchant. After time in Colombia and Ecuador, he travelled to Peru, where he spent the rest of his life.

In Peru he first observed the work of the Dominicans, which inspired him to begin life as a religious. He relinquished all he owned, gave it to the poor and moved to the outskirts of Lima to toil as a shepherd. He gave whatever support he could to the Dominicans until finalizing his vows in 1623.

As a friar, he devoted his life to prayer, penance, and charity, caring for the sick and needy, who sought him out.

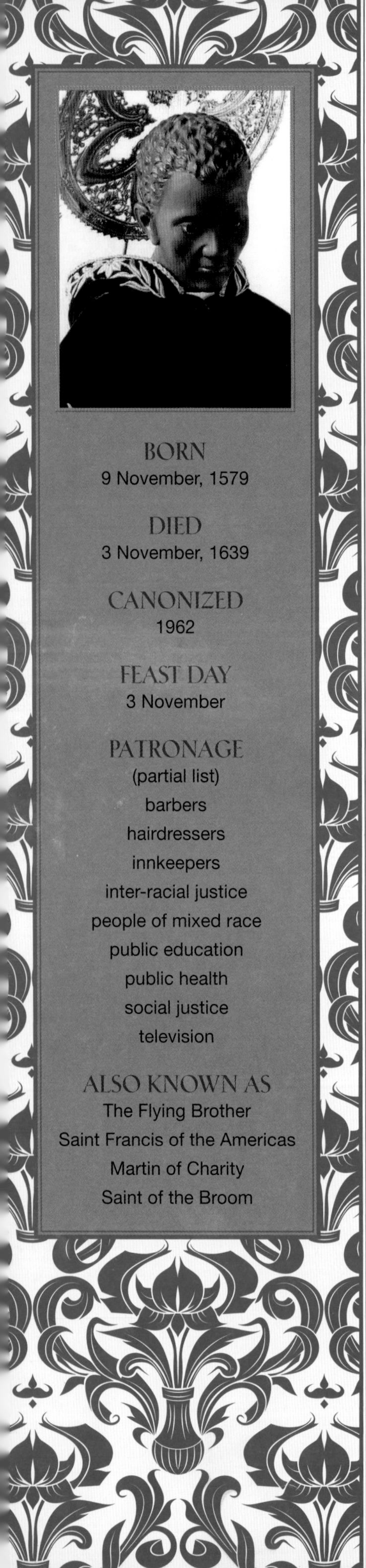

BORN
9 November, 1579

DIED
3 November, 1639

CANONIZED
1962

FEAST DAY
3 November

PATRONAGE
(partial list)
barbers
hairdressers
innkeepers
inter-racial justice
people of mixed race
public education
public health
social justice
television

ALSO KNOWN AS
The Flying Brother
Saint Francis of the Americas
Martin of Charity
Saint of the Broom

Saint MARTIN de Porres

Saint Martin grew up the illegitimate son of a Spanish nobleman, Juan de Porres, and a free black woman, Anna Velásquez, in Lima, Peru, where ubiquitous racism had been institutionalized. When Martin was 15 he joined the Third Order of Dominic; because he was black, however, Order rules prohibited him from taking the habit so he became a lay brother instead, performing the most menial tasks with such alacrity that the Dominicans waived the restriction and admitted him to the order in 1603.

Martin, who had at one point in his youth been apprenticed to a barber-surgeon, became widely known as a healer who would treat anyone, regardless of race or status. He even operated a veterinary hospital for dogs and cats, earning the nickname "Saint Francis of the Americas" because of his great love for animals.

As almoner, Martin raised astonishing amounts of money for the poor and grew fruit trees for their use. He performed many miracles, levitating so frequently that he became known as the "Flying Brother". Efforts to canonize him started as early as 1660; sadly this did not occur until 1962, when the Western world began truly to confront the problem of racism.

Father Thomas McGlynn of the Dominican order sculpted this statue of Saint Martin de Porres. As in most depictions of the saint, Martin holds a broom in honour of the humility he showed even when ordered to perform the lowliest tasks in the monastery.

Saint Vincent de Paul

Vincent de Paul moved in high circles, serving for a time as a royal adviser, working with the famous Cardinal Richelieu, and befriending numerous French nobles, but he and his wealthy followers always directed their efforts to the most needy, raising extraordinary amounts of money for charitable causes.

Charity is certainly greater than any rule.

Saint Vincent de Paul

Saint Vincent de Paul, ably assisted by the Vincentians and the Sisters of Charity, was a tireless worker for the poor and mistreated.

He founded the Congregation of the Mission – priests devoted to ministering to the rural poor and sick – in 1625. They were known as the Vincentians, or Lazarists after they moved in 1633 to the priory of St Lazare. Also in 1633, Vincent founded the Sisters (or Daughters) of Charity, women who nursed the sick and cared for the poor. Vincent founded hospitals, asylums, orphanages, and other institutions to help people in need. He also devoted himself to rescuing and succouring Christian slaves in Africa, and during the Thirty Years' War he raised funds for the victims of the war in Lorraine.

Vincent was greatly aided in these efforts by the Ladies of Charity, a group of wealthy women who raised funds for his work, beginning in 1629. His efforts earned him recognition at court, where he advised both Louis XIII of France and, after Louis's death, his widow, Anne of Austria. By the end of his life Vincent was famous for his charitable zeal, and in 1885 Pope Leo XIII named him the patron of all charities.

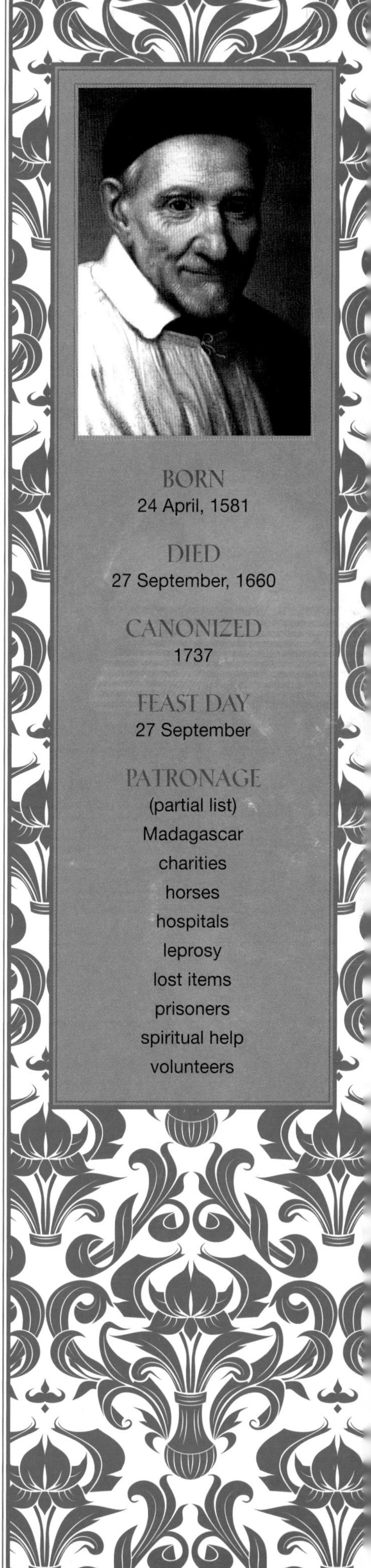

BORN
24 April, 1581

DIED
27 September, 1660

CANONIZED
1737

FEAST DAY
27 September

PATRONAGE
(partial list)
Madagascar
charities
horses
hospitals
leprosy
lost items
prisoners
spiritual help
volunteers

Saint Elizabeth Ann Seton

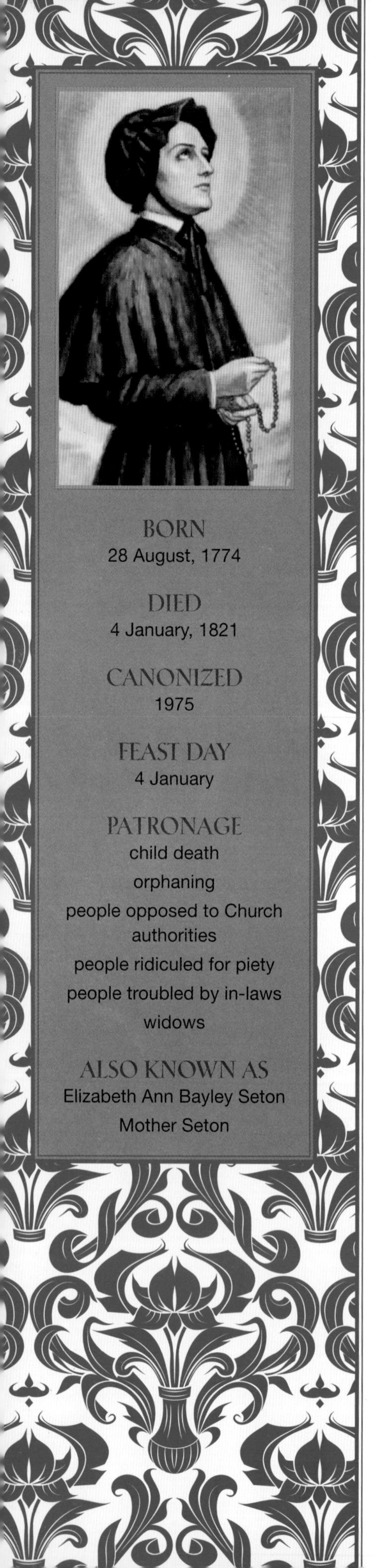

BORN
28 August, 1774

DIED
4 January, 1821

CANONIZED
1975

FEAST DAY
4 January

PATRONAGE
child death
orphaning
people opposed to Church authorities
people ridiculed for piety
people troubled by in-laws
widows

ALSO KNOWN AS
Elizabeth Ann Bayley Seton
Mother Seton

Born into a wealthy New York family and happily married to a successful merchant, Saint Elizabeth Ann Seton nevertheless endured more than her fair share of tragedy. By 1803, her husband William's business had collapsed, his parents had died – leaving William and Elizabeth to care for William's young siblings – and William himself subsequently died of tuberculosis in Italy, where he, Elizabeth, and their oldest daughter had travelled in search of a cure.

Elizabeth, always devout, had been raised Episcopalian, but she felt drawn to the Catholic Church while in Italy and converted in New York in 1805. She was thirty years old, with five young children of her own and three young sisters-in-law to care for. She taught, but intense anti-Catholic feeling in New York resulted in many parents withdrawing their children from her school. Fortunately, in 1807, she made the acquaintance of Father du Bourg, president of a seminary in Baltimore. He persuaded her to open St Joseph's School for Girls in Baltimore in 1808, the first such school in the United States.

Saint Elizabeth organized a group of Catholic schoolmistresses as the Daughters of Charity, which adopted the Rule of Saint Vincent de Paul in 1813 – the first Catholic order founded in the United States. Soon afterward, in 1814, the sisters opened the first Catholic orphanage in the United States, in Philadelphia. Elizabeth posthumously earned another "first", becoming the first American to be canonized, in 1975.

The Shrine of Saint Elizabeth Ann Bayley Seton is located in lower Manhattan on the site of the Seton family home. It sits next to James Watson House, a Federal rowhouse, which matches the former Seton residence.

Saint Mary MacKillop

Saint Mary MacKillop was a determined woman of deep moral conviction, and she has the unusual distinction of having been both excommunicated and canonized.

Born to Scottish parents in Australia, Mary became a teacher but, inclined strongly towards a religious life, became a nun. In 1866, she cofounded (with Father Julian Woods) Australia's first religious order, the Sisters of Saint Joseph of the Sacred Heart. Today, the sisters number about 850 and continue Mary's mission – to educate and care for poor children – around the world.

> *God gives me strength for what is necessary.*
>
> 
>
> Saint Mary MacKillop

In fact, it was this concern for children that landed Mary in trouble: she exposed the abuse of several children by a priest and, in the resulting turmoil, was excommunicated by the bishop of Brisbane, Laurence Sheil, in 1870.

Their faith in Mary MacKillop never wavered and the Josephite nuns elected her Mother Superior-General in 1899, a position she held even through illness until her death in 1909.

Although her punishment was undoubtedly a mighty blow to the pious Mary, she refused to recant her testimony, and after investigating the matter further Bishop Sheil apologized and revoked her excommunication. Some Catholics therefore consider Mary the patron saint of abused children. She is the first Australian saint.

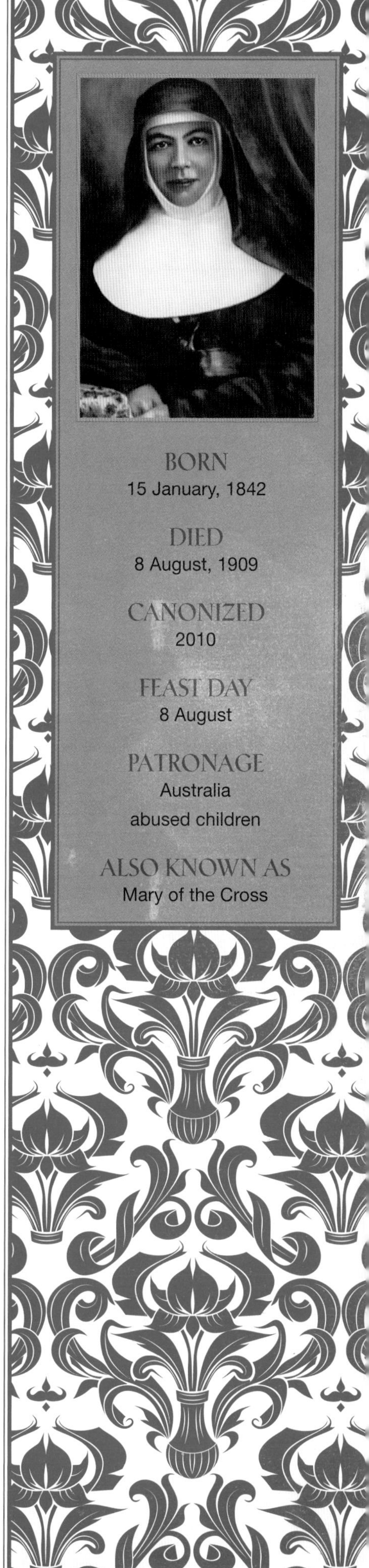

Saints of Mission and Conversion

Ever since Saint Paul's remarkable missionary voyages in the mid-first century, missions have played a large and important role in the history of Christianity. Great missionaries like Saints Augustine of Canterbury, Kilian, and Francis Xavier risked their lives to spread Christ's message, which they believed offered the only path to salvation.

There have been three major points in the history of conversion to Christianity. One arose not from missionary activity but from secular authority, when Emperor Constantine of Rome converted in the early fourth century, taking his Empire with him. The next occurred when Pope Saint Gregory I (r. 590 to 604), sent missionaries beyond the boundaries of the empire with instructions that would shape European conversion for the next five centuries. Finally, with the discovery of the New World in the fifteenth century, there came a flurry of missions to the Americas and the Far East as new trade routes and improved naval technology made travelling easier.

Had it not been for the pioneering activities of these remarkable, adventurous saints, the map of Christianity would today look very different – and would, undoubtedly, be significantly smaller.

BORN
c. 354

DIED
22 June, 431

CANONIZED
Pre-Congregation

FEAST DAY
22 June

PATRONAGE
None

ALSO KNOWN AS
Pontificus Meropius
Anicius Paulinus

Saint Paulinus of Nola

Born into a wealthy Gaulish family, Paulinus served in several public offices and practised law. He married Therasia, a Spanish woman, but they managed only to produce a single child, who died in infancy. Legend has it that Paulinus met Saint Martin of Tours, who cured him of an eye ailment; following these events, both Paulinus and Therasia converted, sold most of their Gaulish estates, and moved to Barcelona, Spain, around 390.

They moved to Nola around 394, having already endeared themselves to the poor of Barcelona with large donations for relieving poverty and in support of the Church. In Nola, Paulinus became very devoted to Saint Felix of Nola, to whom he dedicated several poems and beside whose tomb he built a hospital. Paulinus kept up a correspondence at Nola with Saints Martin of Tours, Ambrose, Jerome, and Augustine, among others. His holiness was so apparent that even in his lifetime contemporaries regarded him as a saint, and in about 409 the Christians of Nola elected him bishop. He was an accomplished musician and poet, and several of his works are still extant.

Paulinus is remarkable for the genuineness of his conversion: since Emperor Constantine's own remarkable conversion, it had become politic for aristocrats to convert, but the Church worried about their sincerity. In Paulinus, however, the Church found a model convert, an aristocrat who abandoned wealth, prestige, and position and dedicated himself to a holy and worthy life.

The bones of Saint Paulinus have been relocated many times. In about 800, a Lombard prince first named them as relics and removed them from their burial place. From the eleventh century, they were kept in Rome. In 1908, they were moved back to Nola, and they now reside in a small church in Sutera, Sicily.

Saint Brigid of Kildare

After Saint Patrick, Brigid of Kildare is certainly the most beloved and famous saint of Ireland. As with Patrick, legends of Brigid abound, and there is reason to suspect that many of her attributes – her name, feast day, and association with cattle, sheep, and fire – stem not from the human saint but rather from a pre-Christian Irish goddess of the same name. Some scholars regard her as merely the Christianized Celtic Brigid; others say the human saint was merely given the name of the goddess.

Traditionally, Brigid converted as a child after hearing Saint Patrick preach. She angered her noble father by giving away her possessions (and his) and refusing to marry. She is said to have founded the important monastery of Kildare. Brigid also worked to convert others: in one famous story, she converts her stubbornly pagan father, who lies dying, by driving away the demons tormenting him with a cross woven from rushes. Now known as Saint Brigid's cross, this kind of cross continues to be made on her 1 February feast day.

ABOVE: *A stained-glass image in a Roman Catholic church in Dublin shows Brigid of Kildare, one of Ireland's most beloved saints.*

LEFT: *An example of Saint Brigid's cross.*

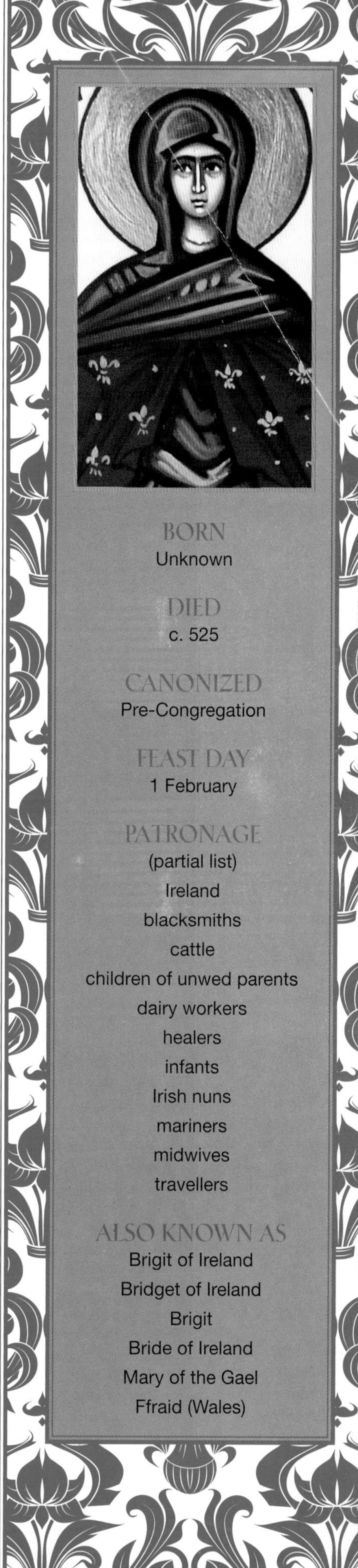

BORN
Unknown

DIED
c. 525

CANONIZED
Pre-Congregation

FEAST DAY
1 February

PATRONAGE
(partial list)
Ireland
blacksmiths
cattle
children of unwed parents
dairy workers
healers
infants
Irish nuns
mariners
midwives
travellers

ALSO KNOWN AS
Brigit of Ireland
Bridget of Ireland
Brigit
Bride of Ireland
Mary of the Gael
Ffraid (Wales)

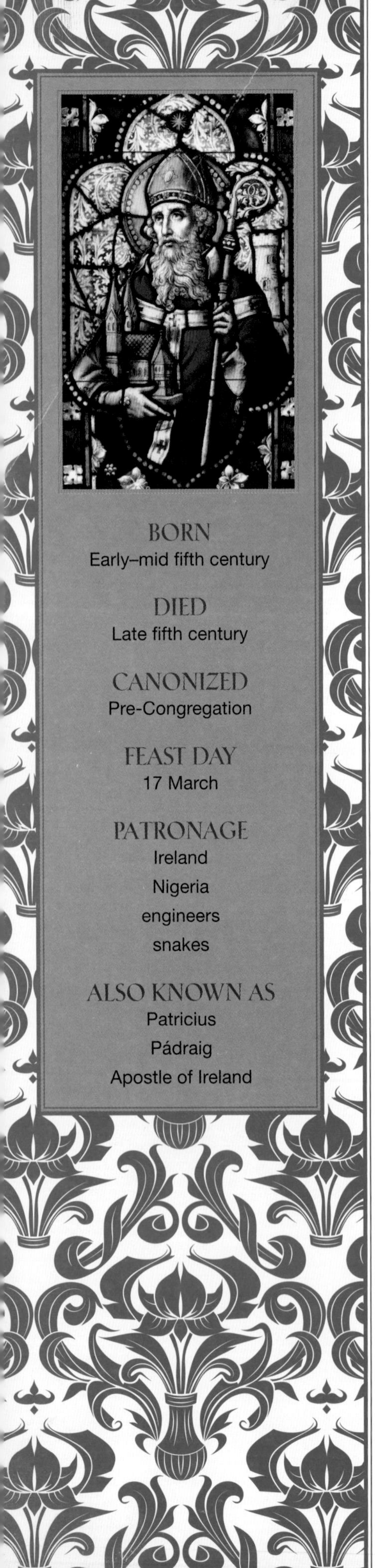

BORN
Early–mid fifth century

DIED
Late fifth century

CANONIZED
Pre-Congregation

FEAST DAY
17 March

PATRONAGE
Ireland
Nigeria
engineers
snakes

ALSO KNOWN AS
Patricius
Pádraig
Apostle of Ireland

Saint Patrick

Few saints have achieved Saint Patrick's renown. He was not Irish by birth: he was born to Christian parents in Roman Britain. Irish raiders captured him as a youth, and for six years he worked as a slave shepherd. During those years, he grew increasingly pious and prayerful, until a voice came to him in a dream, saying: "Behold, your ship is ready."

After several adventures Patrick returned to his family to study for the priesthood. Around this time the pope sent Saint Palladius to Ireland to lead the small minority of Christians. After Palladius left, possibly for Scotland, Patrick travelled to Ireland as his successor.

Apostle of Ireland

Patrick decided not only to minister to his small Christian flock but also to engage the pagan inhabitants of Britain and convert them. He thus became a pioneer, leading the first truly missionary endeavour since Paul went among the Gentiles. It is during this period that his popular but fictitious legends – the banishment of snakes, the confrontation with King Loéguire's druids, the explanation of the Trinity by recourse to the shamrock – were said to have occurred.

Patrick proselytized mainly in the historical northern provinces of Ulster and Leinster, focusing his efforts on the kings and ruling class; in the south, in contrast, in Munster and Connacht, Christianity seems to have risen from below. Conversion was a slow process in both halves of Ireland, but under Patrick's guiding hand the north was a Christian powerhouse, birthing several major monasteries and producing

Saint Patrick is often shown with his staff, which is associated with the fictitious legend that he banished snakes from Ireland.

Saint Patrick and the Druids

In one characteristic and famous legend of Patrick, the saint lights a great fire in celebration of Easter at Slane in violation of a rival pagan custom, decreed by King Loéguire. The king's druids set out to extinguish the flames but fail. The druids then cast a heavy darkness over the area, but Patrick, through the power of prayer, causes the sun to banish the darkness. Finally, one druid rises above the earth in flight – but a rapid prayer by Patrick brings the druid (and, by synecdoche, paganism itself) crashing to the ground and dying. Other versions of Patrick's contest exist as well, but they are late additions to the hagiography, and none are accurate.

ABOVE: A stone carving of Saint Patrick decorates a door to the Chapel Royal of Dublin Castle in Dublin, Ireland.

LEFT: Patrick is said to be buried at Down Cathedral, Downpatrick, along with Saints Brigid and Columba.

several saints. According to tradition, Patrick founded the monastery of Armagh, either in 444 or 457.

SAINT PATRICK AND THE CHURCH OF IRELAND

Although Patrick did not single-handedly convert Ireland to Christianity, as some of his hagiographers claim, he did midwife the Church of Ireland and spur the conversion of the country's ruling class. The Irish Church would later play an enormous role in converting other pagan peoples, and it influenced the development of Western monasticism and the retaining of classical scholarship.

Patrick came under fire for his missionary zeal. We are fortunate in having Patrick's defence, his *Confessio*, along with his other surviving document, *Epistle to Coroticus*, the only definitive sources of information about his life and work. Traditionally, Patrick is said to have died at Saul and was buried either there or at Downpatrick, both of which have since become popular sites of pilgrimage.

A Closer Look: *Pilgrimage*

Pilgrimage, a journey made to a sacred place as an act of religious devotion, has been a part of Christianity at least since the second century.

The New Testament does not specifically instruct Christians to make pilgrimages, but early pilgrims would journey to important places in the life of Jesus Christ, particularly Jerusalem. Later, Rome joined the Holy Land as a common pilgrim's destination. The shrines of saints increasingly drew pilgrims through the Middle Ages, generating virtually an entire international industry. The Knights Templar, to cite one example, was founded in the twelfth century as a military religious order to protect Christian pilgrims visiting the Holy Land.

Particular sites of Christian pilgrimage have waxed and waned in popularity over the years, as the practice has in general. Uncommon for several centuries after the Reformation, pilgrimage did not truly recover until the late nineteenth century, when technology enabled transportation over great distances. Today, shrines can be found all over the world, with the largest – among them, still, Rome and Jerusalem – drawing millions of pilgrims every year.

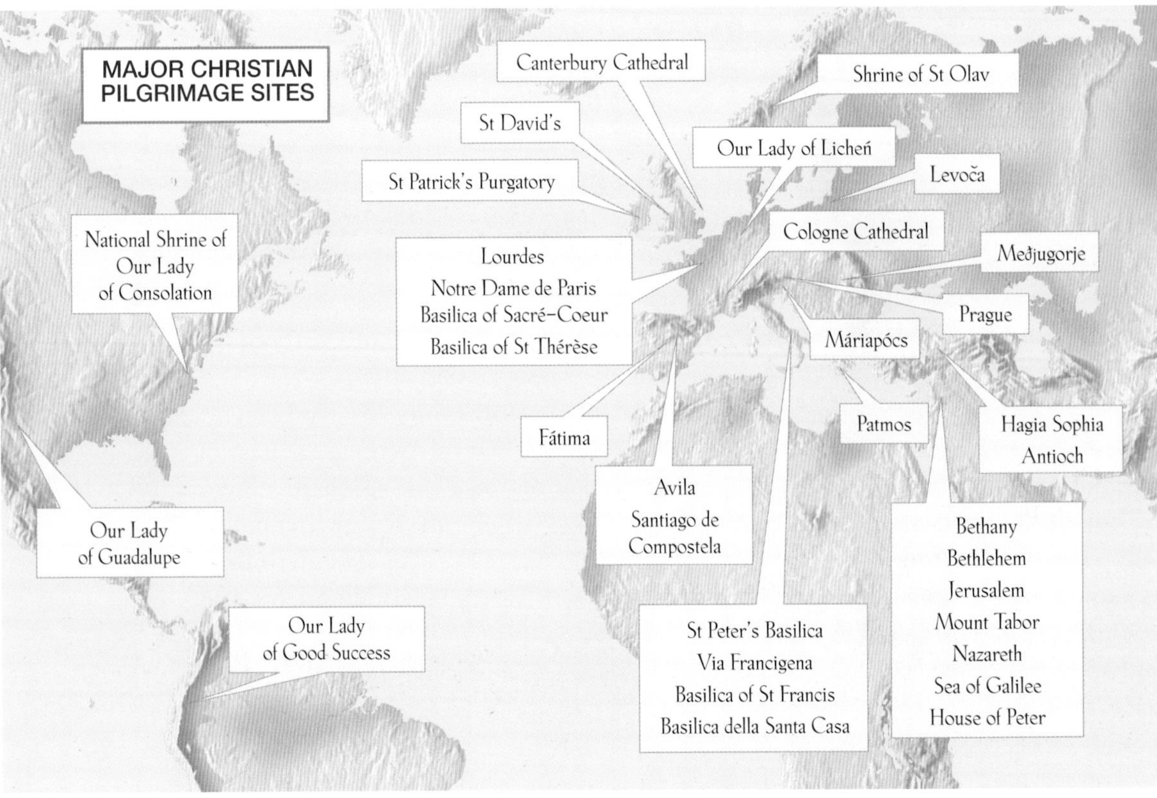

Major Pilgrimage Sites

BOSNIA-HERZEGOVINA
- Međugorje

CZECH REPUBLIC
- Infant of Prague

Since the 1620s, thousands of pilgrims have paid homage to the famous statue of the Infant Jesus of Prague located in the Church of our Lady Victorious in Malá Strana, Prague.

EQUADOR
- Shrine of Our Lady of Good Success

FRANCE
- Lourdes
- Notre Dame de Paris in Paris
- Basilica of Sacré-Coeur in Montmartre in Paris
- Basilica of St Thérèse (Lisieux)

GERMANY
- Cologne Cathedral. Shrine of the Three Kings

GREECE
- Patmos

HUNGARY
- Máriapócs

INDIA
- Vailankanni

ISRAEL
- Church of the Holy Sepulchre
- Bethany
- Bethlehem
- Via Dolorosa in Jerusalem
- Mount Tabor
- Nazareth
- Sea of Galilee
- House of Peter in Capernaum

ITALY
- St Peter's Basilica in Vatican City
- Via Francigena in Rome
- Basilica of St Francis in Assisi
- Basilica della Santa Casa in Loreto

MEXICO
- Basilica of Our Lady of Guadalupe

NORWAY
- Shrine of St Olav in Trondheim

POLAND
- The Basilica of Our Lady of Licheń.

PORTUGAL
- Fátima

SLOVAKIA
- Levoča

SPAIN
- Avila
- Santiago de Compostela in Galicia

TURKEY
- Hagia Sophia in Constantinople
- Antioch

UNITED KINGDOM
- Shrine of Saint Thomas Becket at Canterbury Cathedral in England
- St Patrick's Purgatory in Ireland
- St David's in Wales

UNITED STATES
- National Shrine of Our Lady of Consolation in Ohio

Pilgrimages were a common form of devotion in medieval times. Geoffrey Chaucer's The Canterbury Tales, *written at the end of the fourteenth century, tells the story of pilgrims en route to the shrine of Saint Thomas Becket at Canterbury Cathedral.*

Saint Columba

The third patron saint of Ireland (with Saints Patrick and Brigid) is also the patron saint of Scotland, along with Saint Andrew. This is because Columba, born into the ruling family of the Uí Neill, a powerful and ambitious clan based in Ireland's northwest, spent more than thirty years in Scotland, founding the famous monastery of Iona and, by tradition, evangelizing and converting the Picts.

The pious, yet charismatic, Columba was an active missionary, as well as a scholar and poet.

THE MONASTERIES OF COLUMBA

Saint Adomnan, a descendant of Columba's cousin, wrote the best-known hagiography of Columba around 690. Adomnan draws a compelling image of Columba as a forceful man, resolutely pious but charismatic, an accomplished poet and scholar. In addition to Iona, a chief centre of learning for the next several centuries, Columba also founded the monasteries of Derry, Durrow, and possibly Kells (Ireland's most famous illuminated manuscript, the Books of Kells, takes its name from this monastery, though it may have been written or at least begun at Iona). Scottish tradition speaks of Columba founding a great many more churches in Scotland, but none can be authenticated.

COLONIZATION AND CHRISTIANIZATION

Beginning in the fourth century, the Irish began to settle in colonies in western Britain. The process sped up considerably in the fifth century when the Dál Riata, whose lands were in Ireland's extreme northeast, emigrated and established the first Celtic kingdom in Scotland. The Dál Riata were possibly prompted in this by the Uí Neill, then expanding eastward and attempting to establish overlordship of the north. Nevertheless, it was a king

BORN
c. 521

DIED
597

CANONIZED
Pre-Congregation

FEAST DAY
9 June

PATRONAGE
Ireland
Scotland
bookbinders
computer hackers
plagiarists
poets

ALSO KNOWN AS
Colum Cille
Colmcille
Columcille
Columkill
Colum
Columbus
Combs
Columba of Iona

of the Dál Riata who bestowed the island of Iona on the saint, and it was the Dál Riata in Scotland who formed Columba's primary Christian flock.

Traditionally, Columba served not only as abbot but also as missionary. In one legend, told by Adomnan and possibly Pictish in origin, Columba arrived at the stronghold of King Bridei Mailcon (Brude, son of Maelchon) of the Picts to find the gates shut against him. Columba made the sign of the cross and knocked, and the doors blew open violently of their own accord. According to Saint Bede, King Bridei converted along with all his Picts; Bede also claims that it was this Pictish king who gave the saint Iona. Bede's account is deeply untrustworthy, however, and it is unclear how much evangelizing Columba actually did; yet his legend developed early in Scotland and northern Britain, and has stayed strong.

The ruins of Saint Columba's church in Gartan, Donegal; Gartan is the likely birthplace of the saint.

Columba in stained glass in Saint Margaret's Chapel, Edinburgh Castle.

Columba at the gate of Bridei. When he knocked and made the sign of the cross, the doors blew open of their own accord.

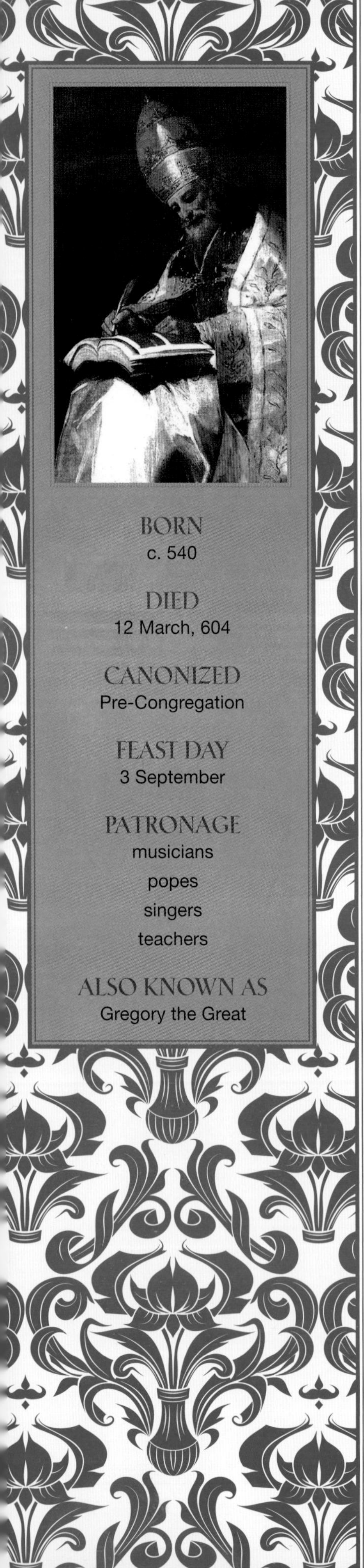

BORN
c. 540

DIED
12 March, 604

CANONIZED
Pre-Congregation

FEAST DAY
3 September

PATRONAGE
musicians
popes
singers
teachers

ALSO KNOWN AS
Gregory the Great

Pope Saint GREGORY I

Pope Gregory I never wanted the office, yet he was so influential that he is one of only two popes known as "the Great". He is also one of the "Four Latin Doctors", joining Saints Ambrose, Jerome, and Augustine of Hippo. He guided the Catholic Church through the transition from Late Antiquity to the early Middle Ages, divorcing it from the shattered Roman Empire and establishing it as a power in its own right.

GREGORY: ARISTOCRAT, AMBASSADOR, ABBOT

Gregory's family was wealthy, pious, and oriented to public service. Gregory must have had a good education, for around 572 he occupied an important civil post worthy of an ambitious young Roman aristocrat. Yet he quickly tired of the worldly life and, in 573, sold his estates and founded seven monasteries – six in Sicily and one, St Andrew's on Caelian Hill in Rome. He entered Caelian Hill himself and spent three years there.

In 578, Pope Benedict I ordained Gregory a deacon of Rome, and in 579 Benedict's successor, Pelagius II, sent Gregory to Constantinople as ambassador. Around 585, Gregory returned to his monastery, where he served as abbot until 590. After meeting Anglo-Saxons in Rome, he became interested in leading an evangelizing mission to England. The incident became famous and appears in subsequent hagiographies. Pope Pelagius II approved Gregory's mission and he set off with several monks, but according to Saint Bede the Venerable, the Roman populace refused to let their popular preacher depart.

The reluctant Gregory, one of the "Four Latin Doctors", became pope in 590. The dove on his right shoulder here symbolizes divine inspiration.

APOSTLE OF THE ENGLISH

After reluctantly becoming pope in 590, Gregory set about organizing a mission to the British Isles headed by his friend and fellow monk, Saint

Augustine. Though Augustine travelled to England, all of his authority flowed directly from Gregory, whom Saint Bede called "our own apostle".

Gregory's instructions not only led to a rapid and painless conversion of the Anglo-Saxon kingdom of Kent, they served as a template for subsequent conversions. Crucially, Gregory told Augustine to avoid head-on clashes with the pagan religion and customs of the Anglo-Saxons and to proceed gently: not to destroy pagan sites of worship, but to re-consecrate them for Christian use; not to deny pagan festivals, but to discover alternative Christian feasts. Wisely, Gregory foresaw that conversion stemming from such tactics, while it might be more gradual, would ultimately be more consensual and genuine, and missionaries would have a better chance of escaping violence.

This type of conversion naturally led to some amount of syncretism between Catholicism and pagan practices. Many beloved elements of Christianity today – the Christmas tree, the Easter bunny, and almost every feature of the now very secular Halloween – have non-Roman roots. Thus, in addition to being largely responsible for producing Western Christianity as we know it, Gregory's highly successful technique spurred the conversion of a continent full of warring nations and pagan religions.

ABOVE: *A manuscript of Gregorian chant dating from the fifteenth century.*

LEFT: *Pope Gregory at work.*

Gregorian Chant

As pope, Gregory expanded his authority over the developing Christian world of the West, encouraging conversion, expanding the role of monasteries, and co-opting the authority of a civil leader as the vestiges of the Western Roman Empire crumbled. In one typical and famous decision, Gregory demanded that music used during Mass and other liturgical rituals be simplified and codified. The resulting form of plainsong, called "Gregorian" after the pope, was used throughout the Middle Ages, greatly influencing subsequent Western music.

Saint Augustine *of Canterbury*

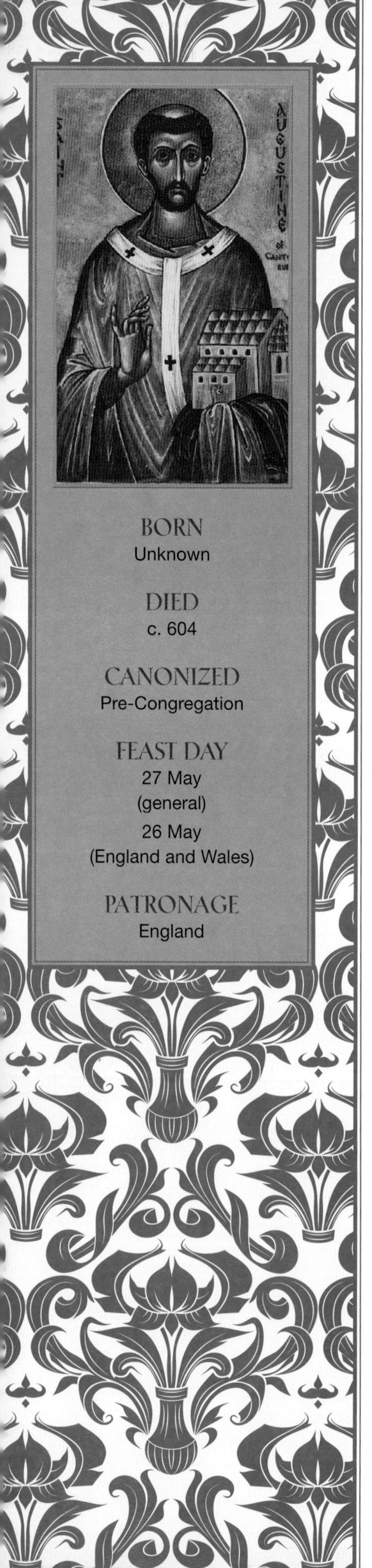

BORN
Unknown

DIED
c. 604

CANONIZED
Pre-Congregation

FEAST DAY
27 May
(general)
26 May
(England and Wales)

PATRONAGE
England

Born in Italy, Saint Augustine became prior of the Abbey of St Andrew's on Caelian Hill in Rome. But this mild-mannered monk was not to lead a secluded life, for in 596 Pope Saint Gregory I sent Augustine, his personal friend, to lead an evangelizing expedition to the Anglo-Saxon kingdoms of the British Isles. The mission did not sit well with Augustine and his thirty monks, who tried to turn back in Gaul; Gregory, however, insisted they continue.

The "St Augustine Gospels" – one of the oldest extant illuminated manuscripts – may have been brought to England by its namesake.

In 597, their ranks now numbering forty, Augustine and his retinue landed in the kingdom of Kent, then one of the oldest and strongest of Anglo-Saxon realms, possibly at Ebbsfleet. King Aethelbert of Kent had already married a Christian woman, a Frankish princess named Bertha, and welcomed Augustine respectfully. It took some time for Augustine to convert the king, but upon his conversion many of his people converted as well.

Augustine established England's first cathedral at Canterbury, with lasting results. He also set up the bishoprics of London and Rochester and a school at Canterbury. He was not successful, however, in uniting the infant English church with the neighbouring Celtic churches, nor could he overcome the liturgical differences that divided them, which remained unresolved until the Synod of Whitby in 664. Augustine was buried in a monastery he founded in Canterbury and dedicated to Saints Peter and Paul. Eventually it became known, as it still is today, as Saint Augustine's.

Saint Gall

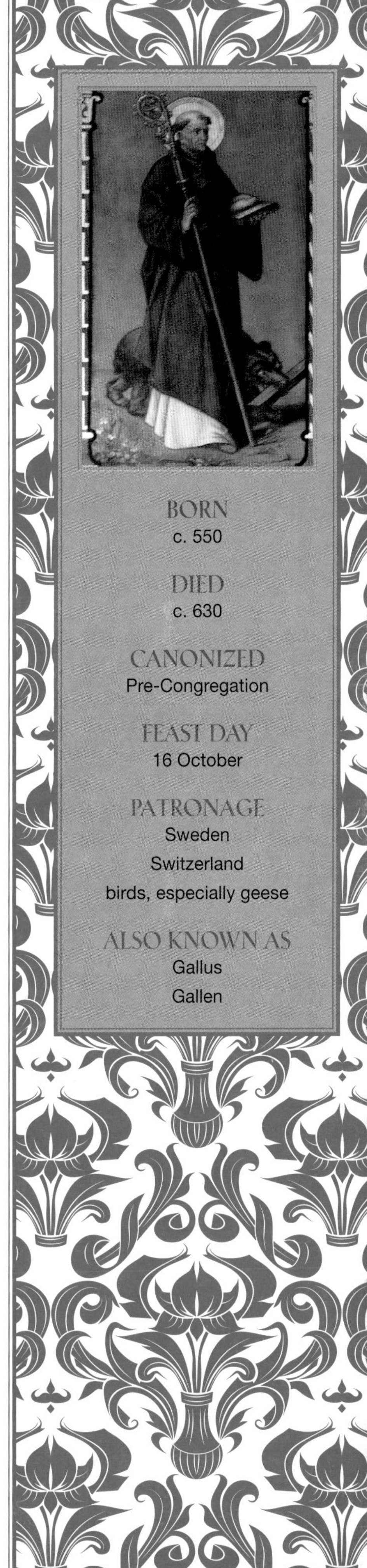

BORN
c. 550

DIED
c. 630

CANONIZED
Pre-Congregation

FEAST DAY
16 October

PATRONAGE
Sweden
Switzerland
birds, especially geese

ALSO KNOWN AS
Gallus
Gallen

Gall was born in Ireland but spent most of his life on the European continent, where, as one of Saint Columban's companions, he helped found several abbeys in Gaul – notably Luxeuil. In 610, Gall and Columban travelled to the region that would later become Switzerland, at the time the kingdom of Austrasia. Gall stayed in the area even after Columban left for Italy, founding several hermitages; he refused to become abbot of Luxeuil when elected by the monks there, and he similarly refused to become bishop when requested by King Sigebert of Austrasia.

In art, Saint Gall is often shown with a bear. A legend relates that at the command of the saint, a bear brought wood to feed the fire that Gall and his companions had kindled in the desert.

The Abbey Library

Indirect evidence suggests that the Abbey of Saint Gall maintained a substantial library as early as 820; it was certainly famous in the Middle Ages for its scriptorium, where the monks produced beautiful illuminated manuscripts. Fortunately, the library survived the long centuries intact, and today, with approximately four hundred volumes produced before 1000 CE, it ranks as one of the world's best examples of a medieval monastic library. Declared a World Heritage Site by UNESCO in 1983, it functions as both a research library and a museum.

Gall is recognized as one of the primary missionaries who converted the Alamanni, a Germanic people, who by Saint Gall's day had become part of the Frankish empire. The famous abbey in St Gallen was founded in 612, about a century after Gall's death.

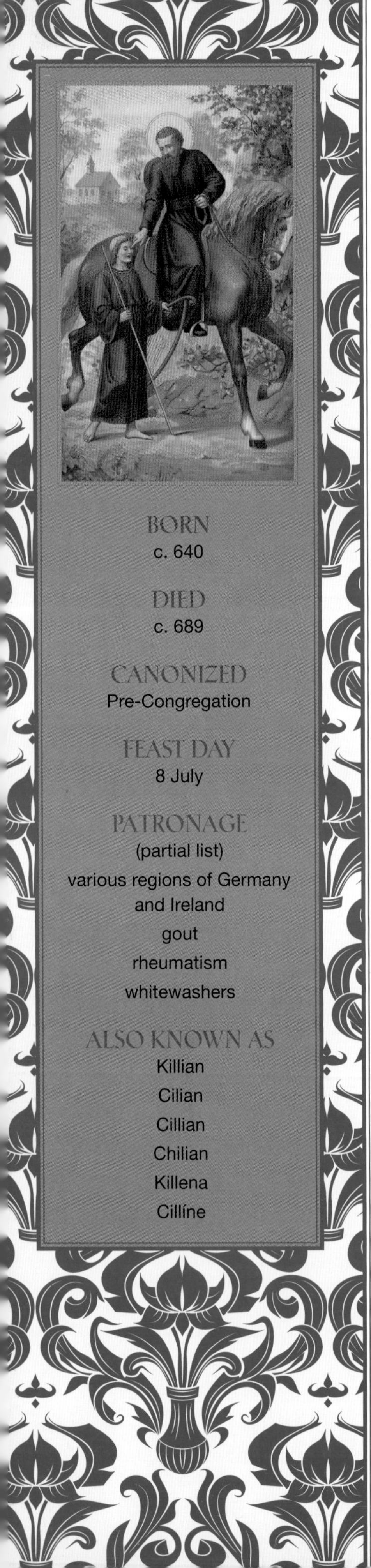

BORN
c. 640

DIED
c. 689

CANONIZED
Pre-Congregation

FEAST DAY
8 July

PATRONAGE
(partial list)
various regions of Germany and Ireland
gout
rheumatism
whitewashers

ALSO KNOWN AS
Killian
Cilian
Cillian
Chilian
Killena
Cillíne

Saint Kilian

Little of historical value is known about Kilian, whose cult nevertheless formed very early and whose feast day, known as Kilianfest, is still celebrated widely today among Germans and people of German ancestry. Even the saint's country of origin is not known with certainty; he probably came from Ireland, but some sources indicate a home in Scotland.

It seems likely that Kilian was ordained a bishop in Ireland, though (as was not uncommon at the time) he had no home diocese to oversee; at one point he may also have been abbot of Iona. As a travelling bishop the desire to become a missionary seized him, and with 11 companions he set out for Thuringia and Franconia (roughly, modern Bavaria). After discovering the pagans there, he travelled to Rome in 686 and met Pope Conon (r. 686–7), who may have bestowed papal authority on the mission; Kilian returned to Germany with only two companions, Saints Colman and Totnan.

Although Kilian succeeded in converting the local ruler, Duke Gosbert, along with several of his subjects, he nevertheless died a martyr along with his two companions. According to legend, Kilian had persuaded the duke to leave his wife, Geilana, who was also his brother's widow. Geilana, still a pagan, resented the interference and had the missionaries murdered. One of the assassins supposedly went insane and confessed; Geilana also went mad.

Saint Kilian was a travelling bishop who, seized with missionary zeal, proselytized extensively throughout Europe.

Saint Boniface

Other missionaries had already evangelized in many of the regions in which Saint Boniface worked, but he is justly remembered as the "Apostle of Germany", for not only did he work tirelessly to convert the many remaining pagans of Thuringia, Saxony, and Frisia, he also combated heresy, instituted reforms, established many dioceses, and became the first archbishop of Mainz. In short, he did much to further conversion, render orthodox the Christianity of the region, and draw Germany into the organized hierarchy of the Catholic Church.

Boniface was born Winfrid (or Wynfrith) in Anglo-Saxon England and educated at Exeter and Nursling. He became a priest around 705 and left on his first mission, to Frisia, in 716. From that point until his death, he evangelized the Germans between trips to Rome and meetings with the Frankish rulers, to whose power he owed much of his success. Germany was unsettled at the time, and the work of several previous missionaries, including Saint Kilian, had been reversed or corrupted by uneducated or unorthodox priests while paganism still claimed the loyalties of many.

The tireless Boniface achieved great success among the pagans, and during the reigns of Carloman and Pepin the Short (whom Boniface himself anointed king in 751), he enacted widespread reforms, including a decree that required all Carolingian monasteries to follow the Rule of Saint Benedict. But Boniface's true calling was missionary work, and shortly after crowning Pepin he returned to Frisia. Now quite elderly, Boniface and his companions were killed there by pagans.

> *Let us stand fast in what is right.*
>
> Saint Boniface

An illumination from the Fulda Sacramentary portrays the baptism of Saint Boniface (top) and his martyrdom (bottom).

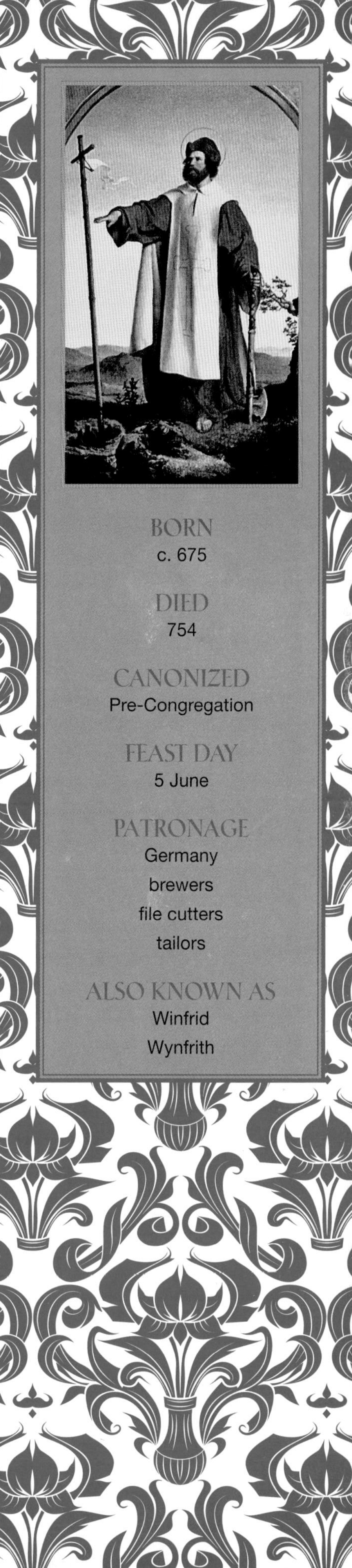

BORN
c. 675

DIED
754

CANONIZED
Pre-Congregation

FEAST DAY
5 June

PATRONAGE
Germany
brewers
file cutters
tailors

ALSO KNOWN AS
Winfrid
Wynfrith

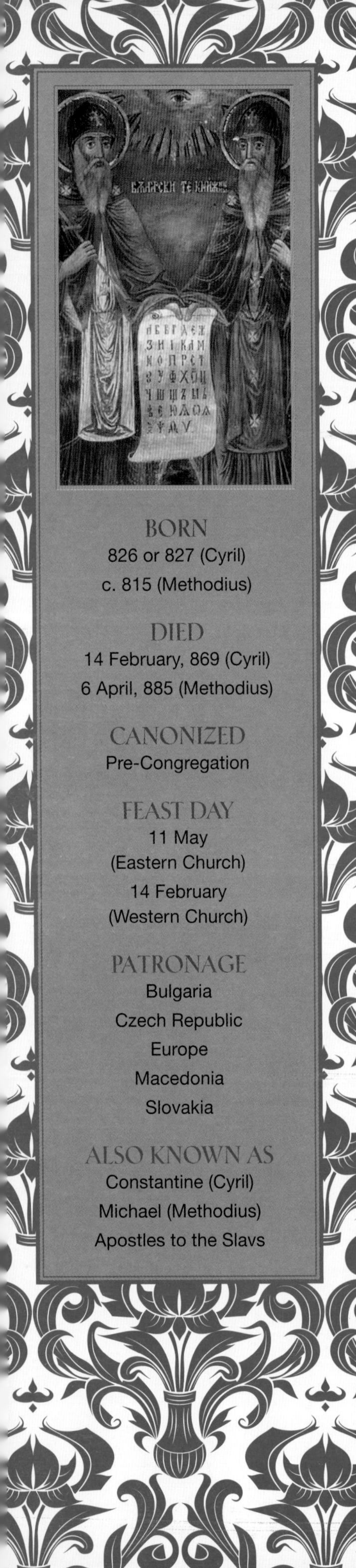

BORN
826 or 827 (Cyril)
c. 815 (Methodius)

DIED
14 February, 869 (Cyril)
6 April, 885 (Methodius)

CANONIZED
Pre-Congregation

FEAST DAY
11 May
(Eastern Church)
14 February
(Western Church)

PATRONAGE
Bulgaria
Czech Republic
Europe
Macedonia
Slovakia

ALSO KNOWN AS
Constantine (Cyril)
Michael (Methodius)
Apostles to the Slavs

Saints Cyril & Methodius

Born into the family of an upper-level bureaucrat in Thessalonica, the brothers Cyril and Methodius (their religious names) are famous today as the "Apostles to the Slavs".

Methodius took his name upon leaving the world for a monastery on Mount Olympus. Cyril, who did not become a monk until very late in life, learned Slavonic as a child – possibly from his mother – and studied at the University of Constantinople, where he later taught. He also worked as the librarian at Santa Sophia before following his brother to Mount Olympus.

Cyril and Methodius were evangelists, teachers, and relentless promoters of the Catholic faith.

Around 861, Cyril (and possibly Methodius with him) travelled to Khazaria, a nation centred on the Sea of Azov, whose rulers had requested a Christian teacher. Cyril succeeded in converting many Khazars, who lived at the crossroads of Islam, Christianity, and Judaism, but the ruling class converted to Judaism. The experience proved valuable, however, and Cyril managed to recover in the Crimea what he believed to be the relics of Pope Saint Clement I (r. 88–97).

MISSION TO MORAVIA

Around 863, the brothers were sent to central Europe, again in response to a request for Christian instruction – this time from Prince Ratislav of Moravia. The country was nominally Christian, but paganism still held fast; Ratislav asked that Slavic-speaking teachers come and explain Christian theology in his people's own tongue.

For more than four years, the brothers enjoyed considerable success in preaching and converting the Moravian Slavs. They met with fierce opposition, however – not from pagans but from Frankish and Germanic missionaries, who resented the encroachment into their territory and feared the influence of Constantinople, whose ecclesiastic relationship with Rome was very tense.

Faced with clerical outrage, Cyril and Methodius travelled to Rome, arguing on the way against those who maintained that only three languages, could be used for religious purposes: Greek, Latin, and Hebrew. In Rome, Pope Adrian II welcomed them (and the relics of Clement I), vindicating their mission and their use of the vernacular. He ordained Methodius archbishop of Moravia and Pannonia, while Cyril, feeling the end of his life approaching, became a monk. He died, still in Rome, on 14 February, 869.

THE STRUGGLE FOR THE SLAVS

Methodius returned to Moravia but despite the pope's support still met with opposition. His own bishops deposed and imprisoned him for three years, from 870 to 873. Released through the power of the pope, he evangelized tirelessly, always having to manoeuvre around the disgruntled Frankish and Germanic clergy, who in 879 managed to charge him with heterodoxy and disobedience, forcing him back to Rome. Once again the pope, now John VIII, vindicated him, and he returned to Moravia. Exhausted, he died in 885, leaving a dedicated band of disciples to continue evangelizing and translating the sacred texts.

ABOVE: *A statue of Cyril and Methodius by the Czech-American sculptor Albin Polasek. The two brother saints are still revered in the Czech Republic today.*

LEFT: *Cyril and Methodius are credited with the creation of the Glagolitic alphabet used to translate the Bible for their followers. The* Codex Zographensis *is an illuminated gospel book found in Bulgaria in 1843. It dates from the tenth or early eleventh century.*

BORN
c. 930

DIED
998

CANONIZED
Locally (Greece)

FEAST DAY
26 November

PATRONAGE
Sparta

ALSO KNOWN AS
Nicon the Metanoeite
Preacher of Repentance

Saint NIKON the Metanoeite

Muslims from the Arabian Peninsula began to expand their territory with enormous success in the seventh century, eating into the Byzantine Empire. In the tenth century, the Byzantines began to push back, reclaiming Edessa in 944 and the islands of Crete and Cyprus by 965. Nikon, born in Pontus (northern Asia Minor), embarked on his own campaign to reclaim former Byzantine territory by reconverting the inhabitants to Christianity.

The people had technically remained Christian in many places, but their faith had been isolated from the rest of Christendom and greatly influenced by Islam. A tireless and fervent preacher, Nikon took it upon himself to revitalize and restore orthodoxy to these areas, travelling through Asia Minor, Crete, and Greece, including the Peloponnese. Everywhere he went Nikon cried "*Metanoeite!*" (meaning "repent"), so that eventually the word became appended to his name.

Nikon is best-known for his many exhortations to repent, as instructed in Matthew 3:2.

Nikon is perhaps best known in Sparta (he is that city's patron), where he died in a monastery he founded after nearly forty years spent travelling and preaching. Nearly everything we know about him comes from the *Life of Saint Nikon the Metanoeite,* written by the monastery's superior some fifty years after the saint's death. Nikon's *Life* is valuable to scholars interested in the reconversion of Byzantium.

> *Repent ye: for the kingdom of Heaven is at hand.*
>
> 
>
> Matthew 3:2

Saint Norbert

Born into nobility, Norbert took holy vows and, for political reasons, became a subdeacon and canon while continuing to lead a life unworthy of a man of the cloth. He eventually became a member of the court of Holy Roman Emperor Henry V, leading a worldly life.

His conversion – in the sense that he suddenly became truly repentant and pious – came in 1115. While travelling through Westphalia one day, a thunderstorm came up around him. A lightning bolt struck, so close to the horse he was riding that he was thrown to the ground. Norbert lay motionless and stunned for almost an hour, the storm raging around him, when suddenly he heard an inner voice telling him to seek holiness and peace.

O Priest!

You are not yourself

because you are God.

Saint Norbert

A statue of Saint Norbert stands at left, with Saint Wenceslas and Saint Sigmund, on the Charles Bridge in Prague.

The episode utterly changed him. Not only did he now abide by the letter and the spirit of his vows, selling all of his property and preaching repentance, but he also organized a clergy-reform movement, which led ultimately, in 1121, to the founding of a new order, the Premonstratensian (or "white canons"), emphasizing pastoral duties as well as austerity.

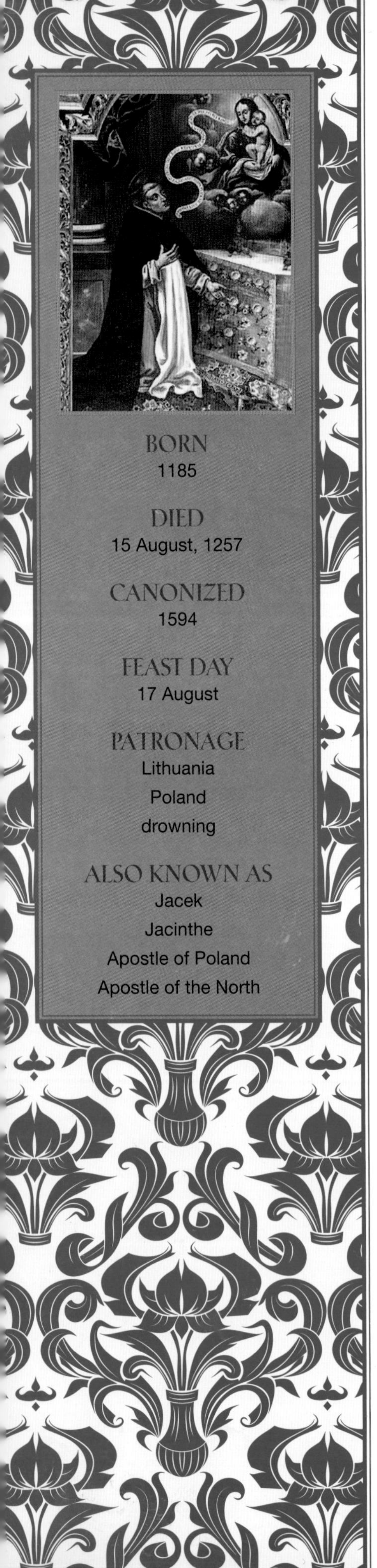

BORN
1185

DIED
15 August, 1257

CANONIZED
1594

FEAST DAY
17 August

PATRONAGE
Lithuania
Poland
drowning

ALSO KNOWN AS
Jacek
Jacinthe
Apostle of Poland
Apostle of the North

Saint HYACINTH

Born into a noble family in Silesia, Hyacinth studied at Cracow, Prague, and Bologna. With his relative Saint Ceslaus and his uncle, the bishop of Cracow, Hyacinth travelled to Rome in 1218. He was very impressed by Saint Dominic, whom he met in Rome, and he joined the new Dominican Order. Hyacinth can, in large part, claim credit for establishing the Dominican order in northeastern Europe; upon leaving Rome he founded Dominican houses in many Polish cities.

Although officially Christian since 966, when King Mieszko I converted, Poland still harboured many pagans and Christians of doubtful orthodoxy, especially in rural and isolated areas, and Hyacinth laboured to bring the Polish into the Catholic fold. He also evangelized in Scandinavia – likewise Christian in the cities and among the elite, but with pagan peoples still living in less cosmopolitan regions – Muscovy, Russia, and Lithuania. The tradition that he reached as far as China and Tibet is likely exaggerated.

Supposedly Hyacinth could walk on water, a feat witnessed several times at both the Vistula and Dnieper rivers.

Hyacinth did much to establish the Dominicans in northeastern Europe. He also evangelized in Scandinavia, Russia, and Lithuania.

An inspired preacher, he succeeded in converting many schismatics, heretics, pagans, and Muslims, and is recognized today as a patron of both Poland and Lithuania.

Saint Francis Xavier

Born not far from the birthplace of Saint Ignatius Loyola, Francis Xavier met the founder of the Jesuits in 1529. He became one of his first companions and was one of the group who, led by Ignatius, formed the Jesuit order in 1539.

From their inception the Jesuits emphasized missionary activity; the evangelizing zeal Francis displayed led some to call him the greatest missionary since Saint Paul. At the request of King John III, Francis travelled to the Portuguese colony in Goa, India, an arduous journey that took 13 months. In Goa he worked hard to correct the lax, unchristian behaviour of the Portuguese there; he also worked hard to convert the Indians. Despite his predilection for seasickness and difficulty in acquiring foreign languages, Francis next spent seven years evangelizing tirelessly in southern India, Ceylon (Sri Lanka), the Malay Peninsula, and the Molucca Islands.

Francis also reached the coast of China and, in 1549, Japan, where he evangelized with such success that by the time he left in 1551 there were some two thousand Christians living there. Francis died without receiving the last sacraments or a Christian burial after a sudden illness overcame him en route to China, where he had planned to evangelize.

Francis Xavier was born in a family castle in the Kingdom of Navarre, but his strong faith led him to a life as a Jesuit missionary in Asia.

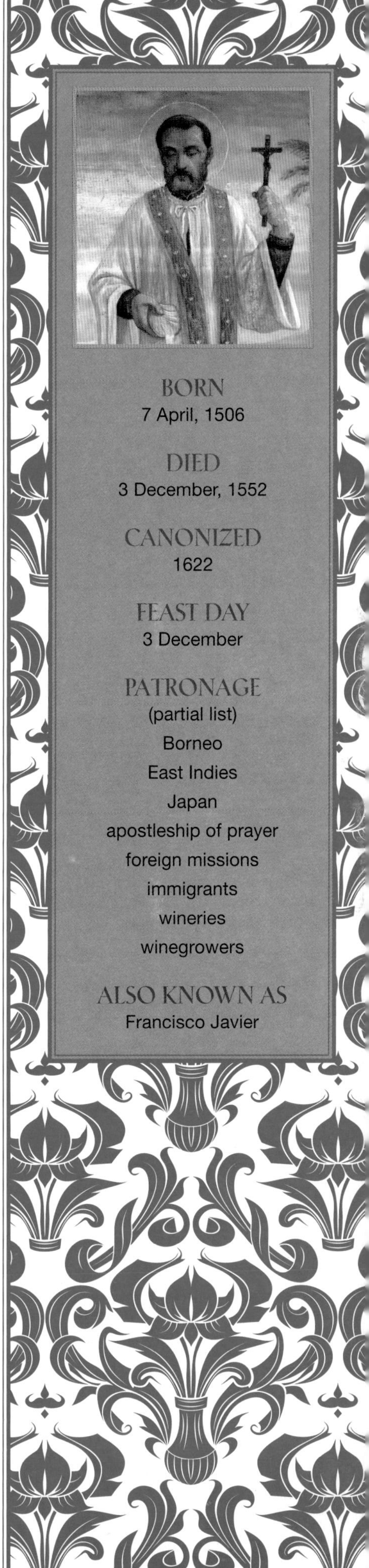

BORN
7 April, 1506

DIED
3 December, 1552

CANONIZED
1622

FEAST DAY
3 December

PATRONAGE
(partial list)
Borneo
East Indies
Japan
apostleship of prayer
foreign missions
immigrants
wineries
winegrowers

ALSO KNOWN AS
Francisco Javier

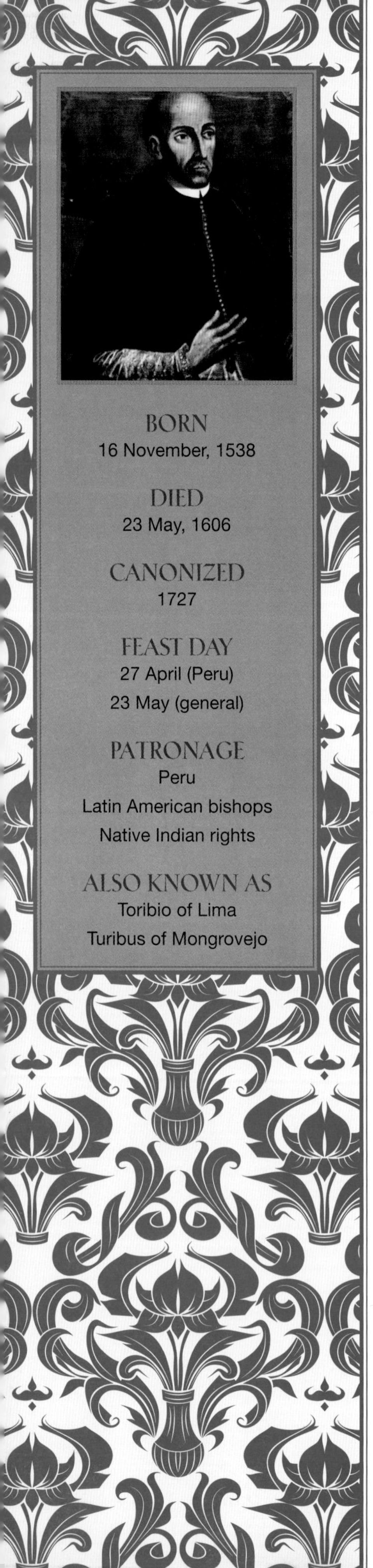

BORN
16 November, 1538

DIED
23 May, 1606

CANONIZED
1727

FEAST DAY
27 April (Peru)
23 May (general)

PATRONAGE
Peru
Latin American bishops
Native Indian rights

ALSO KNOWN AS
Toribio of Lima
Turibus of Mongrovejo

Saint TURIBIUS *Mogroveio*

On his arrival in Lima, where he was posted as archbishop in 1580, Saint Turibius Mogroveio found his supposedly Roman Catholic country in a terrible state of spiritual and moral corruption. Spain had conquered the Inca Empire some fifty years before, subsequently converting thousands of natives. Priests were scarce, however, and Christian instruction almost nonexistent, so that hardly any of the baptized Indians knew anything about their nominal religion. To make matters worse, the Spanish rulers were tyrannical, petty, cruel, immoral, and greedy.

Turibius's vast archdiocese covered eighteen thousand square miles of often very difficult terrain with no roads, yet he travelled to every part of it. His first journey took seven years.

His tireless efforts to reach converts earned the love and respect of the native population. As archbishop of Lima, Turibius baptized and confirmed about half a million people, including two of the best-known saints of South America, Rose of Lima and Martin de Porres.

In Lima, Turibius worked to alleviate the abuses of secular authorities as he set about reforming the lax clergy.

He also became a champion of Indian rights, and he even learned some of the native Quechua dialects to better perform his missionary duties and charitable work. He built churches and hospitals and founded the first seminary in the Americas to train priests. His industry lasted until the day of his death, which occurred after a brief illness during one of his peregrinations.

Saint Francis Solano

Francis Solano was a missionary in the reforming spirit of Turibius Mogroveio, whom he knew in Lima, and travelled to South America after labouring for several years in Spain. Francis studied at a Jesuit school, but he joined the Franciscans in 1569. When the plague struck Grenada in 1583, he distinguished himself by caring for the victims – until he became one himself.

Upon recuperating he expressed a wish to become a missionary. This wish was granted, in 1589, but Francis nearly died en route when his ship ran aground in a storm. Instead of fleeing in a lifeboat as did the rest of the Spaniards, Francis stayed behind to baptize the abandoned African slaves. After the storm, Francis and the Africans somehow managed to sail the remainder of the ship to land.

Francis journeyed throughout South America, paying scant heed to the dangers of poor roads, hostile Indians, and adverse terrain. Blessed with a quick mind, he learned several Indian languages and dialects, evangelizing for twenty years through the western parts of the continent, including areas of modern Colombia, Peru, Bolivia, Chile, Argentina, and Paraguay. He is, therefore, counted a patron of many South American nations.

Saint Francis Solano was dubbed the thaumaturgus, *or "miracle worker", of the New World. He evangelized and baptized extensively throughout South America.*

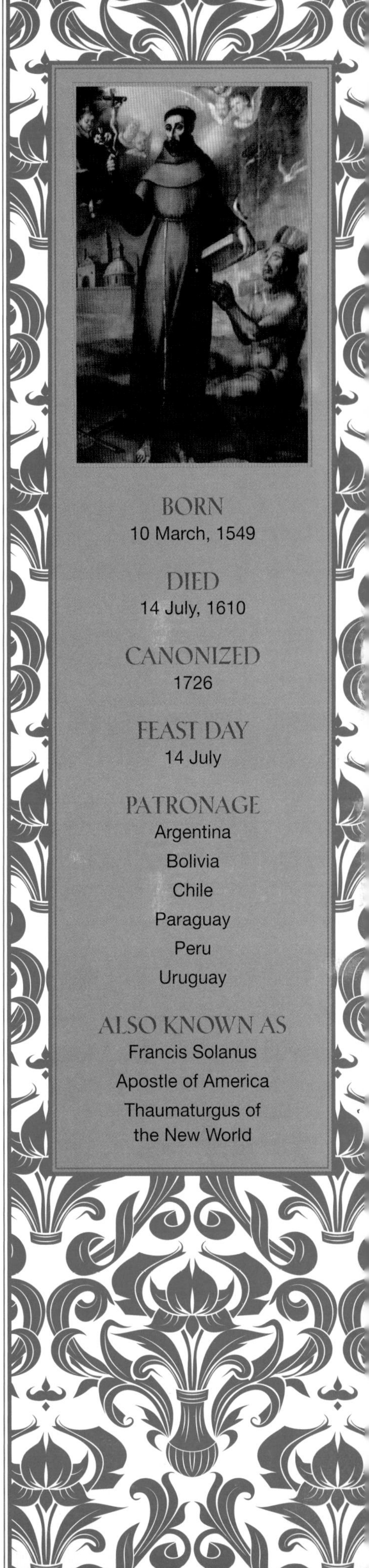

BORN
10 March, 1549

DIED
14 July, 1610

CANONIZED
1726

FEAST DAY
14 July

PATRONAGE
Argentina
Bolivia
Chile
Paraguay
Peru
Uruguay

ALSO KNOWN AS
Francis Solanus
Apostle of America
Thaumaturgus of the New World

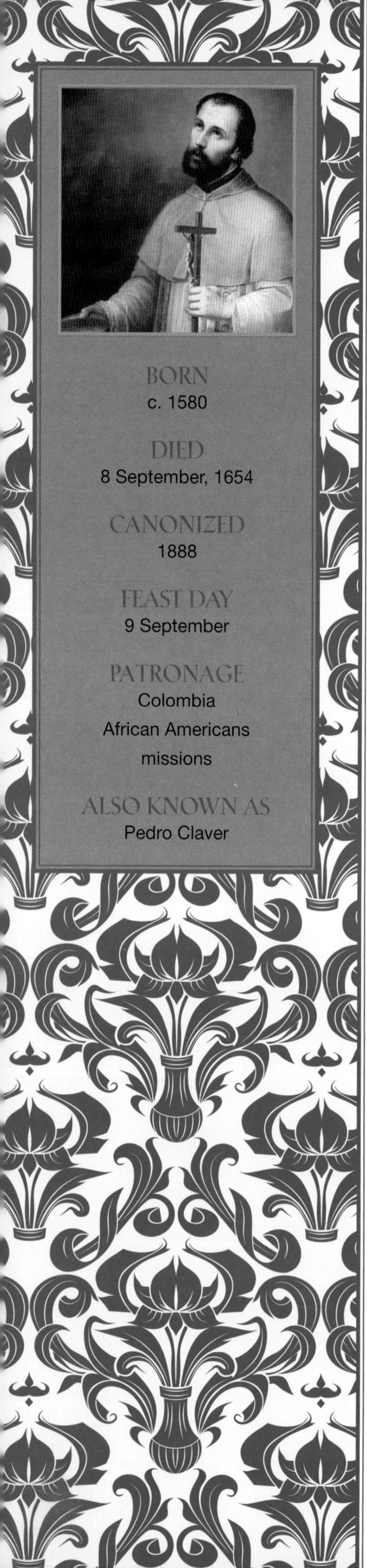

Saint PETER Claver

Peter Claver joined the Jesuits in Spain, quickly deciding to become a missionary in the Americas. He arrived in Cartagena (in modern Colombia) in 1610, where he was shocked by the conditions of the enslaved Africans. The slaves were unloaded after a long voyage packed in terrible, disease-ridden ship holds, separated into healthy and sick packs, and then branded. Their treatment – except for a few kindly hands – was unceasingly, brutally inhumane.

To love God as He ought to be loved, we must be detached from all temporal love. We must love nothing but Him, or if we love anything else, we must love it only for His sake.

Saint Peter Claver

Peter would meet the Africans as their ships came in – Cartagena, Spain's primary slave port, accepted about three thousand slaves a year (as many as ten thousand in "good years", according to some estimates) – and venture into the holds to offer what succour he could, sometimes carrying out the ill on his back. Peter tended the slaves' wounds, healed the sick, and, with the aid of African interpreters and out of pressing concern for their souls, instructed them in Christianity, baptizing perhaps one hundred thousand slaves during his ministry.

Peter declared himself a "slave to the slaves", but he also ministered to the general population, visiting mansions as well as slave huts. His advocacy of slaves, nevertheless, generated umbrage among the Spanish upper class, and when he died of plague, in 1654, the authorities denied him a religious service, giving him a perfunctory civil burial instead.

Saint Katharine Drexel

Katharine Mary Drexel devoted her long life to the conversion, care, and education of Native and African Americans. Born in Philadelphia in 1858, Katharine lived through momentous times in the history of minority rights in the United States, from the Civil War (1861–65) to the beginning of the Civil Rights Movement (1955–68).

Descended from a pious family of great wealth, Katharine expressed an interest in religious life at a young age. Guided by her mentor and pastor, Dr James O'Connor – later bishop of Nebraska – Katharine waited until she was 31 to take her vows as a nun. By then she had already established a school for Native Americans in Santa Fe, New Mexico.

In 1889, she became a missionary to the Dakota tribes, and two years later she founded the Sisters of the Blessed Sacrament, approved by the Vatican in 1913. With the help of her order, Sister Katharine founded missions for Indians, schools for African Americans – including the high school that, in 1925, became Xavier University – and forty mission centres, expending her entire fortune in doing so.

Sister Katharine suffered a heart attack in 1935 and stepped down from her office as superior general two years later, but she continued to pray and work for her chosen causes, even when bound to a wheelchair. African Americans and members of the Indian nations bore the coffin at her funeral.

Saint Katharine Drexel was an eyewitness to history, living through both the Civil War and Civil Rights eras. She is especially renowned for her ministry to Native and African Americans.

ST LUDMILLA

ST METHODIUS

ST WENCESLAUS

Saints of Noble Blood

Despite the ancient proverb that states "It is easier for a camel to pass through the eye of a needle than for a rich man to enter the kingdom of God", there are numerous examples of men and women using their wealth and position for spiritual improvement, whether their own, that of their communities, or – as in the case of the nobly born saints in this chapter – entire nations. Several, like Wenceslaus of Bohemia, Vladimir the Great of Russia, and Olaf II of Norway, played large and conscious roles in efforts to convert their respective countries to Christianity. Others, notably Helena and Edward the Confessor of England, led by example, adopting a humble and pious demeanour all the more admirable for their elevated station.

Still other rulers devoted themselves to the spiritual improvement of their countries: Louis IX of France, perhaps the most famous royal saint, donated huge sums of money for building monasteries, churches, and establishing charitable organizations. These saints of noble blood are, indeed, the exception to the rule in Christ's proverb.

Saint HELENA *of Constantinople*

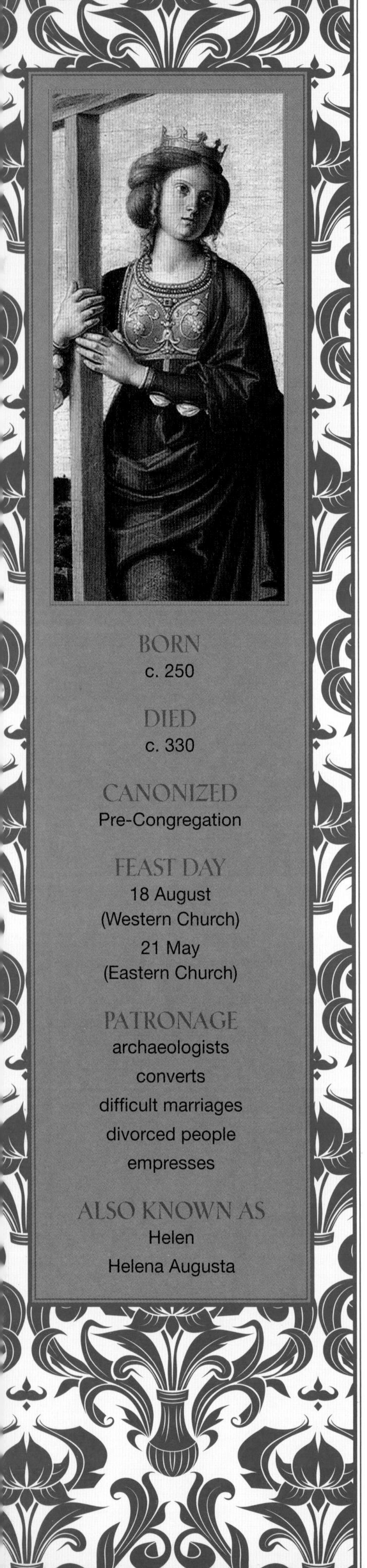

BORN
c. 250

DIED
c. 330

CANONIZED
Pre-Congregation

FEAST DAY
18 August
(Western Church)
21 May
(Eastern Church)

PATRONAGE
archaeologists
converts
difficult marriages
divorced people
empresses

ALSO KNOWN AS
Helen
Helena Augusta

Constantine, the first Roman emperor to convert to Christianity, convinced his mother, Helena, to convert as well. Of lowly birth, Helena was the consort of General Constantius. When he became emperor in 292, Constantius II put Helena aside, but upon taking the throne in 306, Constantine restored her to honour.

Helena must have been middle-aged when she converted around 312, yet so complete was her devotion to Christian ideals that observers believed she had been Christian since birth. She used her wealth to care for the poor, built churches, and visited (and occasionally released) prisoners, all while maintaining a simplicity of dress and lifestyle that did not at all conform to the standards of a Roman empress.

After Constantine defeated his rival emperors to become sole ruler of Rome in 324, Helena, despite her advanced age, took the opportunity to make a pilgrimage to Palestine. In Palestine she visited Christian churches, never failing to make generous donations, founded two churches herself – one in Bethlehem and one on the Mount of the Ascension – and according to legend, discovered the True Cross on which Jesus Christ was crucified. Helena died in the East, possibly in Palestine or Nicomedia, but was buried in Rome.

Shrine to Saint Helena in St Peter's Basilica in Rome.

Saint Wenceslaus I Duke of Bohemia

The son of Vratislaus I, Duke of Bohemia, and Drahomira, a princess of Havolans, Wenceslaus was raised by his Christian grandmother, Ludmila, until Vratislaus's death and Drahomira's assumption of power in Bohemia. Drahomira orchestrated Ludmila's death, possibly to eradicate a rival political power and possibly for religious reasons (a pagan, Drahomira was no friend to Christians), but in any event Wenceslaus became ruler of Bohemia in 922.

Saint Ludmila of Bohemia. Ludmila, who was herself canonized shortly after her death in 921, raised her grandson Wenceslaus. She and her husband, Bořivoj I of Bohemia, were most likely converted to Christianity through the efforts of Saints Cyril and Methodius.

Wenceslaus was a competent king and, as a pious Christian, encouraged the Christianization of his people. Unfortunately, his mother's strict anti-Christian policy found much support among the people, and Wenceslaus's pursuit of conversion made him unpopular among certain pagan elements of the country. Even worse, perhaps, was his recognition of Henry the Fowler, king of Germany, as his liege (thus Wenceslaus is called duke of Bohemia, rather than king).

In either 929 or 935 (sources differ), Saint Wenceslaus's brother Boleslav – who had been raised by Drahomira – had Wenceslaus assassinated. Boleslav assumed the throne, but alarmed by the unexpected strength of veneration for Saint Wenceslaus, he translated his brother's relics to the church of St Vitus in Prague, which almost immediately became a major pilgrimage site. Bohemians venerated Wenceslaus as their country's patron saint within a century.

BORN
c. 907

DIED
September 929 or 935

CANONIZED
Pre-Congregation

FEAST DAY
28 September

PATRONAGE
Czech Republic (Bohemia)
Prague

ALSO KNOWN AS
Wenceslas
Wenzel

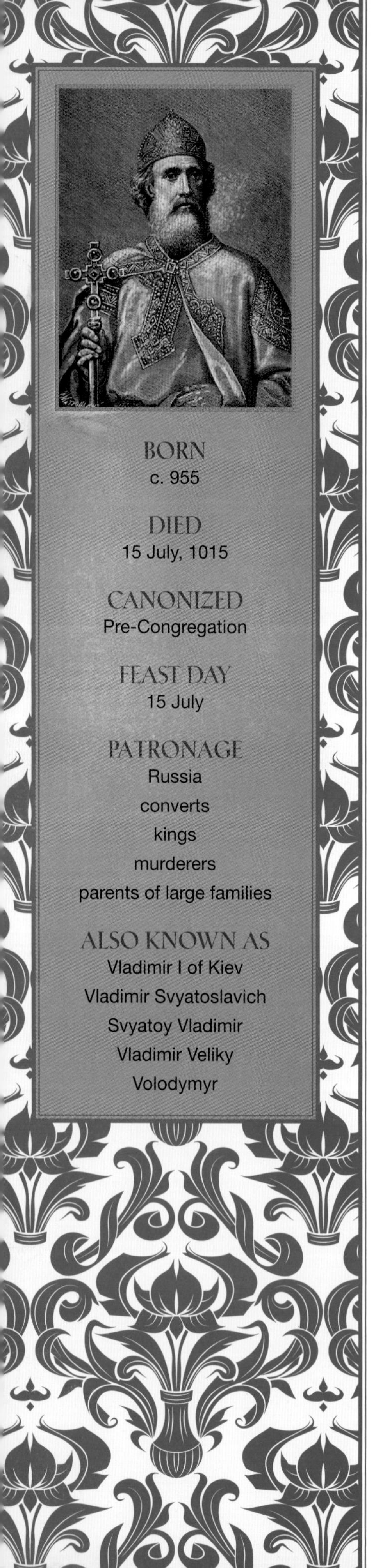

BORN
c. 955

DIED
15 July, 1015

CANONIZED
Pre-Congregation

FEAST DAY
15 July

PATRONAGE
Russia
converts
kings
murderers
parents of large families

ALSO KNOWN AS
Vladimir I of Kiev
Vladimir Svyatoslavich
Svyatoy Vladimir
Vladimir Veliky
Volodymyr

Saint Vladimir the Great

Vladimir the Great ruled the Kievan Rus' during the transformative period when Russia shed its Scandinavian roots and joined the Byzantine Empire's sphere of influence. An important step in this gradual metamorphosis occurred when Vladimir converted to Christianity in 989. His reasons for abandoning his pagan, Scandinavian religion were primarily political – part of a deal in which he allied himself with Constantinople – but the conversion nevertheless was genuine.

The baptism of Vladimir. The Russian ruler's decision to choose Orthodox Christianity as the new faith of the Kievan Rus' was based on the reaction of his envoys to the sheer beauty of the Byzantine Church. Once converted, however, Vladimir became a staunch believer in the faith.

He put aside his several previous wives in favour of his new Christian bride, the daughter of the Byzantine emperor; destroyed pagan idols; and encouraged his people – sometimes forcefully – to follow his example and convert. Although his support of Greek missionaries and his allegiance to Constantinople dictated that Russia would follow the trajectory of the still-nascent Eastern Orthodox Church, the Roman Catholic Church also recognizes Vladimir as a saint, and Vladimir himself welcomed papal legates.

Russia's first Christian ruler, Vladimir is one of the country's patron saints. He expanded the rule of the Kievan Rus' to extend from Lake Onega in the north to the Black Sea in the south, and from the headwaters of the Dniester River in the west to those of the Don in the east. A member of a very contentious family, he died fighting one of his sons near Kiev in 1015.

Saint HENRY II

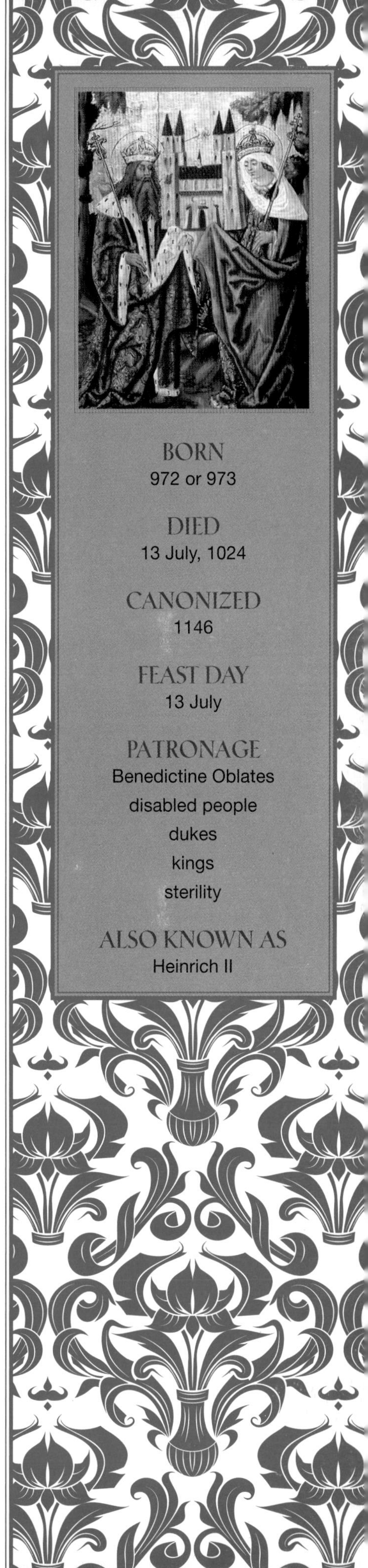

Born into the complicated dynastic struggles of German nobility, Henry became Duke of Bavaria in 995, after his father died, and – with rather more trouble – Holy Roman Emperor in 1002 following the death of his cousin, Otto III. Obliged to struggle with contentious relatives, rebels, and foreign wars, he dedicated his reign to strengthening and unifying the Holy Roman Empire, which perceived itself as Rome's direct successor.

Henry's dedication to Catholicism stemmed in part from political manoeuvrings; his support of the bishops, for example, enabled him to utilize more effectively the stable Church hierarchy, as opposed to the more truculent secular princes. Yet he had, as a youth, studied for the priesthood, and he strongly supported the Cluniac reform movement then affecting the clergy. He established the Diocese of Bamberg with the intention of creating a sort of centre for missionary activity, founding schools, monasteries, and the famous Münster Cathedral in Basel, Switzerland. There can be little doubt that Henry was a pious and devoted Catholic, but it is almost certainly untrue that he and his wife Cunegund (Kunigunde), who were childless, had sworn themselves to celibacy. Canonized in 1200, Cunegund is also venerated as a saint.

Saint Cunigunde of Luxembourg. Cunigunde, the wife of Henry II is the patroness of Luxembourg, and her feast day is 3 March.

Saint Olaf Haraldsson

Pagan by birth, Olaf converted, probably in France, around 1013. Along with his predecessor, Olaf Tryggvason, Olaf Haraldsson is credited with the conversion of Norway to Christianity during his 13-year reign. At the time, Norway was dominated by Danish power and influence, and Olaf spent his youth not in his own country but among relatives in Russia. He took part in Viking raids throughout the Baltic and North Atlantic, which included participating in Danish invasions of England.

In 1015 Olaf began his subjugation of Norway, in part by force and in part by bribing chieftains to obey him; he ascended the throne the following year. Olaf set about Christianizing the country, including the inland regions that were less cosmopolitan and therefore less exposed to Christianity, sometimes using severe force. Several chieftains who opposed Olaf's rule joined Knut the Great when he declared himself king of Norway (he was already king of Denmark and king of England) and invaded. Olaf was forced into exile, in 1029, but returned with an army a year later. This counterinvasion proved short-lived, however, as Olaf fell at the Battle of Stiklestad in 1030. Although Knut was also a Christian, Olaf's cult venerated him as a martyr and spread rapidly, the result of widespread dissatisfaction with Danish rule.

A fourteenth-century bishop's crozier displays Saint Olaf with his axe. The axe is an appropriate symbol for this harsh ruler.

Saint Stephen I of Hungary

Although Geza, Stephen's father and king of the Magyars, converted his country to Christianity in 972, Geza himself only paid lip service to the new religion. Stephen, who assumed power upon his father's death in 997, took his baptism seriously, however, and applied to Pope Sylvester II for recognition of his kingship. When Sylvester complied, it meant that the new Kingdom of Hungary had both apostolic and papal authority–a fact that carried great weight (not to mention political ramifications) in medieval Europe. Stephen received his crown in 1001; Hungarians not only recognize him as their patron but also as their nation's founder.

Certainly, Stephen did much to knit the fractious tribes of his territory together, imposing new laws, structuring a new system of governance, and building a network of royal fortifications throughout the country. Stephen also made a valiant effort to convert his people in truth, founding many monasteries and dividing the realm into dioceses. His devotion to his faith is illustrated by one probably factual character note: he would disguise himself to deliver alms to the country's poor personally, once barely surviving an encounter with thugs.

Unfortunately, Stephen's son, whom he had carefully groomed to ensure his kingdom's Christian future, died in a hunting accident, and the crown passed to decidedly less pious rulers; nevertheless, devotion to Stephen began almost immediately and continues to this day.

Be merciful to all who are suffering violence, keeping always in your heart the example of the Lord who said, "I desire mercy and not sacrifice."

King Saint Stephen I of Hungary, to his son

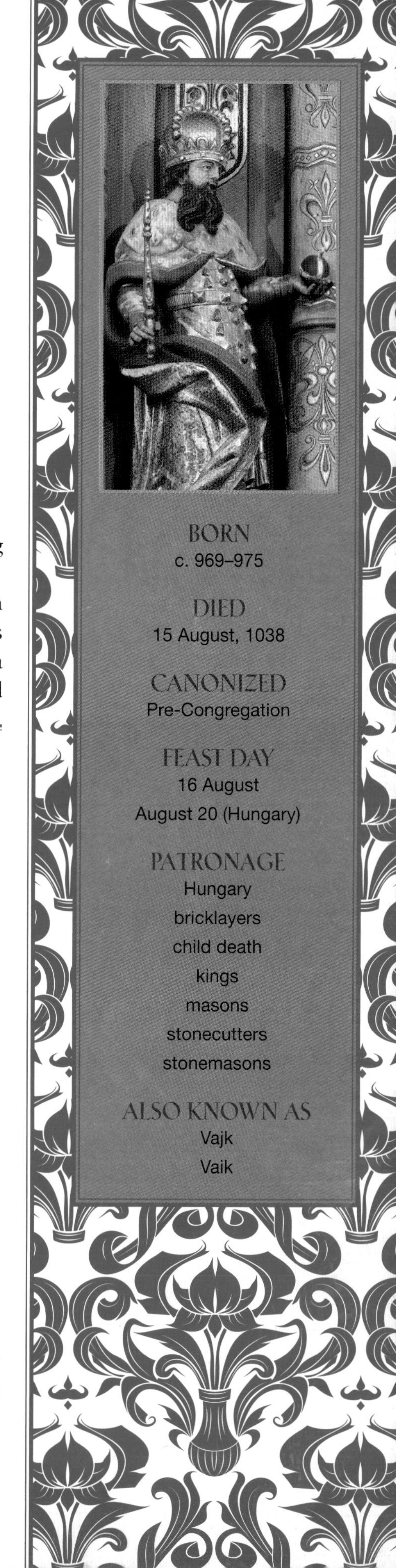

BORN
c. 969–975

DIED
15 August, 1038

CANONIZED
Pre-Congregation

FEAST DAY
16 August
August 20 (Hungary)

PATRONAGE
Hungary
bricklayers
child death
kings
masons
stonecutters
stonemasons

ALSO KNOWN AS
Vajk
Vaik

A CLOSER LOOK: *Relics*

Relics, an important feature of the veneration of saints, both in Roman Catholicism and Orthodox traditions, are objects that once came into physical contact with the saint or – typically of greater significance – the saint's actual physical remains, including bones, hair, or their preserved bodies. In Orthodox churches, veneration of saints usually focuses on the saint's icon, a holy image considered proper for liturgical ritual. The earliest appearance of relics in Christian tradition – though they are not named as such – can be found in the Acts of the Apostles (19:1–12), when cloths worn or used by Saint Paul cured the sick and exorcised demons.

In the Middle Ages, relics were sought-after items; the most impressive tended to draw huge crowds of worshippers and pilgrims, and accordingly produced large profits for the monastery, church, or cathedral that held them. Housed in magnificent reliquaries, often constructed with precious metals and bedecked with expensive gems, relics were the focus in any house of worship that could afford them. Unfortunately, this situation resulted in many forgeries, and during the Reformation, Protestants rejected the veneration of relics altogether. In both Catholic and Orthodox

We do not worship, we do not adore, for fear that we should bow down to the creature rather than to the creator, but we venerate the relics of the martyrs in order the better to adore him whose martyrs they are.

SAINT JEROME

A collection of first-class relics from the shrine of Saint Boniface include a bone fragment from Saint Boniface at the centre and bone fragments of Saints Benedict of Nursia and Bernard of Clairvaux at the corners of the pillow.

RIGHT: *Head reliquary of Saint Martin of Tours from the fourteenth century. By the tenth century, relics had often come to be housed in a container made in the shape of the relic, such as a foot or arm. Others were purely decorative and might hold third-class relics, such as oils.*

BELOW: *A reliquary casket from the twelfth century. Medieval craftsmen produced elaborate and beautiful containers designed to hold the relics of the saints.*

worship, however, relics remain extremely important, sacred objects, and acquisition of a relic is still considered an important event.

CLASSIFICATION OF RELICS

The Roman Catholic Church recognizes three classes of relics.

First-class relics are those items directly associated with the events of Christ's life, such as the cross or shroud, or the physical remains of a saint, such as bone, hair, or body parts.

Second-class relics are items that the saint wore, such as a shirt or an apron, or items that the saint owned or frequently used, such as a rosary or book.

Third-class relics are any objects that are connected to a first- or second-class relic, such as lamp oil or pieces of cloth.

The crown of King Stephen of Hungary, worn by the saint, is an example of a second-class relic.

BORN
c. 1003

DIED
5 January, 1066

CANONIZED
1161

FEAST DAY
13 October

PATRONAGE
British royal family
difficult marriages
kings
separated spouses

Saint Edward the Confessor

Growing up in exile after the Danish takeover of England in 1013, Edward and his brother, Alfred, spent a good deal of time in Normandy, where Edward became enamoured of religious life and, according to later hagiographers, took a vow of chastity. An unfortunate plan to recover the throne in 1035 or 1036 led to Alfred's death; nevertheless, the Danish ruler of England, Harthacnut, named Edward – his half-brother – as his successor, and in 1042 Edward ascended to the throne.

The opening sequence of the Bayeux Tapestry, which dates from about 1070 and depicts the Norman conquest of England, shows King Edward sending Harold to Normandy.

THE CONFESSOR KING

Although he was now king, Edward maintained respect for the Church and actually strengthened its position in England, welcoming papal legates, promoting new bishops, and – most famously – greatly increasing the wealth of Westminster, where he built a Norman church in which he would later be buried. His dedication to Westminster resulted from his vow to make a pilgrimage to Rome; when his royal duties prevented him from fulfilling the vow, the pope allowed him to develop Westminster instead.

In his lifetime Edward accrued a reputation for piety and humility, resulting in his sobriquet, "the Confessor". He endeared himself to his subjects with his generosity, his personal interest in caring for the poor, and by rescinding heavy taxes levied by his Danish predecessors. A popular legend about Edward highlights his beneficence and sanctity: one day in 1063, outside a chapel of Saint John the Divine, Edward took the ring from his finger and handed it to a beggar. Two years later, two English pilgrims travelling through Palestine (some versions say India) met an old man who identified himself as Saint

John. He handed them the king's ring, telling them he would meet Edward in Heaven in six month's time.

1066

Edward had to contend not only with the ambitious monarchs of Scandinavia but also with his own nobles – several were nearly as powerful as he. Of these, Earl Godwin of Wessex was the most troublesome. Canny and as politically astute as he was powerful, Godwin supported Edward in 1042 but resented the influence of Normandy over the king, who, Godwin felt, showed a tendency – among his other perceived faults – to promote Norman bishops over English ones. Despite these misgivings, Godwin married his daughter Edith to Edward in 1045, but their uneasy alliance ruptured in 1051, resulting in the exile of Godwin and his family, including Edith – whose marriage to Edward, it was said, remained unconsummated in accordance with Edward's vow of chastity. Popular sentiment forced Edward to make amends, however, and Godwin returned in 1052.

In 1066, Edward died, childless, setting off a storm of contention among his potential heirs, including Godwin's son Harold, Harald Hardrada of Norway, and William, Duke of Normandy (William the Conqueror), whose successful invasion late in 1066 is recognized as a crucial turning point in British history.

Edward's popularity grew in the later Middle Ages, especially after his descendant, Henry II, took the throne and assiduously promulgated his cult. Pope Alexander III canonized Edward in 1161 largely as a result of Henry's influence.

ABOVE: *Nothing remains of the original Westminster Abbey that Edward the Confessor founded, but one of his descendants, Henry III, rebuilt the abbey in Edward's honour and placed his relics in a shrine in the abbey's sanctuary.*

LEFT: *Edward the Confessor is shown at the centre of one of the panels of the fourteenth-century Wilton Diptich with Edward flanked by Edmund the Martyr and John the Baptist as they stand behind the kneeling Richard II.*

BELOW: *Another section of the Bayeux Tapestry shows the solemn funeral procession for Edward.*

BORN
c. 1045

DIED
16 November, 1093

CANONIZED
1250

FEAST DAY
10 June

PATRONAGE
learning

ALSO KNOWN AS
Margaret of Wessex

Saint Margaret of Scotland

As a granddaughter of the Anglo-Saxon king of England Edmund Ironside, Margaret was obliged, with the rest of her family, to spend the years of Danish rule in exile. She therefore grew up in Hungary, where she received a very good education and became a devout Christian, expressing a wish to live a chaste, religious life.

Saint Margaret of Scotland is buried at Dunfermline Abbey. King Saint David I of Scotland built the abbey to honour his mother. Parts of the original rectory still stand.

She returned to the British Isles after the death of Harthacnut, last of the Danish kings of England, but after 1066 the Norman rulers considered Margaret and her kin personae non gratae, and she fled to Scotland. There she met and fell in love with King Malcolm III, whom she married in 1069. The king, who deeply loved Margaret, let her exercise great influence over the Scottish court, and especially over the Scottish Church.

She instituted Church reforms, read the Gospels and Christian literature avidly, and founded several churches and monasteries, notably Dunfermline, later her burial place. She also revitalized the monastery of Iona and guided the Scottish Church towards a Roman Catholic revival.

Queen Margaret died fairly young, aged 47 or 48, exhausted from a life of religious austerity and from giving birth to eight children – one of whom, David, not only became king of Scotland but was also canonized. Her husband died earlier in a battle against the Norman English king.

Saint King David

Saint David was the youngest and arguably most successful child of Malcolm III of Scotland and his wife, the canonized Margaret, who died in 1093. He ascended the throne of Scotland in 1124, also claiming the English earldoms of Huntington, and rather more ambitiously, Northumbria through the inheritance of his wife, an Anglo-Saxon noblewoman. One of David's sisters had married the English king; their daughter Mathilda claimed the throne upon the king's death in 1135 but was challenged by her cousin Stephen, the eventual victor in a civil war known as "the Anarchy". David supported his niece, largely to support his own claims on his earldoms, and though he lost militarily he nevertheless succeeded in winning Northumbria and Cumberland as well.

King Saint David founded many churches, including Melrose Abbey, which lies in ruins.

As a ruler David showed himself to be energetic and ambitious. He had been reared in England, and as Scotland's king he set about introducing reforms along Anglo-Norman lines, including altering the judicial system and encouraging trade as a means of fostering city growth. Extremely pious, David is remembered chiefly for his efforts to consolidate the position of the Church in Scotland and secure its independence from English or Scandinavian archbishoprics. In this last he failed, but he founded a great many churches and abbeys; he did much to encourage the spread of monasticism and veneration of Mary. Like his mother, Saint Margaret, he is well known for his abundant almsgiving and was venerated soon after his death.

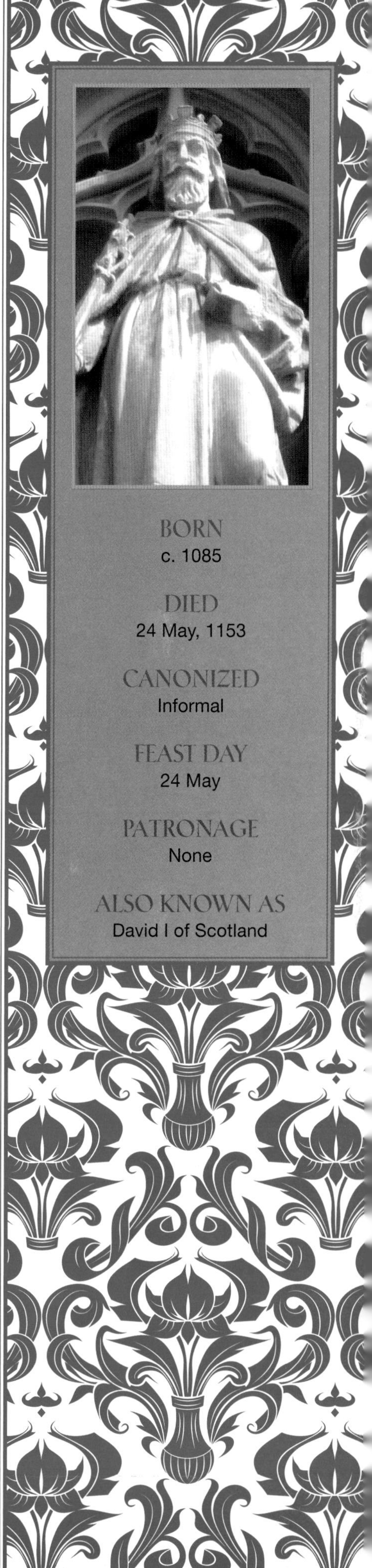

BORN
c. 1085

DIED
24 May, 1153

CANONIZED
Informal

FEAST DAY
24 May

PATRONAGE
None

ALSO KNOWN AS
David I of Scotland

Saint Louis IX

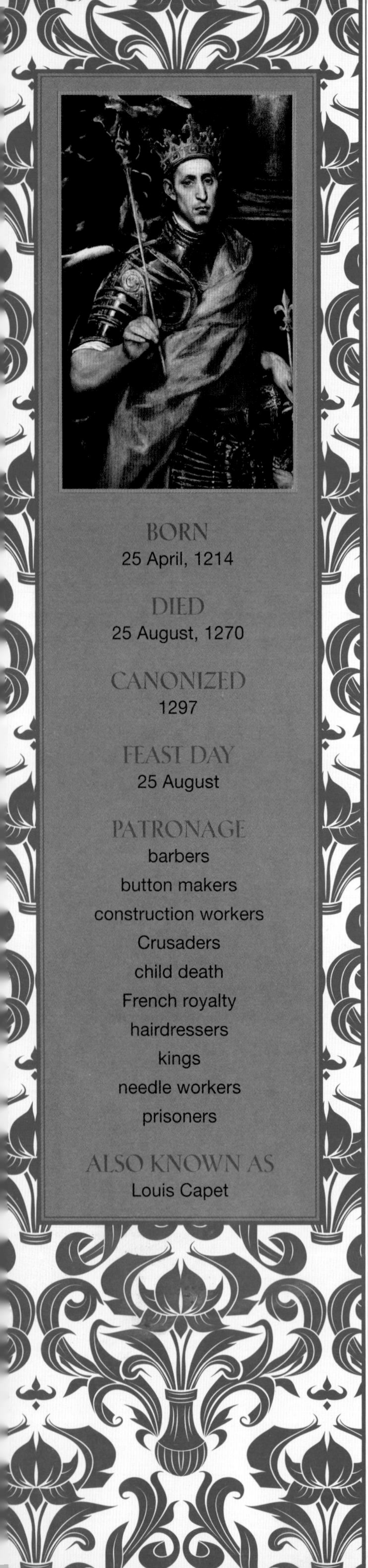

BORN
25 April, 1214

DIED
25 August, 1270

CANONIZED
1297

FEAST DAY
25 August

PATRONAGE
barbers
button makers
construction workers
Crusaders
child death
French royalty
hairdressers
kings
needle workers
prisoners

ALSO KNOWN AS
Louis Capet

Louis IX , one of France's most famous and revered monarchs, reigned over a flowering of French power and culture. A patron of the arts, Louis directly supported the explosion of fabulous Gothic architecture at the time. Interested equally in intellectual achievement, he fostered friendships with Saint Thomas Aquinas as well as Robert de Sorbon, who founded the Sorbonne in 1257 as part of the University of Paris.

THE REIGN OF LOUIS IX

Louis's father died in 1226, leaving the new king – then only 12 years old – and his country in the capable hands of Queen Blanche. It was Blanche who

Louis granting alms to beggars. Even as a very young king he is said to have displayed kindness.

> *In order to avoid discord, never contradict anyone except in case of sin or some danger to a neighbour; and when necessary to contradict others, do it with tact and not with temper.*
>
> King Saint Louis IX

rather adroitly secured papal support for France in the continuing dispute with England over ownership of certain large, wealthy provinces. She also ended the so-called Albigensian Crusade, which had begun as a Catholic attack on heresy in southern France but escalated into a political morass.

Louis took over from his mother when he was around twenty, becoming a model for Christian monarchs, ruling with wisdom, diplomacy, and virtue.

He bestowed funds on churches, supported monastic orders, strengthened the rule of law – even for the poorest of his subjects – and founded a hospital for the impoverished blind, which is still in existence.

In 1259, Louis brokered a deal between himself and his brother-in-law, King Henry III of England, which ended a sixty-year-old struggle over Normandy but unfortunately failed to avert the Hundred Years' War.

THE CROWN OF THORNS

In 1239, King Baldwin of Constantinople, grateful for the monetary assistance bestowed by King Louis, offered to sell his fellow monarch a remarkable relic – nothing less than a piece of the crown of thorns worn by Jesus (Baldwin offered him a piece of the True Cross shortly afterward). The prices were very high, but having at his disposal one of the richest kingdoms of Europe, the pious Louis did not hesitate, and to house the sacred relics he built the Sainte-Chapelle in Paris, his most famous architectural accomplishment and one of the modern world's best examples of extant Gothic architecture.

LOUIS, CRUSADER KING

Khorezmian Muslims ended Christian control of Jerusalem in 1244 (it had been held tenuously by treaty from 1229). Louis declared a crusade to recover the holy city despite a serious illness, and after four years of fund-raising he set sail in 1248, taking the city of Damietta in Egypt in 1249 with little trouble. Unfortunately, this turned out to be the only bright point. The crusaders proceeded to behave abominably, much to the king's dismay. Disease struck, and in

However disastrous the results may have been, it was sincere belief in the rightness of the mission that drove Louis IX to lead two disastrous crusades to the Holy Land.

February 1250 his army suffered a major defeat at al-Mansura, Egypt. Louis was captured but was released with the other prisoners after agreeing to return Damietta and pay a hefty ransom.

Louis travelled briefly through Christian-held areas of Palestine but returned home in 1254 with little accomplished. Undaunted, he launched a second crusade in 1270, and this, too, ended in disaster. He became terribly ill after landing in Tunis and died shortly thereafter. Even on his deathbed the altruistic monarch attempted a pious mission, pleading with Greek ambassadors to seek reconciliation with the Roman Catholic Church.

A statue of Louis stands in the Sainte-Chapelle, commissioned by the saint.

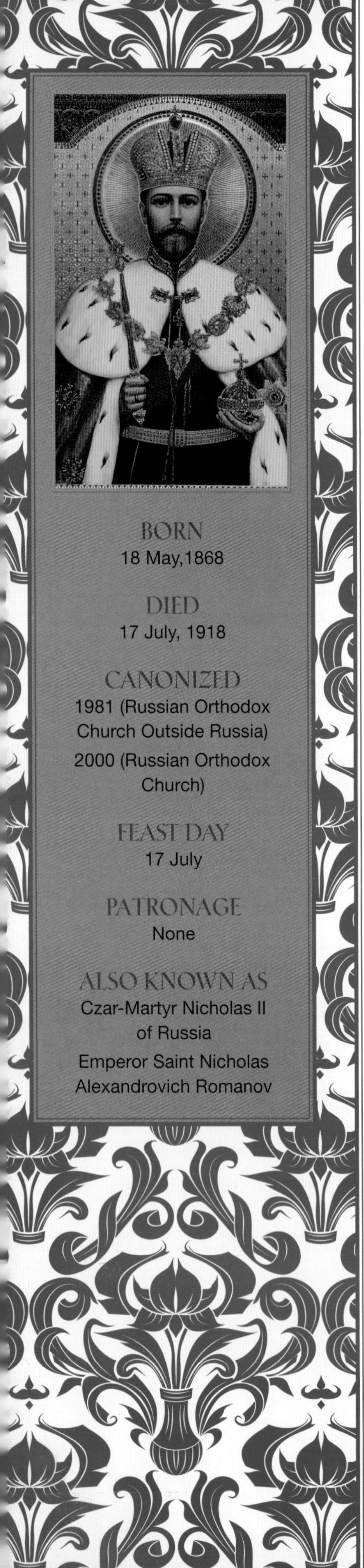

BORN
18 May,1868

DIED
17 July, 1918

CANONIZED
1981 (Russian Orthodox Church Outside Russia)
2000 (Russian Orthodox Church)

FEAST DAY
17 July

PATRONAGE
None

ALSO KNOWN AS
Czar-Martyr Nicholas II of Russia
Emperor Saint Nicholas Alexandrovich Romanov

Saint Nicholas the Passion-Bearer

Nicholas II ascended the Russian throne in 1894. Inexperienced, and rather cowed by his wife, the German-born Alexandra, Nicholas made several unfortunate mistakes during his reign. He was genuinely pious, however, and in no sense did he deserve the grim fate he received at the hands of the Bolshevik revolutionaries who, having forced his abdication in 1917, subsequently murdered Nicholas and his entire family in 1918, ignobly dumping their bodies down a mineshaft.

The remains were discovered decades later; DNA testing confirmed their identity. At around the same time, the question of canonization arose in the church. Controversy, coloured by international politics, surrounded the issue. While nobody doubted Nicholas II's personal piety, critics claimed his incompetent rule and autocratic policies had hastened, or even caused the Russian Revolution; moreover, because he did not die for the faith, Church authorities denied him status as a martyr, though many faithful had venerated him for years. Finally, in 2000, the Russian Orthodox Church canonized Nicholas II as a passion-bearer, one who suffers and dies at the hands of political enemies – as Jesus Christ did. Joining Nicholas for his canonization were his slain family members and 860 other Orthodox faithful, who died as martyrs during the revolution.

Nicholas with his wife, Alexandra, and their five children in 1911. The entire family was canonized as passion-bearers in 2000.

Index

D

E

F

S

T

U

V

W

X

Y

Z

Credits

All images used in this book are public domain, unless noted below.
All maps by Paul O'Brien

Abbreviations Used
t = top; b = bottom; m = middle; l = left; r = right

SS = Shutterstock.com; WC = Wikimedia Commons

SAINTS OF MARTYRDOM

10 br Zvonimir Atletic/SS; 11 Zvonimir Atletic/SS; 12 Zvonimir Atletic/SS; 13bl Vlad Ghiea/SS; 16tl Zvonimir Atletic/SS; 17tr Jose Ignacio Soto/SS; 17bl Renata; Sedmakova/SS; 18bm Kenneth V. Pilon/SS; 19bl Goran Bogicevic/SS; 21tm George Cleminte/SS; 22tl Zvonimir Atletic/SS; 24bm Asier Villafranca/SS; 33m Romary/WC; 34tl Fred.th/WC; 34tr John Lord; 35tr Ludwig Schneider/WC; 36 Immanuel Giel; 38tm Mary Lane/SS; 40tl and 40tr Courtesy of the Holy Transfiguration Monastery, http://www.thehtm.org41tm SFC/SS; 41bn catholictradition.org

SAINTS OF THE BOOK & THE WORD

42r Zvonimir Atletic/SS; 42bl Zvonimir Atletic/SS; 45bl Orf3us/WC; 47br Godromil/WC; 51tr Alfgar/SS; 56tl Zvonimir Atletic/SS; 61tr Jastrow/WC; 62bm Luis García/WC; 63tm Benedictus/SS; 64mr simonekesh/SS; 64l Bocman1973/SS; 65br NicFer/WC; 67tm Zvonimir Atletic/SS; 67tr Zvonimir Atletic/SS; 73bm Willy Horsch/WC; 74br Juhanson/WC; 78bm emei/SS; 79br igor1308/SS

SAINTS OF THE BIBLE

81 Zvonimir Atletic/SS; 85br Bryan Busovicki/SS; 87br Renata Sedmakova/SS; 89tr Zvonimir Atletic/SS; 91bm Zvonimir Atletic/SS; 92bm Fel1ks/SS; 93bm thaagoon/SS; 96tl Zvonimir Atletic/SS; 96bm Zvonimir Atletic/SS; 98bm Zvonimir Atletic/SS

SAINTS OF VISION & ECSTASY

106bm Ωριγένης/WC; 109br Zvonimir Atletic/SS; 110bm ribeiroantonio/SS; 111br iron45/WC; 113bm Bill Perry/SS; 116m Túrelio; 122m Tupungato/SS; 127m BrendanDias/SS; 130m Renata Sedmakova; 131br Foyers de Charité; 132br Rotatebot/WC;

SAINTS OF THE CLOTH

141br Victorian Traditions/SS; 143br vyskoczilova/SS; 148tl Panaspics/SS; 149m Lian Deng/SS; 149tr BasPhoto/SS; 151br Ed Phillips/SS; 152tl Alistair Scott/SS; 153tm Gordon Cable; 154tl BasPhoto/SS; 156tl Zaqarbal/WC; 162br Luigi Chiesa/WC; 167br Joseolgon/WC; 169bl Malgorzata Kistryn/WC; 174bm PHB.cz (Richard Semik)/SS

SAINTS OF MISSION & CONVERSION

178bm MikAnCa/WC; 179bl Culnacreann/WC; 179m Jurand/SS; 180tl Thomas Gun/WC; 180m stenic/WC; 181tr Matt Ragen/SS; 183l Renata Sedmakova/SS; 185bl angusmclellan/WC; 185tr Madame.evangelista/WC; 190m Juri/SS; 193tr Radka1/SS; 195lb Diligent/WC

SAINTS OF NOBLE BLOOD

205 Tiberiu Stan/SS; 207m Evrik/WC; 208m Aiwok/WC; 209tr Zvonimir Atletic/SS; 210l SieBot/WC; 212tl A.C.Jones/SS; 213tr Christian Mueller/SS; 214tl Patrick Wang/SS; 214m jean morrison/SS; 215m Myrna Schwartinsky/SS; 215tr Kim Traynor/WC; 217br World Imaging/WC